SAMURAI

AND

Cotton

7/12/2012

SAMURAI

AND

Cotton

A STORY OF TWO LIFE JOURNEYS IN JAPAN AND AMERICA

TOMOKO T. TAKAHASHI

iUniverse, Inc.
Bloomington

Samurai and Cotton
A Story of Two Life Journeys in Japan and America

A Japanese edition of this book was originally published in 2010 by Fueisha (Osaka, Japan).

iUniverse books may be ordered through booksellers or by contacting:

iUniverse
1663 Liberty Drive
Bloomington, IN 47403
www.iuniverse.com
1-800-Authors (1-800-288-4677)

Because of the dynamic nature of the Internet, any web addresses or links contained in this book may have changed since publication and may no longer be valid. The views expressed in this work are solely those of the author and do not necessarily reflect the views of the publisher, and the publisher hereby disclaims any responsibility for them.

Any people depicted in stock imagery provided by Thinkstock are models, and such images are being used for illustrative purposes only.
Certain stock imagery © Thinkstock.

ISBN: 978-1-4620-4364-4 (sc)
ISBN: 978-1-4620-4366-8 (hc)
ISBN: 978-1-4620-4365-1 (ebk)

Library of Congress Control Number: 2011917190

Printed in the United States of America

iUniverse rev. date: 11/10/2011

For Mom

Contents

1. Family History

2. Youth

3. Home, Sweet Home

4. Parenting

5. Education Papa

6. Growing Together

7. Dad's Dream, My Dream

8. College Junior

9. Farewell, Albertus!

10. The Price We Pay for Love

11. After His Passing

Passing through the round of births and deaths, one makes one's way on the land of the Dharma nature, or enlightenment, that is inherent within oneself.

—*Nichiren*

1. Family History

An Old Photo

I have an old photograph displayed at my home in Southern California. Its sepia color suggests how antique the photo is.

The graceful lady in this photo is my grandmother, Toku. Just like her name, meaning "virtue" in Japanese, she appears to be an honorable person. As a Japanese woman born in the Meiji era (1868–1912), she looks a bit exotic because of her big eyes with double eyelids and her well-built physique.

The baby on her lap is my father, Kiyoshi. He was born on February 11th in the tenth year of Taishō[1] (1921). The photo was most likely taken sometime in the spring of that year. It was shot in a stylish photo studio.

I would assume it was quite a luxury at that time to have such a portrait taken. Overjoyed with the birth of the firstborn son, someone in the family must have taken the mother and her baby out to a neighboring town for a photo shoot so that copies of the mother-and-son portrait could be distributed to close friends and relatives.

The mother, Toku, looks a bit melancholy in the photo, but it was customary at the time not to smile in portraits. That must be why she looks so sober. Or, she might have simply been nervous sitting in a photo studio for the first time.

Looking at this photo of a baby born into a well-to-do family and held by his beautiful and loving mother, people believed they were looking at a perfect family. They might also have readily assumed that many more photos would be taken to record Toku's happy life and the growth of her son, Kiyoshi.

Sadly, this is the only known photo of Toku that exists in the entire world. No other photos depict her life. Strangely, even this sole photo had never been seen by her son, Kiyoshi, until he was more than fifty years old.

One day in the early 1970s, an old woman came to visit my father, Kiyoshi, and gave him an antique photograph. She explained she had received it from his family half a century before.

The woman had deliberated for many long years whether or not she should give the photo to my father. Knowing his complex family circumstances, she hesitated. As she got older, however,

---

[1]   A macron (¯) is used over a long vowel in Japanese words except well-known proper nouns (e.g., Tokyo, Hokkaido, Yoko) and common nouns that have entered the English language (e.g., daimyo, sumo, kendo). Also see notes to the *Glossary*.

possibly sensing her death approaching, she finally decided the best course was to give him the photo. Until then, my father had thought there was not even one photo of his mother left in the entire world. It was a profound and welcome surprise.

When this old photo came home to our family, everyone—Dad, Mom, my siblings, and I—felt a mystical connection with Toku. Up until then, she had only been a name to us, but from that day on, the photo turned her into someone that truly existed. We could now visualize her and feel her as a living being.

When we saw the photo of Toku for the first time, we exclaimed,

"Grandma Toku was gorgeous!"

"Dad, you look just like her!"

My father didn't say much. He went into his office for quiet and solitary reflection. After all, he had just seen his mother's photo for the very first time. Our surprise was nothing compared to his. He was perhaps reflecting upon the fifty-plus years of his life—with many images coming and going in his mind's eye . . . just like a revolving lantern.

December 10th of the tenth year of Taishō (1921) was a gloomy winter day with freezing sleet falling. It was the day when the Tōkamachi Festival was annually celebrated at Hikawa Shinto Shrine in Ōmiya, where people prayed for health, security, and prosperity in the coming New Year.

The entrance path to the Shrine was filled with numerous street stalls, and the year-end fair was thronged with energetic vendors and crowds of visitors. Despite the freezing weather, men and women of all ages walked briskly through the festival site.

Merchants carrying "fortune rakes" strode around proudly, showing off their purchases. The rakes were decorated with many colorful, glittering ornaments—gods of wealth, straw rice-bags, gold coins, cranes and turtles, pine needles, bamboo leaves, plum blossoms, etc.—Japanese symbols of wealth, longevity, good luck, and happiness.

A symbol of prosperity, the fortune rake was a must-have for business owners, as it was believed to "rake in" monetary fortune. Each year, merchants would buy a larger and more expensive rake than the previous year and display it in their home.

The Takahashi family had always had a large fortune rake displayed at home. It symbolized the family's prosperous business. Every year on December 10th, the family visited the Hikawa Shinto Shrine to celebrate the Tōkamachi Festival. In that particular year too, they were to visit the Shrine to give thanks for the good business they had enjoyed and to buy a new fortune rake. It turned out, however, there was no celebration for the family that year.

On that particular day, December 10, 1921, Takahashi's young bride, Toku, passed away after repeatedly calling her baby son's name in a heartrending voice.

"Kiyoshi~, Kiyoshi~"

She was only twenty-one years old. Her baby, Kiyoshi, was only ten months.

After so many years, it might be meaningless to speculate why and how Toku died, but I would assume it was not a long illness. Looking at her healthy appearance in the portrait taken several months before, and considering her youthful age, I would imagine it was an accident or a sudden illness.

It's possible that Toku might have been pregnant with her second child and had a premature labor or a childbirth accident. The death rate from childbirth was much higher at that time, so it's a reasonable assumption. If it was a childbirth accident, another life was lost at the same time, making it doubly tragic.

Whenever I think of Toku's death, I simply do not know how to grasp the fate of her short life. If she had been born in our time, she likely would have been enjoying her new life on a college campus somewhere. Instead, she died young, as many women did then due to the lack of medical knowledge and technology.

Life and death . . . They are indeed close neighbors.

After Toku's sudden death, her ten-month-old baby Kiyoshi, with no knowledge of his mother's fate, was pushed into hell, and a life full of trials began.

With his mother's milk no longer available, Baby Kiyoshi was fed with the water used for washing rice. Powdered milk was not available, and cow's milk was rare and difficult to obtain.

Kiyoshi's father, Kiichi, soon remarried. Evidently, his remarriage was arranged out of the necessity of having a woman who could take care of his baby son. It soon became clear, however, the woman who assumed the role of Kiichi's second wife had forced her way into the well-to-do Takahashi family.

She was, in fact, related to Toku, but was very unlike her gentle, virtuous relative. Not much is known about how it all happened, but this woman became Kiyoshi's stepmother. Because he was still a baby, Kiyoshi grew up not knowing the truth—that she was not his real mother. And his family kept it a perfect secret; Kiyoshi had no reason to believe that this woman was not his real mother.

All the photos of Toku were burned into ashes, and her existence was virtually eradicated. No one spoke of her. This is why we know little about her life and nothing about the cause of her death.

Kiyoshi's stepmother gave birth to a baby girl. After a second daughter, she finally had a baby boy and soon began to wish that he were the heir. Her stepson, Kiyoshi, was nothing but a nuisance and became an obstacle to her selfish ambitions for her biological son. Kiyoshi was, after all, not her flesh and blood. She loved and doted on her own children while treating Kiyoshi coldly. If it had not been forbidden, she would have gladly revealed the secret that she was not his real mother.

Although Kiyoshi was treated badly by his stepmother, he did have family members who adored him. One of them was his great-grandfather Kisuke, whom Kiyoshi affectionately called "Grandpa Baldy." The other ally Kiyoshi had was his grandmother Sui, who was loving and all embracing.

Great-grandpa Kisuke cherished Kiyoshi as the firstborn and the heir. Grandma Sui also poured her love into Kiyoshi, feeling terribly sympathetic to her grandson, who had lost his mother at a very young age.

Wataya Kisuke, the Founder

When summer vacation approached each year, Kiyoshi was told to leave school early so that he could accompany his great-grandfather Kisuke for an extended vacation at the Shima hot springs in Gunma Prefecture. As always, he took Kiyoshi and no one else.

As Kisuke's annual trip drew closer, his servant was ordered to cook a Siam gamecock in a sweet and spicy sauce and to stuff the meat in tea cylinders so that the old man could take it with him to the hot springs.

One summer day, Kisuke left home with his great-grandson Kiyoshi. Upon arriving at the train station, the old man, who had made this trip many times before, began making his way to the appropriate train. Normally, one would have to take stairs to go to the other side of the track in order to catch a down train on Takasaki Line. Boldly, Kisuke took a shortcut by walking on the stationmaster's special crossroad, completely ignoring the "Do Not Enter" sign.

The platforms were not so high back then, and trains were infrequent. Most people thought it would be more convenient to just cross the track right there instead of taking a detour and going up and down the stairs. And yet, no one had done it—except for Kisuke, who was quite accustomed to finding the most efficient way to reach his business goals and to achieve success. Or, perhaps, his old age was making him impatient.

Oh, no! Grandpa is doing it again . . . lamented the schoolboy Kiyoshi, looking down, utterly embarrassed, as he followed his great-grandfather across the track.

Then, the stationmaster came out of his office, stood on the other side of the track, and warned the old man,

"Sir, you shouldn't have crossed the track there. It's dangerous!"

I knew it, thought the young boy, feeling guilty for following his great-grandfather.

Then, the old man replied to the stationmaster,

"So, what do you want me to do now? If I come back to your side, I'll have to cross the track again, and that is apparently most dangerous."

Kisuke's resolute attitude and speech style were somewhat reminiscent of a *samurai* warrior.

The Takahashi family descended from a samurai lineage, but Kisuke, my great-great-grandfather, became a merchant when he was young. Prior to that, the family used to serve a samurai clan called "Ina."

I don't know what roles my ancestors played while serving the Ina clan. All I know for sure is that Kisuke's family and ancestors used to live near the mansion called "Ina Castle" in the Maruyama village of the Komuro section in the Musashi province (present-day Saitama Prefecture).

The Ina family was a samurai clan of the Ashikaga lineage that was descended from the Seiwa Genji, which was founded by Minamoto no Tsunemoto (894–961), a descendant of Emperor Seiwa (850–881). The Ina clan once used its original sir name "Arakawa" but began calling itself "Ina" after receiving a section of the Ina region in the Shinano province (present-day Nagano Prefecture) from the Ashikaga shogunate in the fifteenth century.

The clan flourished, thanks to Ina Tadatsugu (1550–1610), who served Tokugawa Ieyasu (1543–1616) and was rewarded for his dedication and service to Ieyasu with the vast fiefdom yielding more than 10,000 *koku* [about 1,500 tons or 10,000 cubic feet of rice per year] in the Komuro section of the Musashi province. Subsequently, Tadatsugu became a *daimyo* [powerful feudal lord] when he established the Komuro Han [Fiefdom] in the region.

Unfortunately, the Ina clan was later reduced to a *hatamoto* [upper vassal] from a daimyo, but it had kept its samurai lineage until the beginning of the Meiji era.

Kisuke, my great-great-grandfather, was born in 1855, the second year of Ansei during the Edo period (1603–1867). During the Ansei era (1854–1860), a series of three major earthquakes devastated Japan, known as the Ansei Great Earthquakes. One of them, the Ansei Edo Quake, struck Edo (present-day Tokyo) on November 11, 1855—the year in which Kisuke was born.

Moreover, 1855 was only a few years after the arrival of the American Black Ships at Uraga Harbor (1853), which marked the dawn of a new era and the end of the Tokugawa shogunate that had barred Japan from trading with the outside world for more than two hundred years.

Kisuke had a rocky start and grew up in the midst of the turmoil of a chain of events that led to enormous changes in Japan's political and social structure—known as the Meiji Revolution. The entire populace experienced drastic changes; the survival of the samurai was especially threatened.

In 1869, all Tokugawa shogunate lands were seized and placed under the prerogative of the new Meiji government. In 1871, all the daimyo lords, past and present, were summoned before Emperor Meiji, where it was declared that all fiefs were to be returned to the Emperor. This marked the abolition of the feudal system.

The daimyo lords were promised ten percent of their fiefs' production as private income, and payments for samurai stipends were to be taken over by the state. The government soon became financially distressed because of this promise; thus it went on to abolish the samurai class. As a result, many samurai lost their sources of income.

The former samurai became teachers, government officials, military officers, and so forth. Some of them became merchants despite their inexperience in business, and many of them failed and went bankrupt. There were also former samurai who simply could not find employment and fell adrift.

These changes taking place after the Meiji Revolution were also a matter of identity and status, especially for the samurai. For instance, in 1871, the new government abolished a rule that all men must wear a *chon-mage* [topknot]. It was also proclaimed that the samurai would not have to wear swords. This was a precursor to the ban on wearing swords (1873) as well as the eventual abolition of the samurai class.

Samurai's swords were not so much for the purpose of arming themselves, but rather for purposes of identity—symbolizing their privileged class as the samurai. The ban on wearing swords, therefore, meant depriving the samurai of their identity.

The new government went on trying to abolish the four divisions of society—*shi, nō, kō, shō* [gentry, farmers, artisans, and merchants]. The government's efforts to bring "class equalization" led to a series of riots by disgruntled samurai.

In the midst of the turmoil and drastic changes, Kisuke abandoned his sword—the samurai's soul—and looked for some other form of employment. It's hard to imagine what it must have been like for a young samurai to become a merchant.

Around that time, when Kisuke was sixteen, his father, Kisaburō, passed away. Consequently, as the heir to the family, Kisuke had to shoulder the family's fate.

We don't know how Kisaburō died. All we know is that he died in the fourth year of Meiji (1871). As mentioned above, that was the year when the samurai's identity of carrying swords and wearing topknots receded and the feudal system was abolished. Who knows? Disgruntled, Kisaburō might have joined a samurai riot and been punished to death. Or, he might have committed *harakiri*.

Prior to Kisaburō's death, there was a series of arguments between him and his son. The father chose the traditional way of samurai life, while the son chose a modern, liberal path. The generation gap widened between the old-fashioned father and the son who was born into a new era.

The father died. His surviving son, Kisuke, chose to live on and give up his samurai status and several generations of samurai tradition. The pain and suffering from confusion and conflict were indescribable. He could not even afford to mourn his father's death.

Kisuke went from the highest rank of samurai to the lowest class of merchant within the already abolished four divisions of society—"gentry, farmers, artisans, and merchants." But it didn't matter to him. Survival was his number-one concern.

After giving up his samurai status, Kisuke left his home and family in Maruyama and went about ten miles to the west to live in the town of Kawagoe. There he apprenticed with a cotton merchant named Aburashō.

Kawagoe was called *"Ko-Edo* [Small Edo]" being connected with the capital city of Edo via the Kawagoe Kaidō [Highway] and many boat rivers that allowed good transportation. It was also a castle town that had prospered during the Edo period, thanks to the powerful Kawagoe Han. It was a perfect town for learning business.

In the nineteenth year of Meiji (1886), after a number of years of apprenticing, Kisuke opened his own business, *Takahashi Men-ten* [Takahashi Cotton Store], in the Haraichi town of the Kita-Adachi region in Saitama Prefecture. He was thirty-one years old.

The property Kisuke acquired for his new enterprise had been an inn. It was a piece of land known as "an eel house" or "an eel's bed." As its nickname indicated, the property was long and narrow. The width was about that of one house, but length-wise, it stretched long enough to contain several houses.

The Haraichi town was only about a twenty-minute walk from the Maruyama village, where Kisuke had grown up. That is to say, he had started his business, if not in his hometown, then in his home territory. And, he returned home triumphant. As the founder of Takahashi Cotton Store, people began calling him *"Shodai* [the First Generation or Founder]" with much respect. He also came to be known as *Wataya Kisuke* [Kisuke, the Cotton Merchant].

Haraichi was an old town established in the sixteenth century. It flourished as a market town as its name indicates—*hara* [field] + *ichi* [market/fair]. Fairs were regularly and frequently held in the town—six times a month, on the days that ended with 3 and 8—i.e., on the 3rd, 8th, 13th, 18th, 23rd, and 28th.

When I was a child growing up in the 1950s and 60s, although they were not as frequent as they had been before, fairs and markets were still held outdoors in my hometown of Haraichi. I could hardly wait for the start of each fair.

My favorite was the Hina Festival Fair held on March 3rd. There were many street stalls selling *hina* dolls. Not only that, the Main Street was filled with vendors selling goldfish, turtles, cotton candy, *Imagawa-yaki* muffins, and lots of goodies. The fair was thronged with shoppers. When my father bought me a turtle for the first time, I watched my new pet hide its head and legs, extend them again, and repeat. I never grew weary of it.

As soon as each fair opened, I dashed to my favorite Imagawa-yaki vendor and impatiently watched the old man make my fresh muffins stuffed with sweet red beans. My father told me he had always gone to the very same vendor when he was a child. The only difference was that Dad called those muffins *"kin-tsuba,"* whereas I preferred the standard and more modern name "Imagawa-yaki"—Imagawa was the name for the birthplace of the muffin. Since I thought *kin-tsuba* meant "golden spit," I decided not to copy my father in this instance only. (The word *tsuba* is a homonym meaning both "saliva" and "a hand guard [on a Japanese sword]." Many years later, I realized that *kin-tsuba* really meant "golden sword-guard" since the muffin was shaped like a hand guard on a sword.)

In 1881, five years prior to the founding of Kisuke's business, the first privately owned railroad was built in Japan. Two years later, in 1883, the Takasaki Line between Ueno and Kumagaya was inaugurated, which resulted in the opening of Ageo Station in the town of Ageo, right next to Haraichi. Due to the new railroad station, Ageo flourished, while Haraichi gradually became overshadowed by it and fell behind.

At the time when Kisuke opened his business, Haraichi was still a very prosperous market town and was quite well known. What's more, he opened his business right in the center of Main Street.

Takahashi Cotton Store had a *yagō* [special name for trading], which was read "Yama-ki." This was chosen by Kisuke, the Founder. This yagō looked more like a logo, which was a combination of the mountain-shaped sign and the *katakana* character キ [ki]—i.e., *yama* [mountain] + *ki*.

The *ki* of Yama-ki obviously came from the *Ki* of Kisuke. I don't know where "Yama" came from. Maybe, it was the *yama* of Maru<u>yama</u>, the name of his hometown. If so, Yama-ki evidently meant "Maru<u>yama</u>'s <u>Ki</u>suke."

A yagō was used by merchants and wealthy farmers, who needed a name so they could trade their merchandise and crop. Prior to the Meiji era, during the Edo period (1603–1867), no one was permitted to use surnames except for the samurai. That's why merchants used their yagō instead.

Since Kisuke had been a samurai, he already had his surname, Takahashi. Although he didn't really need one, he still chose to use a yagō just like any other merchant. I find this to be an indication of his enthusiasm and desire to become a true merchant. Also, I suspect that he had a flexible mind and was willing to abandon class distinctions.

Kisuke was a talented entrepreneur full of ideas. For instance, he advertised his business by distributing handbills, which was rare at the time. He also created a brand name, *Masukotto-jirushi* [Mascot Brand], for the cotton processed at his plant. The cotton, which was received in raw condition, was treated and made ready for use in *futon* bedding.

The *masukotto* [mascot] of Masukotto-jirushi was a mustachioed gentleman wearing a Western swallow-tailed tuxedo. Apparently,

Kisuke had a good sense of humor. On the label, right next to the comical drawing of this gentleman, it said, "Here I come again!" He presumably had a liking for anything Western and modern. I assume so based on his choice of the English word "mascot" [pronounced "masukotto" in Japanese] and the Western swallow-tailed tux. What else could one assume about the selection of such a brand name and emblem?

The store became a great success. Thanks to thriving business, the Takahashi family gradually became affluent and began to make a good living.

Yōzaburō, the Second Generation

Kisuke was successful in business, but his family always suffered from misfortune.

Kisuke's heir (the Second Generation) was named "Yōzaburō." As his name indicates, he was most likely Kisuke's third son because the name ending -*zaburō* [a variation of -*saburō* meaning "third boy"] was customarily given to a third-born son. It's not entirely impossible, however, that Yōzaburō was named after his grandfather Kisaburō, whose name ended with -*saburō*.

Another indication that he was the third son is that Kisuke was twenty-six years old when Yōzaburō was born—i.e., a bit too old to be a new father, especially at a time when most people got married very young, before twenty.

How, then, was Yōzaburō the heir? I can only assume it was because Kisuke's first and second sons had died young or were taken off the succession line for some (probably tragic) reasons.

Yōzaburō, too, experienced much misfortune. In 1902, still newlywed, and right after his son Kiichi was born, Yōzaburō was drafted into the military and was assigned to the twenty-fifth infantry regiment of the seventh division. This division had been formed based on the army named *Tonden-hei* that focused on the security of Hokkaido, the northern island of Japan, close to Russia. Most of its regiments were stationed in Asahikawa, except for Yōzaburō's regiment, which was stationed in Sapporo.

13

After having been trained as a soldier for two years, in 1904, Yōzaburō was shipped to Manchuria, the hellish battlefield of the Russo-Japanese War (1904–1905).

Yōzaburō's army service history is known to us, thanks to the monument built by his son Kiichi years later:

> *On December 3rd in the thirty-fifth year of Meiji (1902), he was drafted into the twenty-fifth infantry regiment of the seventh division.*
>
> *On September 4th in the thirty-seventh year of Meiji (1904), he was called into military service.*
>
> *On November 13th of the same year, he left the Port of Osaka.*
>
> *On November 25th of the same year, he arrived in Qingniwaqiao.*
>
> *On November 26th of the same year, he participated in the Battle of Lüshunkou; transported the seriously wounded Captain Koide to a filled hospital in the midst of great danger; and was cited for his bravery.*
>
> *On April 1st in the thirty-ninth year of Meiji (1906), he was decorated with the seventh rank of* Kinshi-*bird imperial medal of the eighth class of the white paulownia award for his military merit in the thirty-seventh through thirty-eighth years of Meiji.*
>
> *Founded by Takahashi Kiichi*
> *March 21st in the fourth year of Shōwa (1929)*

Qingniwaqiao, mentioned above, is the district around Dalian, whose name is said to have originated from "Dalny" meaning "far away" in Russian. Lüshunkou, or Lüshun Port, is in the municipality of Dalian in the Liaoning province of then-Manchuria. It was also known as "Port Arthur" in English or "Ryojun" in Japanese.

Port Arthur, located at the southern tip of Liaodong Peninsula, was an excellent natural harbor—the possession and control of which became a casus belli in the Russo-Japanese War.

As described on the monument built by Kiichi, on November 26, 1904, Yōzaburō participated in the Battle of Lüshunkou, also known as the Third Battle of Port Arthur, one of the worst battles of the Russo-Japanese War. The army officer whom he is said to have transported to a field hospital was Second-Lieutenant Koide Masakichi, who is recorded in history as the bravest member of the *Shirodasuki-tai* [White-sash Corps].

The Shirodasuki-tai was a suicide corps formed as the last resort when the Japanese military army reached a dead end. It consisted of 3,105 volunteers from several different army regiments. Members of this corps wore white sashes crossed on their upper torsos so that they could recognize one another in close combat.

The Japanese army at the time made it a rule not to draft eldest sons and family heirs into a suicide corps like this one. Regardless, many of these soldiers knowingly volunteered to join the Shirodasuki-tai corps. This they did despite the fact that their death could lead to the extinction of their family name.

Yōzaburō, the heir to the Takahashi family, was one such soldier. He volunteered to take part in the Shirodasuki-tai suicide corps, perhaps pretending that he was a third-born son, conveniently using his name, which ended with -*zaburō* [third son]. He wished to devote his life to his country, firmly believing that dying for his country was the greatest virtue and the best way to bring honor to his family and newborn son. Yōzaburō became a member of the Shirodasuki-tai suicide corps, joining Captain Koide.

One record indicates that 1,565 solders out of the 3,105 in the corps, more than a half, came from the twenty-fifth infantry regiment of the seventh division. This is the regiment to which Captain Koide and Yōzaburō belonged.

(Above) A group of the Shirodasuki-tai soldiers photographed a few hours before the deadly attack (1904); the soldier pointed at with the arrow is assumed to be Yōzaburō, my great-grandfather (see the enlarged photo of him attached—left).

On November 26th of the thirty-seventh year of Meiji (1904) at 4 p.m., General Nogi gave a short speech to raise the morale of the Shirodasuki-tai soldiers, and offered barrels of *saké* [rice wine] mounted on a horse. The offer was rejected by all the soldiers, excepting some commanders.

At 6 p.m. and in freezing temperatures at 14° F, the corps left their position, and at 9 p.m., they began an assault on the Russian fortress on Shōju Mountain near Port Arthur. What was to have been a surprise attack was thwarted by the presence of land mines, which were everywhere, triggering and exploding. Strong beams from the Russian army's powerful searchlights illuminated the Shirodasuki-tai soldiers, and the rain of bullets began falling on them. Nevertheless, the Japanese troops refused to retreat and continued their attack.

While many commanders and soldiers were killed one after another, there was one soldier who singly led the troops and jumped into the Russian fortress, using a cannon for cover, holding a Japanese sword high above his head. It was Captain Koide. After a mighty struggle, however, he was isolated from his troops and completely surrounded by enemy reinforcements. Finally, he was killed in action.

This is the story of the Shirodasuki-tai and Captain Koide's brave combat recorded in numerous historical documents.

According to those documents, Captain Koide was killed in the battle. According to the monument commemorating Yōzaburō's military service, Captain Koide was seriously wounded and taken to a field hospital. It is possible that the expression "seriously wounded" engraved on the monument was used euphemistically and really meant "fatally wounded" or "dead." In other words, Yōzaburō presumably found and transported Captain Koide's corpse to a field hospital, and the army, not Captain Koide himself, rewarded Yōzaburō with a citation for his merit.

It is also indicated in historical documents that the Russian army was so impressed and moved by Captain Koide's brave combat that they later returned to the Japanese army his sword that had been left behind on the battleground.

The Shirodasuki-tai lost more than 2,000 men while storming with bayonets and swords into the modern fortress of the Russian army. On the following day, November 27th, before dawn, General Nogi ordered his Japanese troops to cease the assault. That morning, after dawn, they found a mountain of dead bodies and rivers of blood. The Japanese army asked its Russian counterpart to have a short cease-fire so that it could collect the corpses of the fallen soldiers. One record states that it was not unusual to have a cease-fire after fierce combat in order to collect corpses, and during the Russo-Japanese War, it was frequently done.

During the battle or the cease-fire, Yōzaburō found Captain Koide and frantically transported him (or his corpse) to a field hospital. Having been able to find Captain Koide, Yōzaburō undoubtedly fought close to the Captain and witnessed his brave combat with his own eyes. Sometime after taking Captain Koide to the field hospital, perhaps immediately or perhaps after more ghastly battles, Yōzaburō became mentally ill.

The Shirodasuki-tai was destroyed, but its spiritual damage to the Russian army was grave. A journal kept by a Russian army officer described the battle as follows:

> *The battle on this day was so furious and gruesome that no past Russian literature could offer an appropriate adjective to describe its intensity. [. . .] Thousands of white-sashed soldiers came storming like a flood. We all turned pale at the sight of those masses of troops swarming, wearing white sashes stained with blood, holding swords aloft. We were caught at once dumbfounded and speechless. In spirit, we completely surrendered.* (Author's translation of excerpts from *Nogi Maresuke* by Okada 2011)[2]

The Japanese army eventually seized Port Arthur, which resulted in victory for Japan. Even though Japan won the Russo-Japanese War, both armies had sacrificed and lost countless precious lives.

In spite of miraculously surviving the war and returning home, Yōzaburō was no longer able to play with his young son or even recognize him as his own child. The medal he later received from the Emperor meant nothing.

---

[2]   Okada, Mikihiko 岡田幹彦. *Nogi Maresuke: Kōki-naru Meiji* 乃木希典: 高貴なる明治 [Nogi Maresuke: the Noble Meiji]. Tokyo: Tentensha, 2001.

Scars of the Russo-Japanese War

We have a photo of Yōzaburō, my great-grandfather, probably taken sometime after he returned from the war. It used to be displayed on the wall in the family Buddhist-altar room at my home.

My great-grandfather Yōzaburō (ca. 1905)

When I was a child, I used to look up at the photo hung high on the wall every day. Because of the old-fashioned *kimono* jacket, it gave me the impression that it was a photo of an old man. Many years later, I looked at it closely and realized that the man in the photo was not only young but quite handsome. It was a fresh surprise.

No one knows, however, when and where this photo was taken. It was presumably shot at a hospital, as implied by his Red-Cross cap and what looks like hospital clothes. Back then, taking a portrait was such a big deal that people normally dressed up. If so, why was Yōzaburō wearing hospital clothes and why was he holding a stick that looks too thin to be a cane?

A document about Japanese military history indicates that the Asahikawa Hospital in Hokkaido was opened as an army hospital for the seventh division in the thirty-fourth year of Meiji (1901), four years prior to the end of the Russo-Japanese War. An army hospital at that time was intended to serve its assigned army division permanently in the respective region and to treat its garrison and keep them healthy.

It's most likely that Yōzaburō was sent to this Asahikawa Hospital after becoming mentally ill during the war. The photo gives an impression of a cold climate; one might be correct to assume it was taken somewhere in Hokkaido, the northern part of Japan.

Now, why was Yōzaburō dressed as a patient? Maybe because he refused to change, or because it was the hospital's regulation not to allow patients to change into regular clothes while under hospital care. Then, why was Yōzaburō photographed at all? Here is my guess.

- Yōzaburō's father, Kisuke, traveled all the way to Asahikawa to visit his son at the hospital. At one point Kisuke had thought Yōzaburō might have been killed in action, but then he learned that he was still alive. Overjoyed, Kisuke traveled to Asahikawa to visit him.
- Kisuke wanted to prove to his family that Yōzaburō was alive and had no physical defect. He hired a photographer and took him to the hospital to have him take a photo of Yōzaburō.
- There was no place appropriate inside the hospital, so an outdoor spot was chosen and set up for a photo shoot. It was freezing outside.

- Yōzaburō only had his white patient clothes on, so Kisuke dressed his son in the dark kimono jacket and gloves he had brought from home.
- Yōzaburō came outside holding a stick; he liked drawing pictures on the ground with this stick.
- Kisuke finally persuaded his emotionless son to be photographed.

Conceivably, Yōzaburō was released from the hospital and sent home sometime after this photo was taken.

Records indicate many of the patients had to be released from army hospitals around that time because there were so many mentally ill patients that the hospitals became overcrowded.

We don't know whether Yozaburō's release was due to the hospital's overcrowded conditions, or because his father had asked the hospital to release him. Even if it was the former, Kisuke must have welcomed his son home with open arms, telling himself and others, "I will cure my son's illness."

And yet, it was still quite difficult to have a mentally ill patient living at home.

At my childhood home, I remember, there was a small cottage used for storage. It was like an annex detached from the main house. I heard that Yōzaburō had once been confined there. Kisuke had that cottage built for him, thinking that it would be better for his son to live there than living in a far-away hospital.

A talented artist, Yōzaburō could draw pictures despite his affliction, the intensity of which is unknown. Horses in his drawings, for instance, looked vividly alive as though they would jump off the page.

Gradually, Yōzaburō became the talk of the town. Although he was a war victim and someone the townspeople had known before his time away, still the whispering began,

"That family has a crazy man."

"Insanity runs in that family."

The family was stigmatized . . . unfairly.

21

More misfortune befell the family. Right after Yōzaburō returned from the war, in July 1905, Kisuke's wife (Yōzaburō's mother), Hana, passed away. And a year later (1906), his mother (Yōzaburō's grandmother), Chō, passed away. We don't know the cause of their death, but most assuredly, the plight of Yōzaburō must have played a part.

A year after losing his wife and mother, Kisuke built a monument that recorded his life's history—that he had left Maruyama alone to become a merchant and returned home to resettle in Haraichi with his family. While reminiscing about the time when he had lost his father at the young age of sixteen and had become a merchant, he understandably wanted to honor his wife and mother who had shared the pain and struggles with him for all those years.

About fifteen years later, in 1921, Kisuke's family was blessed and overjoyed with the birth of Kiyoshi (the Fourth Generation), whose mother was Toku and father Kiichi (the Third Generation). Kiichi was Yōzaburō's son born in 1900, right before Yōzaburō was drafted. Kisuke (the Founder), in place of his ailing son Yōzaburō, had himself raised Kiichi, his beloved grandson.

Needless to say, the birth of a son to his grandson was such a great joy to Kisuke. But his joy was short lived. The young mother, Toku, died on that freezing December day, leaving behind her ten-month-old baby, Kiyoshi. Then, to make things even worse, Yōzaburō passed away several years later, without regaining his sanity.

Kisuke was able to build monetary fortune with his talent and hard work, but he had no control over his and his family's destiny. He utterly hated having no control.

My great-great-grandfather Kisuke
(Year unknown)

As for Kisuke, he lived an extremely long life, as you could guess from those episodes about his trips to the Shima hot springs with his great-grandson Kiyoshi. Longevity for him, however, was nothing to be thankful for since he sadly outlived his wife and sons, and many other family members. Still, he chose to live. That was the determination and choice he had made at age sixteen.

"Grandpa Baldy lived for more than eighty years," my father used to say about his great-grandfather.

It was quite rare to live such a long life at that time. Kisuke lived through four epochs—born in the Edo period, he lived during the Meiji, Taishō, and Shōwa eras. The average life expectancy in Meiji and Taishō was only about forty years.

He watched over the store he had established for half a century. It was undeniably his strong determination that enabled him to accomplish a great deal. He lived on for the sake of his ancestors and descendants, while he kept telling himself: *I'm going to become absolutely happy. I'm laying the foundation for it now.*

Kisuke lived a heroic eighty-three years through all the turmoil and the series of misfortunes without giving up.

The Secret

Why is my mother so cold to me? Kisuke's great-grandson Kiyoshi often wondered when he was a young boy.

Although he was puzzled and troubled by it, he grew up to be a gentle and kind boy, thanks to Great-grandpa Kisuke and Grandma Sui's loving attention.

Kiyoshi was straightforward and righteous. He was also very bright and athletic. Kisuke's pride and joy, he was indeed good at *kendo* [Japanese fencing]. Maybe it was because of his samurai lineage, or he was simply talented. He practiced kendo diligently at a *dojo* [training hall] called Kōdō-kan.

Decades later, my father's kendo teacher closed the dojo and opened an osteopathy clinic named Kōdō-kan. In the late 1960s, when I was in junior high school, I injured my knee from playing too much basketball, and Dad took me to his old kendo teacher's clinic to have my knee treated.

The *sensei* [teacher/doctor] remembered my father's youthful days clearly, and said to me,

"Tomoko, you look just like your father when he was young."

And after welcoming us into the dark clinic room, he treated my knee, while chatting with Dad.

The sensei was reminded of the great lapse of time—my father used to practice kendo in his youth and now his daughter was into basketball, a Western sport. I still remember the sensei's warm gaze and voice, which I have kept next to the memories of my father.

My father, Kiyoshi, as a young boy
(Drawing—production year unknown)

Young Kiyoshi studied hard. He wanted everyone in his family to be proud of him as the eldest son and the heir to the family. He never even complained about any hardships. One day, however, fate came knocking.

On this day, Kiyoshi, a preadolescent boy, came across a quarrel in the neighborhood. The man bullying his much weaker victim looked at Kiyoshi, who was attempting to step in and end the fight. As soon as the man recognized the boy as the eldest son of the Takahashi family, he said,

"Oh, is that you? Motherless you? Your mom is your stepmother. She's not your real mother!"

The secret was revealed. It was the man's dirty trick to hurt the boy who had bravely challenged him.

Kiyoshi was shocked and stunned. His mind went blank. He completely forgot about the trouble he had come to settle.

Once he became himself again, he felt anger welling up from the bottom of his heart.

Everybody has been deceiving me! She's my stepmother! I don't have a mother. I can't believe in anyone. Not even Grandpa Baldy. Not even Grandma Sui!

It was a sensitive age. He thought about protesting by ignoring his family's honor and becoming a delinquent. For someone who had always been dutiful, it was a painful time.

But who would really suffer if I became a delinquent?

Myself!

After wondering to himself, Kiyoshi decided to accept his fate and continue living strong. He learned to look at life rather philosophically because of this experience.

Kiyoshi never went astray. He continued to live earnestly. He also kept his polite and kind attitude toward his stepmother no matter how coldly and badly she treated him.

Since my father, Kiyoshi, told me this story several decades ago, I have often wondered how a preadolescent boy was able to remain so cool-headed and rational at the turning point of his life like that, and never go astray.

Well, that reminds me . . . my father would always calmly consider a problem from every angle before making a decision based on his sharp observations. He often used military expressions such as "Know your enemy's position." He began looking at his own weaknesses as his enemy from a young age. And he continued to win over that enemy—himself.

Dad also loved quoting from *The Analects of Confucius*. And, as I remember, he was good at applying what he learned from books to his own life. He was evidently good at it even when he was very young.

If you cannot use your knowledge to "know yourself," your learning is meaningless. In that sense, my father's learning was outstanding.

2. Youth

The War

Kiyoshi graduated from elementary school in the eighth year of Shōwa (1933) and then went on to middle school under the old system of education—equivalent to today's junior and senior high schools combined. Middle school at that time was considered a gateway to success for elites. Especially in the Meiji era, those who attended middle school were from the aristocracy, former samurai, and the wealthy landowner class.

During the time known as the Taishō Democracy, which is usually distinguished from the preceding chaotic Meiji period and the following militarism-driven first half of the Shōwa era (1926–1989), more people became enthusiastic about middle-school education. And yet, it was still unattainable for most of the general public.

Since the education Kiyoshi received from middle school was regarded as a privilege, people naturally thought that it was more than enough for a merchant's son, and assumed that Kiyoshi would start working for his father's business after graduation.

Kiyoshi wished, however, to go on to enter the next stage of education. He was smart and rather a scholarly type, and naturally, he wished to continue studying.

My father once told me that he had been accepted to, and had almost enrolled in, the Yokohama Higher School of Commerce under the old system of education, known as "Yokohama Kō-Shō," the predecessor of the present-day Yokohama National University's Economics Department. The school offered a program in international trade, which interested my father.

Going to school in Yokohama really sounds like something my father would have longed for in his youth. Yokohama is a port city located less than half an hour south of Tokyo by train, and is the capital of Kanagawa Prefecture. Toward the end of the Edo period, during which Japan maintained a policy of self-isolation, Yokohama was one of the first ports to be opened to foreign trade in 1859. Consequently, it quickly grew from a small fishing village into one of Japan's major cities, especially known for international trade and exchanges, as well as its exotic atmosphere. Yokohama was a perfect place to learn about business.

Both trading and Yokohama well symbolized my father's dream of going overseas. In my youth in the 1960s, I remember, he loved watching those American TV shows, such as *Bonanza*, which were imported to post-war Japan. He especially loved John Wayne's cowboy movies too. He doubtlessly cherished a dream of going to America as a young man—going to a far-away country possibly because he could not find his own place at home. But his dream never came true.

When Kiyoshi turned sixteen in the twelfth year of Shōwa (1937), the Second Sino-Japanese War broke out. Before then, China and Japan fought in small, localized engagements called "incidents," but the two countries, for a variety of reasons, had refrained from fighting an all-out war. The 1937 Lugouqiao Incident is historically regarded as the opening of Japan's comprehensive invasion of Mainland China.

Militarism became increasingly stronger each day in Japan. When Kiyoshi graduated from middle school at age seventeen, he had to give up his dream of studying at Yokohama Kō-Shō despite his admission to the school. Presumably, the time was not right for going to college to study business.

My father used to tell my siblings and me to study hard by saying,

"Because of the war, I couldn't go to college, but I would have loved to. You are lucky because you can go to college if you want to. So, study as hard as possible when you can."

He was very enthusiastic about our education, which I mischievously took advantage of when I needed pocket money. I would say to him,

"I want to buy books."

This strategy was extremely effective.

In actuality, however, the primary reason why my father could not go to Yokohama Kō-Shō was not the war. There were a number of students who attended the school even during the war, so he, too, could have attended.

Having applied to the school and been accepted, he was supposed to enroll in the school. But it was turned upside down at the last minute.

In April 1938, right after Kiyoshi graduated from middle school, he was supposed to go on to Yokohama Kō-Shō. In the same month, there was a death in the family—Kisuke, the Founder, passed away.

When Kiyoshi was struggling with his decision about school, his great-grandfather had already been ill in bed. If Kisuke had been well, he would have backed up his great-grandson's desire to continue his studies. In other words, Kiyoshi was unable to go to college because he had little to no support from anyone. His stepmother, in particular, was strongly against his going to college and told him to give up, saying,

"Do you really want to go to school during the war? What would people say about us?"

His father, Kiichi, was unable to stand up for Kiyoshi in the presence of his wife (Kiyoshi's stepmother) and other children. Or, maybe, Kiichi, himself, was questioning why a merchant's son should become so educated, privately expecting his eldest son to start working for his business and eventually taking over.

In any case, it was all over for Kiyoshi since no one in his family supported his decision to go on to school. And yet, he simply could not go to work in his father's business and become a cotton merchant. Clearly, he had no genuine desire to do so. The reality is, however, that he was born into a merchant's family.

Despite his yearning to leave home and become involved in international trading, Kiyoshi gave up his dream due to socio-political and family circumstances. Rather than working for his father, he found employment with a textile company in Nihonbashi, Tokyo. This was a compromise made between him and his father.

It is unfortunate that his era and family did not have the capacity to allow him to pursue his dreams. When children try to break out of the tradition that their parents and ancestors have long followed, they will inevitably experience friction. A great deal of understanding and tolerance is required for parents to allow their children to freely choose their own path. Such tolerance was not to be afforded Kiyoshi.

Kiyoshi began working as a salaried worker while still questioning his life's path. In the meantime, Japan was plunging deeper into war.

All men at age twenty were required to take a physical examination for conscription. In 1941, when Kiyoshi turned twenty years old, he did so too. He passed the exam with a "Grade A" evaluation.

Kiichi gave his son Kiyoshi a military saber made out of a traditional samurai sword. Nobody had seen such a magnificent saber, Kiyoshi thought. Rather reserved, his father expressed his affection for his son in that manner. Kiyoshi left home with much appreciation for his father's silent encouragement.

On December 10, 1941, which was by coincidence the twentieth anniversary of his mother Toku's passing, Kiyoshi was drafted into the army and joined the seventeenth corps of the Eastern region army as a soldier on active service.

On December 23rd, he left Tokyo to be shipped out of the country to serve at the war front in China. He then departed the Port of Hiroshima for the Hebei province in China via Pusan in Korea. Hebei 河北, as its name—河 [big river] + 北 [north]—suggests, is located north of the Yellow River and holds the Cities of Beijing and Tianjin.

On January 1, 1942, Kiyoshi passed the fortress of Shanhaiguan at the eastern end of the Great Walls and finally reached Qinhuangdao in the Hebei province.

In April of the same year, Kiyoshi was transferred to the twenty-seventh regiment of the transport corps. At the same time, he was selected to be a military cadet. He was then soon promoted to a Grade-A military cadet, and in May 1942, he began his training at the Military Preparatory School in Baoding in the Hebei province.

My father, Kiyoshi,
as a young army officer (1942)

Japanese military preparatory schools were established at various locations starting in 1939. Students were selected from the Grade-A military cadets who were graduates of middle school or above and were evaluated as fit to be military officers. They were then trained to become junior officers so that there would be more of them in the first reserve.

The establishment of those military prep schools was triggered by the expansion of the war, which had resulted in a shortage of junior officers, who were lost at the highest death rate. It thus became necessary for the Japanese militarist government to drastically increase their number. There had also existed regular military academies that produced army officers on active service, but there were limits on how many they could produce. Therefore, more military prep schools became necessary and were established at various locations.

After completing his six-month military training in Baoding, in late October 1942, Kiyoshi graduated from the school and was promoted to the rank of Sergeant Major. He was soon transferred to the army on active service, and on December 1, 1943, he was appointed a Second Lieutenant.

Evaluated as "Grade A" at the physical exam for conscription, Kiyoshi was tall and healthy. He was also quite handsome even with his head shaved. Even so, he had two "flaws."

One was that he had sloping shoulders. Because of that, the shoulder pads of his uniform jacket had to be doubled. A military officer with sloping shoulders might not look sufficiently masculine.

The other flaw was that he had flat feet, a more serious problem than having sloping shoulders. Presumably, as a result of his flat feet, he was assigned to a transport corps, which allowed the soldiers to ride horses.

Transport corps transported weapons, fuels, food, etc. to combat troops. They worked behind the scenes and dealt with logistics.

In modern days, this is a corps that is regarded as absolutely vital, but back then during wartime, people used to look down on transport corps as they did not directly participate in combat. In retrospect, however, some critics today regard such shallow-mindedness as a cause of the Japanese army's defeat. (I would say that true shallow-mindedness is found in the act of starting a war itself.)

My father never looked at his assignment to the transport corps as something to be ashamed of. He was rather grateful for the assignment (as well as for his flat feet) because he was able to ride a horse, which helped him survive the war.

I heard that Dad had received horseback-riding lessons even before joining the army. I wonder if he knew that his flat feet would become an obstacle in the army, or if he had a dream of joining a cavalry division. (By the time he joined the army, however, the cavalry corps had already been diminished, being absorbed into tank and infantry corps and becoming armored corps.)

How do I know this much about his "flaws"? Well, I heard the episode about his sloping shoulders when my dad took me to a tailor to order my junior-high-school uniform. The tailor took my measurements and wrote down, "Note: sloping shoulders—extreme."

Looking at the tailor's note, Dad said, "Just like me . . ." and he told me about his military uniform.

Not only that, I was also born with flat feet. My father and I used to gauge whose feet were flatter.

"Your flat feet are pretty bad too," said Dad, looking innocently happy.

As a child, I had no idea why he would be so happy about his daughter's flat feet and other traits that resembled his.

Army Buddy

My father had a friend who was drafted into the army in the same year and became his classmate at the military prep school in Baoding. His name was Yuji Yoshimura. He was quite a unique person.

As his given name Yuji [酉二]—酉 [Rooster] + 二 [two]—indicates, he was a second son born in the Year of the Rooster, the same year as my father—in the tenth year of Taishō (1921). In addition, Mr. Yoshimura was born only two weeks after my dad—on February 27th.

The two were close friends as well as friendly rivals.

"Yoshimura was the second from the bottom, and I was the second from the top," boasted Dad, talking about a chemistry exam. (He was good at chemistry.)

Whenever my father reminisced about the army-school experience, he spoke of Mr. Yoshimura as if he were his younger brother. He brought up his buddy so often that I felt quite attached to Mr. Yoshimura as though he were indeed my uncle.

Before I was born, I was so active in my mother's womb kicking and moving all the time that my parents came to believe that they would be having a boy—their second son. My dad soon came up with the idea of naming me Yuji. This name was obviously chosen in honor of Mr. Yoshimura. I don't know, however, which Chinese characters Dad was thinking of using.

Then, I was born. To my parents' surprise, I was a girl. (Today, of course, people can easily find out the baby's sex before birth. In those days, however, folks used to have a perhaps more thrilling experience because of the greater potential for such surprises.)

After this unexpected turn of events, my mother came up with an alternative, Tomoko, which was the name of her favorite schoolteacher. The Chinese characters 朋子 were chosen by my father—the 朋 of 朋子 is that of the word 朋友 meaning "friends studying together or comrades." He was again thinking about his army buddy.

Mr. Yoshimura was born as the second son to his family, but his elder brother died in childhood. Consequently, he was brought up as the heir to his family. His father being a renowned garden designer and *bonsai* artist, Mr. Yoshimura began receiving training in the art of bonsai when he was still a young child.

A few years after graduating from the Tokyo Horticulture School, a middle school, Mr. Yoshimura was drafted at age twenty, just like my father. The Yoshimura family also came from a samurai lineage.

After the war, Mr. Yoshimura resumed his activities as a bonsai artist. In 1953, he was invited by the Brooklyn Botanic Garden to give lectures. He extended his teaching and lecturing beyond the East Coast to the West Coast and Hawaii. In 1962, he returned to New York to root himself there to teach the art of bonsai for the rest of his life.

His talent blossomed, and he eventually became internationally known as one of the most respected bonsai artists in the world. He also authored a number of books and articles.

My father admired his buddy's courage to move to America despite his status as the heir to his family. It's also possible that Dad felt envious of his friend and might have even thought, *I've lost to my former rival.*

Decades later, in 1970, as a college student, my brother, Hiromi, traveled around the world. While in the States, he stayed for a short period of time with Mr. Yoshimura in Terrytown in New York.

Fifteen years later, in 1985, accompanying my brother and mother, I had the very first chance to meet and visit with Mr. Yoshimura, who lived in Briarcliff Manor in New York at the time. Hiromi was so happy to see him again that he was moved to tears. We enjoyed chatting with Mr. Yoshimura, who was so upbeat and cheerful. We indulged ourselves in his stories about the good old days.

At one point, Mr. Yoshimura laughed and said to me,

"Tomoko, you remind me so much of your father. The way you've just teased your brother is so reminiscent of your dad when he was young."

Although we had met for only the first time, Mr. Yoshimura talked to me with great affection as if I were his niece. I also felt good about being told by someone who had known my father in his youth that I resembled him.

Mr. Yoshimura appeared to have become so American that I simply could not believe he had once been in the Japanese army. He really looked cool, casually dressed in an old flannel shirt and jeans and wearing white sneakers. His house and its atmosphere also suggested he had become fully American.

When my mother, brother, and I had to leave, we said goodbye with great reluctance. Mr. Yoshimura also looked as if he were missing us already.

More than ten years later, in 1998, I happened to find out about Mr. Yoshimura's passing as I read *The New York Times.* I was shocked and saddened as though I had lost my real uncle.

He was seventy-six years old. The photo of Mr. Yoshimura in a kimono published with the obituary was quite striking—in the photo he looked truly like a samurai. He looked more Japanese than any Japanese living in Japan. Considering the fact that he had taught the beauty of Japanese culture through the art of bonsai in the United States, I reaffirmed that he was and had always been Japanese as much as, or more than, the Japanese living in Japan.

What a unique and fascinating person Mr. Yoshimura was! I think I know why he and my father got along well. He was a perfect friend for Dad.

The Battlefield

My father spent more than four years on the battlefield in China between ages twenty and twenty-five excluding a short period he spent in Japan as a chemistry student. In China, he witnessed a great deal of misery and brutality.

He once told me how cruel Japanese soldiers had been to the locals.

"Japanese are so evil."

This was his honest opinion.

And yet, he confessed to me: he once cut a civilian's bicycle tire on the street to see how sharp his saber was. He felt so guilty afterwards that he found the owner of the bicycle and paid for the repair without letting the other officers find out about it.

My father didn't consider himself an angel or without blame, but his slashing a tire was innocent compared to the atrocities that he saw others commit. And, he never forgot his sense of guilt.

Dad also told me another enthralling episode.

One high-ranking officer said to a large group of troops,

"Do we have a volunteer who's courageous enough to sing a folk song in front of everyone here?"

"Yes, I will sing!"

My father as a young soldier raised his hand immediately and without thinking. All the high-ranking officers were staring at him and hundreds of soldiers were standing straight as if they were not even breathing.

"I volunteered just like that, but I soon got so nervous that I felt my insides freeze up," Dad described his experience and laughed.

Now that he had already raised his hand, he could not retreat. He soon made up his mind and started singing a variation of the "*Hakutō-san* [White-head Mountain]" song.

> "On the mountain of Hakutō
> Snow has fallen thick.
> Crossing the Sea of Genkai
> Here I come
> To melt the snow.
>
> Don't cry for me.
> I promise to come home . . ."

In the middle of the song, the high-ranking officer who had requested a song grimaced. The lyrics began to imply a longing for home. Although the singer noticed the officer's reaction, he continued to sing.

Soon the officer smiled and looked at him as if he were saying,

"You clever so-and-so . . ."

My father explained,

"I changed the lyrics to say, '[I promise to come home] in a small wooden box wrapped with brocade,' meaning that the best way to return to Japan is to be sent home dead after devoting your life to your country."

This part of the story didn't make much sense to me as a child born in a peaceful era.

"I think it would be much better to come home alive," I objected to Dad, who in turn agreed with me.

"We were all brainwashed at that time and believed dying for our country was the greatest virtue," he admitted quite easily.

My father, Kiyoshi, as a young army officer
visiting home as a chemistry student during WWII (1944)

My father also used to talk about contracting malaria on the battlefield. At one point, he told me, he didn't think he would survive after becoming so weak and emaciated. He hovered between life and death.

Each time I heard this story, I asked the same question,

"Does that mean we wouldn't have been born if you had died there?"

Luckily, riding a horse, because of his assignment to the transport corps (again, perhaps due to his flat feet), my father was able to advance with the rest of the troops despite his compromised physical condition.

He became, however, increasingly weaker and eventually too frail even to ride a horse. Then, one of his subordinates caught a snapping turtle and gave my father its blood.

"He cut the head off the turtle, squeezed its blood out, and let me drink it. And the live blood immediately made me feel stronger." It was quite a graphic description.

Thanks to this snapping turtle, it was made possible for my siblings and me to be born into this world as Dad's children.

My father survived the malaria. Not only that, as he often boasted,

"I survived the battlefields, passing under the rain of bullets."

His conclusion was that there was nothing to be fearful of after having so many life-or-death experiences on the battlefield.

I once received a letter from my father that described his wartime experience in more detail. As I read it again, I realized that he had truly felt helpless coming face to face with death.

Excerpts from my father's letter dated August 14, 1977

To reminisce about the past again . . . I remember, it was in April 1944. After spending 3 months at the Narashino Chemistry School on the homeland, I was ordered to go back to the battlefield.

I left alone for China and tried to catch up with my corps. After two weeks of pursuit, I had finally arrived at the point where my group was stationed.

The day after finally reaching my corps, we went down south as a combat corps. Two months had already passed since I left Japan. Due to the stress of pursuing my corps all alone, I was exhausted even though I was young. Then the corps was reorganized and went into combat. Not being able to rest even for a moment, I came down with malaria when we reached Changsha in Middle China. With a fever higher than 40°C [104°F],[3] my liver gave up and I vomited everything when I tried to eat. All I could take was water and tea for three weeks. I became emaciated rapidly and so badly that I began to think I might not make it.

My corps continued to advance in combat, never allowing me to rest or sleep. I continued to suffer from the high fever caused by the malaria while still clinging onto the back of my horse. In my dreams, came and went the images of my great-grandfather, grandmother, father, and my mother (whom I never knew)[4] as I suffered from the high fever. After two months of fighting the illness, I survived. I remember it as if it were only yesterday.

From this letter it was confirmed that my father had always carried his loved ones in his heart—Grandpa Baldy (Kisuke), Father (Kiichi), Grandma (Sui), and Mother (Toku) whom he never knew.

Kiichi, the Third Generation

Life on the battlefield was intense. And yet, for Kiyoshi, his real battle was not on the battleground, but rather at home.

Kiyoshi was promoted to the rank of Second Lieutenant in December 1943, and in January 1944, as touched upon in the aforementioned letter, he was sent back to Japan to receive training as a chemistry student at the Narashino Chemistry School in Japan.

During the two months and a half of training, Kiyoshi was allowed to visit his family once. So, he went, but the only person who welcomed him was Grandma Sui.

"Grandma, where is Father?"

Sui was at a loss for an answer.

---

[3]   Information in square brackets [ ] that appears in excerpts of a letter is provided by the author. […] indicates that one or more sentences or paragraphs are omitted from the original.

[4]   Information in parentheses ( ) is original—provided by the writer of the letter.

This was how Kiyoshi learned of his father's death. About a year prior to that, in April 1943, Kiichi had died of an illness at age forty-two.

My grandfather Kiichi
(Drawing—production year unknown)

Sadly, another one died very young in the family. Just to count only the heads of the family, everyone except for Kisuke (the First Generation) died when they were in their forties—i.e., Kisaburō (Kisuke's father), Yōzaburō (the Second Generation), and Kiichi (the Third Generation). That's three out of the four generations!

The average life expectancy in the Meiji and Taishō eras is said to have been about forty, so some might argue that dying in their forties was normal in those days. At the same time, however, the life expectancy was lowered during that period by infant deaths and mothers' deaths due to childbirth accidents. If so, dying in one's forties still seems rather young and quite unfortunate.

There was a dark and vexing episode surrounding Kiichi's death. Upon hearing about it, Kiyoshi was flabbergasted.

The relationship between Kiichi's wife (Kiyoshi's stepmother) and the family doctor taking care of Kiichi was the talk of the town—they were having an affair. And several months after Kiichi's death, his widow (Kiyoshi's stepmother) gave birth to a baby boy.

That is, in addition to his father's death, Kiyoshi found out that he now had a baby brother. And everybody knew it was not Kiichi's son. The stepmother became pregnant when Kiichi was gravely ill and dying. The baby born to his stepmother was not related to Kiyoshi by blood.

Indisputably, the baby was not a Takahashi. Nevertheless, Kiyoshi's grandmother Sui (Kiichi's mother) said to the family,

"The child is innocent."

She allowed the baby to be recognized as a member of the Takahashi family and his name to be entered in the family register.

"At age twenty I left home for Manchuria. When I visited home during the war, I found out my father had died long ago and everything at home was a big mess," said Dad decades later, describing the family situation at that time.

As described in the aforementioned letter, my father went back to join his regiment in China in April 1944. Just imagine how he must have felt while traveling back to the battlefield with the knowledge that his father had died and after saying goodbye to his aged grandmother. The suffering from the battle in his head must have rivaled his struggles on the battlefield.

My father described his experience from around that time in another letter he wrote to me.

Excerpts from my father's letter dated April 10, 1977

Allow me to talk about the wartime again. April 8 was the day, and it was 33 years ago (in 1944), when I was ordered to go back to China to join my army corps after completing the training

*at the army chemistry school (that taught us about poison gas),
and I left for Manchuria alone. On April 13, I finally reached
Jinzhou, where my corps had been stationed. But it turned out that
it had already departed. I again pursued the troops down south and
finally caught up with them on April 21. On the following day
(April 22) I departed with my corps. I had never imagined, and
no one could ever imagine, that this would only be the beginning of
a long battle that would last until I was finally discharged from the
army and returned home after the end of the war.*

*Pondering upon this and that of what happened during that
time, I really appreciate how peaceful today's Japan is.*

My father left Tokyo by himself, departed from the Port of
Hakata, and headed for Manchuria. What was on his mind when he
crossed the rough waves of the Genkai Sea? He never mentioned
anything about the death of his father in this letter, but the expression
"pondering upon this and that" seems to imply a great deal.

Then, he caught malaria right after he reached his corps to
linger on the verge of death. And, the war situation worsened.

The battles against his own mind and emotion, and against the
malaria... In the midst of all the struggles and pains, he had participated
in a series of combat missions from April 1944 until July 1945.

Defeat

My father used to say,

"I entered Manchuria, and then went down from Northern
China all the way to Southern China."

His footprints on the battlefield were from the fortress of
Shanhaiguan located at the end of the Great Wall to down south.

In August 1945, he saw the end of the war in Jiujiang along the
coast of the Yangtze River in the Jiangxi province.

"I threw my saber into the Yangtze River," Dad told me.

He was probably so fed up with the war that he threw the blade
away. Or, he might have thought he would be taken prisoner and his
sword would be confiscated now that Japan had lost the war.

And yet, it was the sword given by his father, Kiichi. It had been a treasured keepsake. It took a great deal of courage to give it up. Maybe, my father threw away his past along with the sword in order to become a new person.

Right after the end of the war, Kiyoshi was promoted to the rank of First Lieutenant. And he continued to serve in the army in the provinces of Jiangxi and Jiangsu for more than half a year.

At his home in Japan, on the other hand, the family had no idea what had happened to Kiyoshi. Grandma Sui believed that he had been killed in the war since she had heard nothing from him for a long time. She, of course, wanted him to be alive, but she couldn't help thinking the worst because there was no news from him and also she heard that Japan had been defeated.

Ahhh . . . Kiyoshi must have been killed in Manchuria . . . Sui had lost her hope and energy to live. If Kiyoshi had been alive and discharged from the army, he should have come home long ago. Sad autumn winds started blowing. The cold winter weather arrived. And, spring was just around the corner. Still, no Kiyoshi . . .

On March 26, 1946, Kiyoshi left the Port of Shanghai and headed home. On March 30th he arrived at the Port of Hakata and was discharged from the army there. Fortunately, he didn't have to return home "in a small box covered with brocade."

Eight months had passed since the end of the war, and finally, one day in April 1946, Kiyoshi, who was believed to be dead, came home unexpectedly.

"First Lieutenant Takahashi here."

Kiyoshi gave a military salute. At the sight of him, his grandmother Sui stood there with a look of utter amazement. Then, as she realized it was really her grandson, she broke down in tears.

"Kiyoshi . . ."

She tried to call his name barely straining her voice.

Recall that it was her husband, Yōzaburō, who had returned home with serious mental problems from which he never recovered after the Russo-Japanese War. Considering that, she felt it was simply a miracle that her grandson arrived home both mentally and physically sound.

Through her teary eyes, Sui saw a bright aura around Kiyoshi, who looked stronger than ever. She still could not believe her eyes; she was dazzled by Kiyoshi's big smile. She wiped at her tears again and again. She was then finally able to regain herself to realize it was not a dream.

Kiyoshi, too, was overjoyed to find out his grandmother was well, and he gave thanks from the bottom of his heart. His great-grandfather Kisuke had been deceased for several years already, and his father, Kiichi, had died three years before. The only other surviving family members were his stepmother and her children. So, Sui was the only ally Kiyoshi had. And, Grandma Sui was alive and well!

It was the same for Sui—her only hope was Kiyoshi. Just imagine her joy when he came home unexpectedly, especially after losing her own son Kiichi to an illness and while believing her grandson Kiyoshi had been killed in action.

Here is another letter from Dad:

Excerpts from my father's letter dated April 9, 1978

April 8, 1944—it was [34 years ago] yesterday, and I couldn't help reminiscing about the war again. After graduating from the military chemistry school, I left Tokyo Station to rejoin my corps in China—on a slow train, alone, carrying a single military wicker suitcase. The tide of the war was turning against Japan, so I thought I might not make it home again this time. I prepared myself for the worst. Like this spring, it seemed the flowering of cherry blossoms started later than usual that year. I can still picture those cherry flowers in full bloom as well as the white sashes worn by the women of the National Defense League that I saw as I passed through Shizuoka Station.

After a while, the war ended, and my wishes were granted. I came home in 1946. That was also in April.

45

My father's youth began and ended with the war. Although war is evil, soldiers who fought together became bonded with strong friendships. Another letter I received from my father while in college described the army reunion he had attended.

Excerpts from my father's letter dated October 12, 1975

> *I'm writing this letter, thinking about the most enjoyable comrade reunion I attended yesterday. I was seated next to the [former] company captain—it was, of course, the seat of honor. We all went back 30 years. I was even called "Mr. First Lieutenant" in an old-fashioned way. We had a ball, singing military songs together as if we were 23 or 24 years old again. But the company captain is now 68 years old. Other fellow comrades had lost a lot of hair or had gray hair. I could see the history of the past 30 years on each one's head and face. There were some fellows I had trouble recognizing—I questioned in my mind, "Is this that fellow who was always so vigorous?!" As for me, I'm very happy and grateful that everyone was commenting on my appearance: "You are so youthful. You are so young looking." I'm truly thankful. I guess I'm young because I'm so active.*

My father was fifty-four years old at that time. I wonder what he was really thinking at the reunion, looking back on those thirty-plus years after the war. Beneath the enjoyable atmosphere of the reunion, there were, I'm sure, great depths of pain, grief, and countless other emotions. He and his comrades had experienced such turmoil, continuous violence, and eventually defeat, which must have resulted in a disruption to their value system. Their statuses as military officers also came to mean little.

Who could have imagined the many consequences of the war to which they all had devoted their days as young men? What the war had cost them was simply immeasurable.

My father, however, neither begrudged nor complained about the past. He had no time to spare. Rather, he advanced forward, wishing to become happy. He lived a full life with strong resolve and all his might. Instead of looking back, he focused on the future, seeking an answer to the question: "How shall I open the next chapter of my life?"

Just like his great-grandfather Kisuke, who had lived through his own turmoil, my father chose to live positively.

3. Home, Sweet Home

Arranged Marriage

After the war, my father went to work for a textile company in Tokyo that dealt with silk and fabrics. It was the same company (or its affiliate) that he had worked for after graduating from middle school and before going to the war.

My father, Kiyoshi, as a "*salary man* [salaried worker]"

Dad used to tell us that he was a proud graduate of "Horidome University"—Horidome is the name of the business district where he worked. His returning to this business district of Nihonbashi in Tokyo apparently meant that he had his heart set on learning business outside his hometown.

His great-grandfather Kisuke learned the business trade in the Kawagoe town nicknamed "*Ko-Edo* [Little Tokyo]." Likewise, my father learned the ins and outs of business in Nihonbashi in "*Ō-Edo* [Big Tokyo]."

Kisuke transitioned from a samurai to a merchant during the Meiji Revolution. Likewise, my father transitioned from an army officer to a businessman. Mystically, each of them made this transition and fresh start after losing his father in the midst of the turmoil—i.e., the Meiji Revolution and World War II, respectively.

There were, however, other reasons why my father had to go to work in Tokyo now that he was the head of the household with his father deceased. Why did he leave the cotton store to be run by employees rather than running it himself? It's true he never wanted to take over the store, but that was not the reason. It's likely that the business at the store was suffering because goods of every description were in short supply right after the war.

In other words, my father's salary from the Tokyo company was supporting his entire family. This is again reminiscent of Kisuke, who had supported his family by working as an apprentice in Kawagoe.

And yet, my father was the owner of the store, so he oversaw the family business while working in Tokyo. That is, he had two full-time jobs. That must have required superhuman effort and strength.

There are some photos of my father as a young man working in Tokyo. He was quite stylish and handsome, with the looks of a movie star. Who would have guessed from his appearance that he was commuting to Tokyo from a remote countryside in Saitama?

In those days, transportation systems were so inefficient that it easily took two hours to travel just one-way from home to his office in Tokyo. My father rode a bicycle for about two and a half miles from home to Ageo, left his bike at his friend's house, walked to the train station, took a Takasaki-Line train to Ueno, and then headed for Nihonbashi on another train. It's simply mind-boggling, but he loved Tokyo, and he continued commuting to Nihonbashi.

49

Because his company dealt with silk, Dad had contacts with the US Occupation Army's PX. I heard he used to bring home a lot of Hershey chocolate bars. Contacts with the US Occupation Army must have revived his dream and longing for trading and for America.

My father, Kiyoshi, as a young man

One day, his neighbors set up an *omiai* [a meeting for an arranged marriage] for Kiyoshi. At the meeting, he was introduced to a young woman from a wealthy farming family in the Shima village. Her name was Sachiko.

This was Sachiko's first *omiai* . . . and to be her last. Kiyoshi's too. Prior to this, Sachiko had turned down several invitations to arranged meetings. But when she saw Kiyoshi's photo, her eyes were riveted—she had to meet the man.

The arranged meeting took place the day after Kiyoshi had participated in his company's athletic meet, and his face was so sunburned that his skin looked pretty dark. Sachiko, on the other hand, made a sharp contrast with Kiyoshi, as her skin was so fair that people would have wondered if she had ever been under the sun.

Sachiko politely sat there without saying a word. Kiyoshi hit it off with her father, Shinsaku, and they were enjoying their conversation. Shinsaku's clean baldhead and big earlobes were quite striking. His warm round face with countless laugh lines was reminiscent of Daikoku, the god of farmers.

Sachiko's mother, Tema, was petite and looked fragile, with her beautiful black hair set up impeccably. Her slender face also had wrinkles from smiling and laughing. She looked elegant and was full of motherly gentleness.

Simple and honest, Sachiko's parents seemed to be a couple of lovebirds.

I wish I had parents like them, Kiyoshi thought.

Then, servers brought his favorite—ice-cold beer. He was so thirsty that he finished off his drink in one gulp. Then, surprisingly, the matchmakers proposed a toast as though they were celebrating the couple's engagement.

Drinking alcohol at such a meeting actually meant acceptance of the arranged marriage. My father, Kiyoshi, only learned this after the fact. It's almost laughable.

Reminiscing about it, Dad said,

"Without knowing it, I finished off the beer. And then I saw Mr. and Mrs. Kataoka, the matchmakers, smiling. I couldn't believe it!"

My mother, Sachiko, then added,

"And, I didn't even know what your father looked like. All I saw were his big eyes on his tanned face."

We all laughed.

"Matsutomi" was the name of the horse my father had ridden in the army during the war. My mother learned this name on the first date with Dad after they got engaged. I happened to find this out in 2005.

My brother sent me an e-mail after visiting Mom, who was in the hospital after having a mild stroke.

51

Excerpts from Hiromi's E-mail dated August 20, 2005

"What's Dad's horse's name?" → "Matsutomi"
I have confirmed Mom's memory is going strong. She heard
the story about Matsutomi on her first date with Dad!

If it was a story heard on her first date, that means she had remembered it for nearly sixty years. She never forgot it! How sweet! How romantic!

When I was in elementary school, I learned that there were two types of marriage—arranged marriages and love marriages. I asked my father,

"Dad, did you and Mom marry by arrangement or for love?"

"It was arranged, but we are now in love," he answered.

What a cool answer! My parents' marriage was arranged, but they really liked each other from the beginning.

My parents on their honeymoon in Atami (1947)

On their first date, Mom listened to Dad's stories while her heart fluttered with excitement. Dad always described Mom as "an eternal eighteen-year-old schoolgirl." Having remembered the name of the horse Dad had ridden in the army, Mom has indeed remained an eighteen-year-old at heart . . . still today. When they went on their honeymoon to Atami, Mom tried to catch up with Dad, who walked fast. The romantic love for Dad she developed from that point will never change. I'm sure of it. Mom is so lucky to have met and married such a wonderful man, and he was equally fortunate.

Sachiko, the Cinderella

In November 1947, Sachiko married into the Takahashi family. Her life drastically changed. Just imagine—a well-educated young woman from a nice family raised comfortably by her loving parents to marry into a family with her husband's stepmother and stepsiblings. It was like falling from heaven to hell on earth.

The young bride, Sachiko, worked hard for the business owned by the family, believing that it was her duty as Kiyoshi's wife. Until then, she had never even touched cotton or *futon* materials. A young woman brought up with tender care, she now had to help manufacture futon bedding and take care of her husband's stepmother and stepsiblings. She was forced to work like a slave.

The stepmother and her children enjoyed their comfortable lives, eating and resting whenever they wanted to. Sachiko, on the other hand, was bullied by them and treated like their disrespected servant, just like Cinderella. And yet, she endured the pain.

Each day seemed endless until her husband came home. The only ally she had during the day was Grandma Sui. But being an old woman, Sui was also treated like a second-class citizen in this peculiar household.

A few months later, Sachiko noticed a change in her physical condition. She was pregnant but was still treated as badly as ever by the stepmother and her children.

"One day, they boiled lots of corn in a huge pot. But Grandma Sui and I were given only this much," said my mother, indicating with her thumb how small the piece of corn she was given.

"Stepmother and her kids ate the ears of corn to their hearts' content. Then, they took a nap on the veranda . . ."

Mom looked vexed while talking about the adversities she had experienced back then.

Sachiko's mother, Tema, often brought a whole chicken cooked in sweet and spicy sauce in order to provide her pregnant daughter with good nutrition. Unfortunately, however, Sachiko's in-laws finished it in a moment without letting her have a single bite. She was not even allowed to taste her own mother's home cooking. Yet, she continued to help manufacture futon bedding despite her pregnancy.

The Takahashi Cotton Store at the time was manufacturing mosquito nets too. Electric sewing machines were unavailable in those days, so Sachiko used a foot-operated machine, which was heavy and hard on her feet. Sweating away, she continued to sew the nets.

The monstrous rough materials tormented her and stained her sweaty hands green. She felt like crying from the pain resulting from her feet stepping repeatedly on the sewing machine. Oh, how much she wished she could go home to her loving parents . . .

Actually, Sachiko escaped to her parents' home once when she could not bear it any longer. She left for her hometown late at night on a bicycle. Being very pregnant, she pedaled rapidly but awkwardly. She was almost there . . .

When she reached a Tōhoku Line railroad crossing, the gate came down right in front of her. It was pitch dark. As she hurried to go underneath the gate to cross the railroad, a train came dashing toward her. She came close to being run over.

She almost fainted with fear.

What a horrible thing I've done . . . I almost got my unborn baby killed . . .

Sachiko was so sorry that she felt shattered. Her life was not just her own any longer. If she had died there, her baby wouldn't have been born into this world . . .

The next day, Sachiko was brought back home by her father—to the house full of her in-laws. She resumed her hellish life there.

Despite such hardships, Sachiko never complained. Every day she sent her husband off to work with a smile. Kiyoshi knew, however, what might be happening at home while he was away at work, so he rushed home every evening, terribly worried about his young wife.

My father once told me that he had fallen off his bicycle on a dark street on his way home from Ageo Station because he was in such a hurry. He hit his face, but fortunately it didn't turn out to be a serious accident.

According to Dad, his cheekbone was slightly caved in. He used to say, "Before that accident, I was a lot better looking."

In November 1948, Sachiko gave birth to a baby boy. The baby was quite healthy despite all the bullying his mother had experienced from the stepmother and her children. Having become a father, Kiyoshi was so elated that he felt like running around the entire town telling people about his newborn son. He now had a new family member of his own. His real family . . .

The baby was named "Hiromi [寛美]."

The Takahashi family had a tradition in which male successors were all given a name starting with the character 喜 [ki] meaning "joy"—the Founder's father was "Kisaburō [喜三郎]," the Founder "Kisuke [喜助]," the Third Generation "Kiichi [喜一]," and the Fourth Generation "Kiyoshi [喜儀]." The Fifth Generation could have also been given a name bearing the same character.

Why did Kiyoshi not give his son a name following that tradition? It's because he thought: *Despite the happy name, the Takahashi family has never been filled with joy. To hell with the family tradition!*

Boldly, he gave his son an entirely different type of name.

Kiyoshi was broad-minded enough not to be bound by traditions and customs. He took it to heart that people's happiness was far more important than traditions, customs, formalities, and superficial appearances.

Mom and my brother, Hiromi (1949)

As my father watched Hiromi grow up to be the brightest child in the entire town, or so I heard, he was preparing himself for the possibility that his son might not succeed him in the family business. Rather than being swayed by traditions, Dad was ready to see it closed down if it was for the sake of his son's happiness.

My father obviously felt it unbearable to see Hiromi go through the same pain he himself had experienced from not being able to pursue his dreams as a young man. Because he had suffered so much himself, Dad had developed absolute generosity and a warm heart, with which he embraced not only his family but also people around him.

Evidently, the character he chose for his son's name, the 寛 [read "hiro"] of 寛大 meaning "tolerance," was a symbol of Dad's life philosophy to be "tolerant" and "broad-minded."

Incidentally, it was rather rare to give a boy a name ending with the character 美 [read "mi" and meaning "beauty"] at that time. It was only a few years after the war, so boys' names often ended with masculine-sounding characters such as 雄 [read "o" and meaning "courageous"] and 男 [read "o" and meaning "man"]. And yet, my father dared to choose the character for "beauty," wanting his son to grow up to love peace and beauty.

A few days before Hiromi's birth, Japan celebrated Culture Day for the first time. Dad might have gotten an idea from that special holiday, which was celebrated on November 3rd. On the same day in 1946, the Constitution of Japan was promulgated. Since the Japanese Constitution focused on "peace and culture," November 3rd came to be celebrated as Culture Day starting in 1948.

Dad must have heard the words "peace and culture" as he anxiously waited for his son's birth. And he chose the character meaning "beauty" to express "peace and culture."

I can picture him spending hours thinking about his son's name, and then calligraphing it with a brush and ink. (Compared to this, however, it seems, my sister and I were given names that were decided rather easily. I guess the firstborn always gets more attention.)

Hiromi, unfortunately, didn't like his name because it sounded like a girl's name, but that was only until he entered junior high school. One day, he found out how his name had been chosen and learned about Dad's wishes. Hiromi then came to appreciate and love his name.

Speaking of girls' names, the name "Hiromi" given to girls is typically pronounced without a pitched accent, and it sounds like "hi-roMI" while Dad called my brother's name more like "HIro-mi" with an accent on the first syllable.

Different meanings of Japanese homonyms are often distinguished by pitched accents—e.g., the homonym *ame* could be "*amé* [candy]" and "*áme* [rain]." It seems that Dad used this so-called "supersegmental" distinction to characterize his son's name as a boy's name. I can see how the emphasis on "Hiro" rather than "Romi" makes the name sound more masculine. This is such an intriguing idea from a linguistic point of view.

No Chasing After the One That Leaves

Kiyoshi's stepmother never stopped bullying Sachiko even after Hiromi was born. Actually, it got worse. The stepmother wasn't happy at all now that the heir (Kiyoshi) had his own successor.

Kiyoshi and Sachiko were convinced that it was not a good environment to raise a child and soon decided to give up everything and move to Tokyo. Kiyoshi had a job there. He had no regret giving up the family business in the first place.

When they were just about to move to Tokyo, Grandma Sui refused to go.

"Grandma said she wanted to die in Haraichi . . ."

Her refusal called a halt to Kiyoshi's plan to move to Tokyo.

Still, Kiyoshi felt it unbearable to live with his stepmother and her children. The family relationships at home were increasingly getting worse.

Then, to Kiyoshi's delight, his stepmother and her children decided to move out . . . but on the condition that they take all the monetary and material possessions with them.

"All we need is one *tatami* mat for each to sleep on!" said Kiyoshi. He was so calm as if he were saying, "please take everything with you."

He wasn't even left with a single mat.

"No chasing after the one that leaves!" said Kiyoshi.

He was happy to see the house emptied, and feeling refreshed, he appreciated his newly found freedom. It was 1950.

Kiyoshi's stepmother literally took everything—all the machines from the cotton factory, all the merchandise from the store, all the furniture and material and monetary possessions, and everything else she could find and take. All that was left was the land and the frames of the house, the ancestors' mortuary tablets, and personal belongings of Kiyoshi's family.

The medal Grandma Sui's husband, Yōzaburō had received from the Emperor was also taken away. All the memorabilia from Kiyoshi's father, Kiichi, and great-grandfather, Kisuke, were also taken away and lost. Kiyoshi reminded himself that what really mattered was the heart, not material possessions.

Since all the *tatami* mats [padded floor coverings] were taken away, Kiyoshi covered the bare floor with thin *mushiro* [straw] mats, which were rough and stingy. Baby Hiromi innocently played on the straw mats wearing a sweater knit by Sachiko that became covered with straw needles.

I can't believe I'm letting this happen to my son . . . Sachiko felt terrible seeing that even her baby son had to experience such a rough living.

Baby Hiromi had an innocent smile on his face. He gave abundant hope to Kiyoshi and Sachiko, who both said to themselves, "We'll bear it and make it better for Hiromi's sake."

They felt courage and energy welling up and challenged their testing days with hope.

Grandma Sui, on the other hand, was terribly worried after finding the house and store completely empty. Kiyoshi told her, "Grandma, don't worry about anything at all."

Even so, Sui was still vexed because everything was gone. There was nothing in the store to sell.

"How are we going to make a living?" She was at a loss.

Kiyoshi then came up with an idea after giving much thought to what to do to ease her worries. He went to a bank to have a portion of his salary from that month changed to coins and put them in a sturdy cloth bag. He gave the bag to Sui and said with a big smile, "Grandma, look! We've got a lot of money."

Relieved, Sui slept with the moneybag every night.

In order to make Sui truly at ease, Kiyoshi had to restore the family business. It might have been so much easier if they had moved to Tokyo, but Sui's wish "to die in Haraichi" made Kiyoshi decide to reestablish the family business. His challenge began.

Out of the Frying Pan and into the Fire

Things didn't go easily. Kiyoshi faced tremendous challenges, one after another. For instance, his stepmother tried to steal his real estate property by illegally transferring the title. After taking all the movable property with her, she then tried to take his real estate as well. Kiyoshi had inherited all the land as the eldest son according to the old civil law, which his stepmother despised.

His stepmother tried many tricks, but without success except that Kiyoshi had to give up the 2,000 square feet he had acquired as additional land to be used in the future.

She even refused to pay for electricity at the new location, just to make Kiyoshi have to pay for it; the bills were forwarded to him, and he continued to pay so that his stepmother and her children wouldn't have to go without power.

Sachiko simply could not understand how her husband could be so tolerant and generous. She even felt angry. His stepmother left them to please herself, and after abusing Kiyoshi's kindness and generosity, she would come back when things weren't going well and throw the problems at him. *What nerve!* Sachiko thought.

One day, Kiyoshi was summoned to court, accused of being "a delinquent son" by his stepmother. Not only that, his stepmother claimed he kicked her out of the house although she had voluntarily left and taken all the valuable property with her. Because she could not steal the real estate away from Kiyoshi, she now sued him so that she could get the land as well.

Sachiko was extremely concerned. Kiyoshi smiled and got on his scooter named Rabbit. He said,

"Don't worry."

And he left for the court in Ōmiya City.

Kiyoshi should have come to the court with an attorney, but he stood alone in front of the judge. He hadn't committed any crime, so he thought he didn't need a lawyer.

"You came without an attorney?

No wonder . . . As your mother claims, you really are a delinquent son." The judge began attacking Kiyoshi.

The plaintiff grinned and thought, *Hurray!* Her eyes behind the spectacles glittered.

Kiyoshi, composed and dignified (and more than a little clever), said to the judge,

"Your honor, I was appointed to the rank of First Lieutenant in the army by the Great Japanese Empire during the war. If the Empire had made a delinquent an army officer, then I think you should also accuse the Japanese Empire."

The judge turned pale and asked,

"Is that true? Do you have any proof that you were an army officer?"

"I have it at home," Kiyoshi replied. And he was told to bring it.

Kiyoshi rushed home to fetch the proof. Unfortunately, the letter of appointment for the First Lieutenant had been lost, but that for the Second Lieutenant had been well kept at home since Kiyoshi had brought it home when he attended the chemistry school during the war. Kiyoshi hurried back to the court with the letter.

Upon seeing the letter, the judge bowed deeply and said,

"I did not know you were an honorable army officer of the Great Japanese Empire. I apologize for my rudeness. A former army officer, you cannot possibly be a delinquent."

He then turned to Kiyoshi's stepmother and said,

"You must apologize to your son."

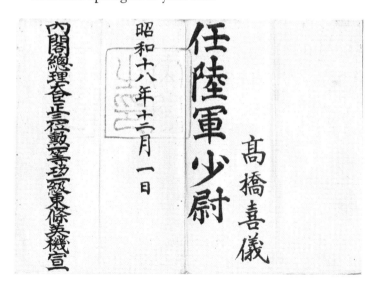

Letter of appointment to the rank of
Second Lieutenant (Dated December 1, 1943)

You may call it authoritarianism, but it was really the last resort my father had since the judge wouldn't even listen to him. Using the officer title from the war was effective. Such was the time.

Former army officers are normally quite reserved and they would not even talk about their army service history—especially responsible officers who felt they were the ones who had led the country to defeat.

My father never boasted about his army service history. In this one instance, he understandably had to resort to it to prove his innocence to the judge, who unjustly treated him as a criminal.

This is how my father was abused by his stepmother, for whom he had always cared. What unfortunate family circumstances he had grown up in! But he was never defeated. Rather he faced his own destiny, believing that not being defeated meant victory.

Rebuilding

Confronting all those obstacles, Kiyoshi and Sachiko devoted themselves to the rebuilding of the family business. It was literally a start from scratch. It was extremely challenging.

Kiyoshi also felt a bit sad saying goodbye to Nihonbashi, to which he had commuted for so many years, but he couldn't afford to be sentimental. He had to get the store ready with merchandise.

Fortunately, the wholesale dealers were helpful to Kiyoshi since they had dealt with his predecessors in the past. Moreover, because he had worked for a textile company in Nihonbashi, he was able to get sophisticated merchandise from Tokyo wholesalers.

Not only did he have excellent merchandise, Kiyoshi also focused on marketing by distributing handbills. This was a tradition he adopted from his great-grandfather Kisuke.

One day, Kiyoshi came up with the idea to decorate the delivery truck with flowers made out of tissue to turn it into a "flower automobile" with big store signs on both sides, and to drive it around the town periodically. It soon became one of the attractions of the town; children and adults would excitedly flock around the truck.

Kiyoshi's marketing led to big success. The store became exceedingly busy and even short-handed during sales. Sachiko was so skilled with her hands that no one made better futon bedding than she did. She was such a perfectionist that the impeccable futon mats she made were favored by all customers and sold like hotcakes. Kisuke's Mascot Brand cotton was revived too.

Big-hearted and forward-thinking, Kiyoshi served his customers well and for their benefit. The store was finally reestablished and was well under way. It also began hiring a number of employees.

Once Kiyoshi's business got going, his stepmother began visiting again occasionally, to spy on his store . . . and to sneak out some goods. What nerve she had to even show up after concocting a ridiculous lawsuit! Shameless, she had no sense of decency.

One day, the stepmother was leaving after a visit, and passed in front of the family Buddhist altar. She then dropped a role of fabric, which she had stolen from the store and was hiding under her kimono jacket.

"Our ancestors must have made it drop," Sachiko said to Kiyoshi.

Each time the stepmother came to visit, Kiyoshi and Sachiko's young son, Hiromi, would hide in a closet and read a book with a flashlight until she left the house. Even though the young Hiromi didn't know who that "spectacled aunty" was, he knew his mother was always upset each time the woman came to visit.

"Justice always wins, Mommy." Hiromi encouraged his mother.

The store was revived and more successful than ever. Several years later, it was incorporated and Kiyoshi became the CEO. Although he kept "Takahashi Cotton Store" as its corporate registration name, the store was renamed "Takahashi Bedding Store," which sold a wide variety of bedding goods. The foundation of the newly incorporated business was laid during this "rebuilding" era.

In September 1952, a baby girl was born to Kiyoshi and Sachiko. She was their second child and first daughter, named "Reiko." The family was elated.

As soon as life had started looking up, Grandma Sui fell ill. And on July 20, 1953, she passed away. She felt finally at ease witnessing the birth of Reiko, and Kiyoshi's family blossoming.

For Kiyoshi, Sui was like his mother—probably more than that. On the night she passed away, Kiyoshi laid his futon next to her corpse and slept there . . . and the next night, again. And the following night too. How painful it was . . . Kiyoshi sent his grandmother off while hiding his tears and wails of grief.

My great-grandmother Sui
(Drawing—production year unknown)

Sui was seventy-two years old. She had lived relatively long compared to other members of the family, but Kiyoshi, of course, wanted her to live much longer.

I thought I could finally make her life better, but she's gone . . . Kiyoshi was remorseful.

All he could do was to hold for his grandmother the biggest funeral ever seen in the town. Indeed, it was grandiose. Reflecting

Kiyoshi's business success, the main street was covered with numerous floral wreaths sent by his friends and business associates. Still, it would not bring back his grandmother. Kiyoshi felt empty.

To Sachiko, too, Sui's death brought immeasurable grief. Sui had been her only ally when Kiyoshi was away at work in Tokyo. It was like losing a war comrade.

"Grandma Sui was plump and had a big belly." My mother reminisced.

"When I was pregnant with your brother, there was a little girl in the neighborhood, named Hisae. I believe she was a first-grader. Looking at Grandma Sui and me, the girl said, 'The house across the street has two big-bellied women.' Hearing that, Grandma and I looked at each other and couldn't stop laughing."

The episode about my father coming home from the war had been told by Grandma Sui to my mom. That's how we know the story.

Mom also told us that Grandma Sui had scolded her whenever she scolded her son, Hiromi.

"He is not only your son. He was born to our family," said Grandma Sui.

Hiromi was quite young then, but he also remembers how much he was adored by his great-grandma Sui. She was very patient even when he threw tantrums. She also took him to the swamp near home to play with him.

Sui poured her love into her grandson Kiyoshi and his family. She cherished Sachiko as if she were her own daughter and embraced Hiromi with immeasurable love.

Why does misfortune always strike when things finally seem to pick up? But the survivors must keep going. They must continue living.

Complaining and questioning, "Why don't the good days last?" wouldn't change anything. It wouldn't make the deceased any happier either.

Kiyoshi and Sachiko could only start moving forward again, step by step by step, to nurture a happy family.

65

4. Parenting

4 − 1 = 3

In January of 1955, Kiyoshi and Sachiko welcomed their second daughter, Tomoko (author). Blessed with three children, the couple felt that spring had finally arrived at their home.

By that time, Japan was said to be "no longer a post-war country." It had already built itself up from the ashes of the devastating war and was gradually making a comeback in the international community. With the arrival of a peaceful era, the strength of the Japanese economy was steadily emerging.

Tomoko [author] held by Mom (1955)

A year and a half later, in July 1957, Sachiko gave birth to another baby girl but tragically lost her during childbirth.

Earlier that day, Sachiko was working at the store, which kept her so busy that she even forgot that the due date had already passed. She later noticed that she was bleeding a little and began to feel anxious about it. Then, her sixty-five-year-old mother, Tema, came to visit unexpectedly; she had likely not forgotten her daughter's due date.

As soon as Tema heard about Sachiko's condition, she ordered, "Call a midwife immediately!"

When the midwife arrived and took a look at Sachiko, she said, "This is beyond my expertise."

She then called a doctor and a nurse from a nearby hospital. The doctor tried his best but was unable to save the baby. The mother also hovered between life and death. Until . . .

"She's gone," the doctor announced Sachiko's death.

"Sachiko~, Sachiko~!"

Tema kept calling her daughter's name.

Then, after a short while, the middle finger on Sachiko's left hand faintly moved. Quickly catching it, Tema screamed,

"She's still alive!"

Miraculously, Sachiko came back to life.

If Tema had not come to see her that day, Sachiko might have died along with the baby.

"It was pitch dark when I arrived at a river. It was probably the river Sanzu [Styx]. And when I was just about to cross it, I heard your grandma Tema's voice," said my mother describing her "near-death experience" years later.

Each time I heard this story, I was terrified—I thought it was rather karmic. My father lost his mother when he was only ten months old, possibly due to a childbirth accident. I, too, almost lost my mother in the same way when I was only a year and a half. Since I resembled my father in many ways, I often wondered if my karma was similar to his as well.

My mother didn't die. Was it my luck or hers? I wonder . . .

With great sadness, the baby was laid in the family grave. Mystically, the day the baby died, July 20th, was the anniversary of Grandma Sui's passing.

My mother used to say,

"Maybe, Grandma Sui was so lonely that she took the baby away."

She was comforting herself, thinking that the baby would be fine if Grandma Sui was with her.

Mom also said to me,

"Your grandma Tema told me the baby's nose started bleeding when she held her in her arms. The baby must have tried to tell her grandma she was happy to be embraced by her. I didn't get to see the baby's face, but I heard she looked just like you, Tomoko."

My mom never forgot about the baby. Neither did my dad. Every morning he would offer incense for the baby, who died without even being given a name. Since the baby's *kaimyō* [posthumous Buddhist name] included the character 夏 [read "natsu" meaning "summer"], Dad decided to call her "Natsuko [夏子]." And he offered incense every day as if he were talking to Natsuko at the Buddhist altar.

Mr. Mom

My mother became sickly after the childbirth ordeal and was down quite often. She looked pale all the time. She frequently broke into a cold sweat and looked as though she was going to faint at any moment.

Since my mom had been so busy at the store, even before she became sickly, we had always had a housemaid or two who took care of us as young children.

When I was a baby, we had a live-in helper named Toyomi. Nicknamed "Toyo-chan," she was everyone's favorite. Her main job was to babysit me. Gentle and loving, she took really good care of me. When I woke up, she was always there for me, except for one time I didn't see her and I cried. I clearly remember the view of the ceiling when I cried that day.

(From left) Tomoko [author], Mom,
Reiko, and babysitter Toyomi (1956)

One family story involves an incident when I was still a baby just crawling around. Toyo-chan left me in a room and came back after a few minutes. She could find me nowhere in the room. She screamed,

"Baby Tomoko is missing!"

She and my mother looked for me everywhere. A small baby, I was unable to walk. They wondered where in the world I could have gone.

Then, they heard someone playing the toy piano upstairs. They looked at each other and said,

"No way . . ."

Dubious, Toyo-chan and Mom went upstairs. Then what did they see? It was me playing the toy piano.

"She crawled up those stairs?"

Looking at the staircase, which was made of extremely steep hardwood steps, they both shuddered with fear. (I guess I was already a tomboy.)

When I was in kindergarten, my parents told me Toyo-chan would be getting married, so we had to say goodbye to her soon. I was devastated. I was so sad that I wrote graffiti on the bathroom wall with a crayon,

"Toyomi stupid."

That was my protest to Toyo-chan, whom I loved dearly.

After Toyo-chan left our home, my father played a mommy's role and took care of us even more. Back then, child rearing was in general assumed to be a mother's job, but he didn't care and looked after us, sparing no pains.

My father had grown up being told, "No man should enter the kitchen." He ignored that and cooked meals for us if Mom wasn't feeling well. He even went grocery shopping.

I don't know where he learned it, but one day he made pancakes—a novelty at that time—for us to snack on. I still remember the sweet smell and taste of the syrup poured over the layers of pancakes.

The traditional New Year's dish *o-zōni* [soup with rice cakes] was one of Dad's specialties. The soup for this dish is cooked in various ways according to regional customs, and Dad's was a *Kantō* [Tokyo and surrounding areas] style—he made soup by boiling chicken bones. He added to this soup a lot of sliced *daikon* radishes and carrots as well as small taros and boiled them together. Then he poured the soup with the vegetables onto the savory toasted, piping-hot *mochi* [rice cakes], and added lots of aromatic *mitsuba* leaves on top of the soup bowl. It was superb and exquisite.

One day, when I was in elementary school, I needed a book bag to take to school. Mom was under the weather that morning. Then, to my surprise, Dad happily made a bag for me. He chose a nice futon fabric with pretty flowers printed on it, and sewed it on a sewing machine. He even put a lining in it. It was so nicely made that I thought it was easily marketable.

I had never seen Dad use a sewing machine before, so I was astonished and totally impressed.

"Dad can do anything!"

He was just like the title of the American TV show we used to watch—*Father Knows Best*. Dad knew virtually everything. Little had I dreamed that he was even able to sew and make a book bag!

Different but Equal

My brother, sister, and I were quite different in terms of personality as well as facial and physical features. The youngest child, I took after Dad, my sister resembled Mom, and my brother was a mixture of both parents with a bit of resemblance to Kisuke, the Founder.

My father tried to help develop each of his children's individuality. For instance, when Dad found out my brother liked reading books, he created a quiet environment where Hiromi could indulge himself. When he discovered my sister liked cooking, Dad taught her how to cook and took her grocery shopping. When he found out I showed interest in his old camera, he bought me a kid's camera.

Dad, however, never spoiled us by simply buying stuff to please us. On the contrary, he taught us the importance of exercising economy and frugality. He even created a poster and put it up on the laundry room wall:

Three "Avoids" lead to a bright family budget—

- *Avoid excessiveness.*
- *Avoid inconsistency.*
- *Avoid wastefulness.*

Naturally, he never allowed us to live a life of luxury.

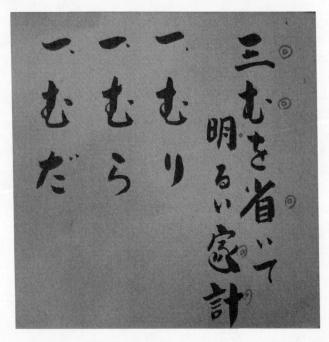

The poster that Dad made and posted on the laundry room wall.
It actually says, "Avoid Three *Mu*'s" in Japanese because "excessiveness,
inconsistency, and wastefulness" are "*muri, muda, mura*" in Japanese.

When we needed to buy something, Dad would carefully make
a selection based on the principle of always purchasing high-quality
goods that would last a long time. He would wisely spend money
on what was needed. He also reminded us not to waste water and
electricity.

My mother shared the same ideas and attitudes toward shopping
and spending money. Because she grew up in a farm family, she
hated wasting food. She would preach to us repeatedly how much
labor and care had gone into each grain of rice. She also often
mentioned that her father had always bought high-quality goods
that lasted a long time. For instance, he had his children wear leather
shoes even in the 1920s and 30s.

My parents valued each child's individuality and uniqueness. They never compared one to the other. They never said, "Like your brother, you should . . ." or "Like your sister, you should . . ." Instead, they seemed to be constantly asking, "What is unique about this child? What is his or her strength?"

Dad never said anything confining like, "Girls should be this way . . ." On the contrary, he always seemed to enjoy watching me play at sword battles with the boys. He allowed me to grow up freely without such restrictions.

On the other hand, both parents were very strict with us when it came to etiquette and manners. Mom hated us to use rough or sloppy language. I was always told by her to mind my language.

While Dad wanted to value each one's uniqueness, he also tried to treat all of us equally. He knew how detrimental to children's wellbeing it would be if some were given preferential treatment, and, especially, how hurt the one would feel if treated badly or coldly by his or her parent. If children were treated unequally, they would never grow up close to one another.

My father knew all that because of his own experience. He wanted his children to grow up to feel cherished individually and close to one another. Since my sister and I were near in age, he paid special attention to us and tried to treat us with the same care. He was extremely considerate. I have an episode to illustrate this point.

One day, I was playing with my classmate at my father's store. I think we were playing hide-and-seek. While playing, I happened to find that month's issue of the magazine that I eagerly awaited each month hidden on the back of a shelf.

"Dad! Why is my *Third-Grader* magazine hidden in such a strange place? If it has come, you should give it to me! You know how much I look forward to reading it each month? Why didn't you give it to me right away?" I protested to him.

Then Dad explained,

"Your sister's *Fifth-Grader* magazine didn't arrive with yours. I felt bad for her, so I decided to hide yours until hers arrived."

He was apologetic. I was so moved by his thoughtfulness that I could not say a word. Having witnessed this exchange, my classmate said to me with a lot of feeling,

"Tomoko, you are lucky to have such a great father. My dad would never think of doing anything like that. He always shows favor to my sister, and he doesn't even care how I feel about it!"

I would have been elated if my father had given me the magazine right after it was delivered, but my sister would have felt jealous. It would have been easy to make one of us happy, but if the other one had become unhappy, then everything would have been meaningless. Always looking for ways to do what was both fair and harmonious, cleaver Dad had hid my magazine and planned on giving it to me upon the arrival of my sister's magazine, so we might enjoy reading our magazines together.

When I think back on it, my magazine and my sister's had always arrived on the same day, but those magazines could have been published and made available on different days. Maybe, my father had always been adjusting the timing of the delivery by hiding one of them even before my discovery; or, perhaps, it just so happened that the secret was revealed that day.

I pledged that I would never forget that incident for the rest of my life. As an educator today, I make it a number-one rule to treat my students fairly and equally. It's not easy to make everyone happy. I sometimes have to be strict with my students in order to be fair and for the sake of their own happiness and wellbeing. I learned the importance of being fair and equal from my father through many experiences like the episode described above.

Closed on Sundays

No matter how busy his business, my father kept the store closed on Sundays so that he could spend the entire day with us children. Back then, we had school half a day on Saturdays, so Sunday was the only holiday we had.

Every weekend, Dad would take us for a drive, to the zoo, etc. We always looked forward to a day of fun with him each Sunday.

(From left) My sister, brother, and father at Ueno Zoo (1956)

Nagatoro River in Chichibu was a perfect place to go for a drive and we have a number of wonderful memories there. We would load Dad's station wagon with a picnic meal such as rice balls and lots of drinks. And we headed for Chichibu, the northwestern part of Saitama Prefecture surrounded by isolated mountains.

The rainbow trout Dad caught were breathtakingly beautiful. And how tasty they were after being barbequed on the dry riverbed! I will never forget that sight and taste.

Dad loved fishing. My sister and I would float in swim rings on the river, while trying not to interfere with his fishing. One time, the river suddenly began to flow faster, and we almost got washed away. Dad immediately threw his fishing rod down, jumped into the river, and saved us. Sundays were always filled with fun and good adventures.

Our family had a tea field that had been handed down from generation to generation, which, thankfully, had not been taken by Dad's stepmother. In early summer each year, the entire family together with my father's store employees would spend a whole day picking tea leaves there. We children would just goof around pretending we were also picking leaves.

> "The eighty-eighth day
> From the beginning of spring,
> Summer is almost here.
> Young leaves are growing thick
> On hills and fields . . ."

We sang and threw ourselves onto the mountain of new shiny tea leaves piled up on a truck. Lying on it made us feel as if we were floating, and the aroma of the young leaves made us feel comfy and dreamy. As we watched the blue sky, lying on the tea mountain, we felt as if we were about to be sucked into the white clouds swimming by above. It was heavenly.

The tea leaves picked by the happy folks would be taken to the tea store in town and roasted. The tantalizing aroma of the tea leaves being roasted would fill the entire town.

Dad's store was closed on Sundays although it was the most convenient day for customers to shop. It was impossible for many to even imagine not opening for business on Sundays—the most profitable day. Business would suffer without Sunday transactions.

One day, a customer told my father she wanted to come back to the store on Sunday.

"We are closed on Sundays," said Dad.

"My goodness, you work like a daimyo [king]," remarked the customer sarcastically.

Dad decidedly responded,

"Sundays are the only days I can spend the whole day with my children. So, we are closed on Sundays."

Listening to their conversation in the back of the store, I was filled with appreciation for my dad.

I spent a considerable amount of time with my father, and not only on Sundays. As everyone knew, I was "Daddy's girl." I loved being around him. I would even ride in his truck when he went to deliver store merchandise to his customers.

Delivery was normally done by store clerks, but Dad was flexible and did not mind going out to deliver goods if necessary. Especially if the delivery was for the old customers, he volunteered to go himself.

When I was still in kindergarten, I was waiting for Dad in the passenger seat in the truck, which he had left idling. I was suddenly stricken with the thought that the truck might start moving on its own, and I was terrified. After that incident, I had always gotten out of the truck and accompanied Dad to his customer's house.

I was rather shy when I was a youngster. I would hide behind my dad, who was very friendly and a good conversationalist. I would quietly watch him enjoy talking with his customers.

The long-time customers would not treat my father simply as a deliveryman. Some, remembering he used to be an army officer, would bow deeply as if they were apologizing for having troubled him to deliver their orders. But my father was modest and polite. He had become a futon-store owner through and through.

The new futon set delivered was displayed nicely on the *engawa* floor.[5] Then the customer would serve green tea and *kashi* [confectionary]. Dad would sit on the *engawa* and sip the tea but never stayed too long. At the right time in the conversation, he would thank the hosts for the tea and stand up. Then, the customer would wrap the untouched *kashi* in a piece of white *hanshi* [calligraphy] paper and give it to me. That was the routine.

Looking at me holding the goodies in my tiny hands, Dad always looked happy for me and said,

"You've got some snacks. Aren't you lucky!"

Then he would add,

"You're going to share that with your sister, right?"

Horrors of the *Miso* Room

My mother was born in the Year of the Tiger, and she used to say,

"The tiger is a cat, so I'm a cat-like doter."[6]

Mom would rub her cheek against mine as she gave me a piggyback ride to the bath, saying,

"Cheek, cheek."

In the 1950s and 60s in Japan, having such physical contact between mother and child was rather rare.

Equally affectionate, Dad would give us piggyback rides or put us on his shoulders. He even wore a *nenneko* coat when carrying one of us on his back. This short coat was stuffed with cotton to keep the baby warm, but it was normally worn by women back then.

---

5   *Engawa* is a wooden strip of floor extending at one side of a traditional Japanese house, facing a yard or garden and serving as a passageway and sitting space. It's similar to a roofed veranda, but the engawa is a raised floor immediately adjacent to the *tatami* [matted] rooms inside the house. Half inside and half outside the house, the engawa space allows visitors to sit there without taking off their shoes.

6   There is an expression in Japanese, 猫可愛がり, meaning "doting on children like cats."

Dad didn't care about other people's perception and would carry us around in the *nenneko* coat.

My father had erect posture as a result of his kendo practice and military training.

"He looked like a straight telephone pole with a tiny cicada on it," Mom described Dad with one of us as a baby on his back.

I certainly remember, as a small child, I always tried to hang on to his sturdy and strong back to keep myself from sliding down when he gave me a piggyback ride. I also remember how prickly his shaved beard felt when I rubbed my cheek against his, and the fragrance of the *Pomade* [brilliantine] on his hair and the smell of cigarette smoke. They are still vivid in my mind.

My father was really a doting parent, and yet, he didn't spoil us. When it came to discipline, he was still like an army officer. He was strict—even merciless.

When I was in kindergarten, I was scolded and punished by Dad for doing something bad. He carried me on his shoulder and took me to one of the storehouses all the way beyond the backyard. My siblings and I were especially afraid of that particular storehouse, as we believed ghosts lived there.

This storehouse was called the *"miso* [soybean-paste] room" because my great-great-grandfather Kisuke (the Founder) used to have miso made there. By the time we were born, there was no need to make miso at home, and this building had been turned into a storehouse.

Being carried on my dad's shoulder, I was terrified, saying to myself,

Oh, no! He's going to throw me into that dark miso room!

I cried loudly.

Because Dad was so tall, being carried on his shoulder, I had a good view of the neighbor's backyard beyond the tall fence. I could even see Dr. Suzuki sweeping the ground.

"Tomoko, what did you do this time?" Dr. Suzuki asked, smiling, looking at me crying loudly.

Our property was more than seventy yards from the house to the rear gate. The storehouse in question was located close to the gate. We passed by the bathhouse, backyard, two persimmon trees, the cotton factory, and we finally reached the cotton storehouse. The miso room was behind this cotton storehouse. What a long journey that was!

With me crying on his shoulder, Dad opened the door and stepped into the storehouse. I could smell a strange odor from the room used for making miso in the past. I was too scared to say a word. Then Dad put me down.

Noooooooooooooooo! I screamed inside my head.

Immediately, I noticed something strange. I was astonished. I thought Dad was going to push me in and leave me there, but he stayed. He closed the door from the inside and stood next to me without saying a word.

Dumbfounded, I didn't cry. Petrified, I stood quietly next to him in the dark storehouse.

After a while, which felt like an eternity, Dad said to me in the darkness,

"You won't do it again, will you?"

"No, I won't!" I answered.

"All right!" said Dad, and opened the door.

It was getting dark outside already. We walked hand in hand, and headed for the main house.

"Dinner is ready." Mom welcomed us back warmly.

The dining room lights looked brighter than usual that evening.

5. Education Papa

No Angel

The Haraichi town, where I grew up, didn't have a kindergarten when I was a child. There was a daycare, so my parents could have sent us there, but they sent us all the way to a private kindergarten in the neighboring town of Ageo. Why did they send us there? According to one opinion, it was because the school was Christian.

Tomoko [author], Age 4 (1959)

Although our family belonged to the Pure-Land sect of Buddhism, my father liked everything Western. He would say at Christmas time each year,

81

"We are not Christians, so you shouldn't ask for Christmas presents. When kids beg for presents, *Kurisumasu* [Christmas] turns into Papa *Kurushimimasu* [suffer], you know?"

This was his pun in Japanese. His puns were always unique and creative.

Also, whenever he heard the song "Silent Night" sung in Japanese, he would say,

"How could people use my first name (Kiyoshi) so casually? That's why I don't like Christmas."

This song in Japanese begins with *"Kiyoshi* [pure/clear] *kono-yoru* [this night]."* Since adults were never addressed by their first names, it really bothered him.

Although he declared his dislike for Christmas, Dad was the first one in town to buy and decorate a Christmas tree. And once Christmas cakes and stockings became popular in Japan, he bought them for us every year without fail.

Christmas stockings sold in Japan are different from those you see in America. Decades ago specialty candy stores in Japan began selling them stuffed with goodies, and they were not stockings, but boots made of paper or plastic. Dad always bought one each for my sister and me when we were young girls. One year, he discovered the contents of the two boots were different. He went all the way back to Ōmiya City to ask the store manager to re-stuff them to make the contents exactly the same.

The kindergarten we attended had a school bus, but it didn't come as far as our town to pick us up. We had to ride a public bus to commute. Despite our parents' worries, my brother and sister commuted by bus with no problems. (It's hard to believe now, though, that five-year-old kids would ride public buses without guardians. I guess it was a safe and peaceful time then.)

My sister Reiko, in particular, loved kindergarten. She would get up in the morning, get ready by herself, and go to her friend's house, cheerfully call out "Yumiko-chan!" accompany her to the bus stop, and get on the bus with her. She was such a trouble-free child.

Being the youngest, on the other hand, I was totally the opposite of her. I hated kindergarten. I just wanted to stay home. I remember I always felt like screaming, "Leave me alone!"

Well, imagine. I had just turned four when my parents sent me to a two-year program at kindergarten. I was born in late January and the school year in Japan starts in early April, so I was younger than most of the other kids when I entered kindergarten. My brother and sister were sent to a one-year program and were five and a half when they started the program. There is a significant difference between four years old and five and a half. I had a lot of disadvantages and passed them on to my folks.

My parents were understandably worried about sending their four-year-old child (me) to kindergarten by bus. Sure enough, I refused to go like this. I hated kindergarten itself. Who would happily ride a bus (other than my sister!)? I would oversleep every morning and get fretful. As a result, I would miss the bus. Then, Dad would chauffeur me to kindergarten.

Dad drove his store's delivery truck to take me to kindergarten for a while, but when it became an everyday ritual, he bought a compact car. I remember its color was a pinkish light brown. Dad called it "Tomoko's private car."

The private car ownership rate at that time was quite low. Japan was more than forty years behind the United States in terms of so-called "family motorization." Japanese automobile companies began manufacturing cars for private use in the late 1950s, and family motorization only began after the Tokyo Olympics in 1964. In my hometown, for instance, in the late 1950s, there were only a few families that owned a private car. The cars and trucks that you saw back then were mostly for commercial use.

You can imagine how rare it was for a Japanese family to own a private car in 1959, when I started kindergarten. And, it was unusual (or unheard of) for a father to drive his child to school every day, let alone to buy a car for that purpose!

Thanks to Dad, I commuted to kindergarten without missing a day. Or, I must say, he forced me to commute without missing a day. Consequently, I received a "Perfect-Attendance Award" at graduation.

My teacher, Miss Naito, smiled and said to me,

"This award is for you and your father."

She handed me the certificate and a drawing board as the prize. Because the drawing board was pink, I wondered,

Why do I have to share this with Dad?

It never crossed my mind that his driving me every day was a big deal.

I commuted to kindergarten every day, but I never came to like it. All the games, songs, and class activities were boring to me. Things got even worse before Christmas because we were made to memorize incomprehensible lines to perform in the Nativity play. I had a good memory, so memorizing those words was not a problem. I just hated being dressed as an angel and being forced to practice the play with other children.

I don't know how she was selected, but the girl who played the role of Mary got a lot of the spotlight. Those who played angels were made to line up and stand in the back, looking more like a backdrop. They were secondary and minor—simply "many others."

Being one of the angels, I was doing my role out of obligation, utterly bored and uninterested. Calling it "my role" sounds a bit grand; I had only one speaking line and then had to stand there for the rest of the play.

I'd rather be playing in the swamp, I said to myself.

I was such a critical child and so hard to please. What's more, I would wear my displeasure right on my face. I was such a difficult child to deal with.

Born Free

If you look at my photo album from those early days, you will find no photos of me smiling. I was always sulking. By contrast, my sister, Reiko, was friendly and always smiling, showing her cute dimples.

Reiko was feminine and lovely, whereas I was not only moody and unfriendly, I was a tomboy. She liked dress-up dolls and would play house with her girlfriends in the neighborhood. I would play with boys only, making swords out of bamboo for battles, and going to the nearby swamp to catch frogs, crayfish, carp, killifish, and so forth. Having grown up like a wild child, I always had rough and dirty hands, which got chapped in winter.

Dad used to call me "Moko-suke" because I was like a boy—the -*suke* of Moko-suke is an old-fashioned male name ending in Japanese. "Moko" was my childhood nickname—it was from Tomoko, of course. The -*suke* ending might have been taken from Kisuke (Dad's great-grandfather). In any case, what a funny name Dad had come up with for me!

Even after I had grown up, Dad often reminisced about the good old days when I was a child. In the letters I received from him years later, he often mentioned that he reminisced about my childhood days.

Excerpts from my father's letter dated September 26, 1976

9/25 (Sat) Fair Sky—I found a little bit of spare time, so I went to check out the garden plants. Then, I discovered the gardenia's leaves had been eaten by worms and spotted with tiny holes. Just as I feared, the gardenia has been attacked. Only about 4~5 days ago, I saw an unfamiliar-looking butterfly on those leaves. I took a closer look and found that the butterfly was laying tiny eggs about the size of a pinhole. I wanted to see what the worms from those eggs would look like, so I left them untouched. Then, I got so busy that I forgot to observe them. By the time I remembered, those leaves had been worm-eaten. Those tiny caterpillars even have horns and are vigorously eating the leaves. It was rather comical. But, sorry to say, I had to spray insecticide over them. I was then suddenly reminded of the dark night from many years ago when you, Moko-suke, with a flashlight in your hands, were gazing fixedly at a mantis laying eggs.

I do distinctly remember that night when I watched a mantis laying eggs. I also remember I used to observe "doodlebugs [ant-lion larvae]" that lived under the floor of the Inari shrine in the backyard at home. As I stirred up the sand with a thin stick, a doodlebug would emerge and soon crawl back into the sand in a spiral, leaving a cone-shaped depression. It was fun to watch, and I never got bored of it.

One time, there was a toad hiding under the floor. As I accidentally poked him with a stick, the toad came out abruptly. When I saw that, I almost had a heart attack!

I loved animals and insects so much that I enjoyed playing in the swamp and fields, forgetting myself, which resulted in many problems.

For instance, I often didn't come home until after it got dark. I once brought home a bucket full of tadpoles and poured them into the pond at home. Several weeks later, those tadpoles turned into frogs all at once, causing an uproar. I also made Mom, who hated lizards and snakes, almost faint several times. I would bring my pet beetles to the dining table, which put everyone off. My pet turtle Kame-suke was often missing, and the entire family had to go in search of him.

I also had a uniquely memorable incident. I found a skylark nest in a field one day. Naturally, I brought it home.

Dad told me I would never be able to raise wild birds and tried to talk me out of it. But those skylark chicks were so adorable that I told him I would raise them by myself. He continued insisting that only the parent bird could feed those chicks, but I stubbornly would not listen to him.

Dad gave in. He began helping me prepare food for the chicks, crushing and softening some vegetables and grains in a mortar. He then put a little bit of food on the tip of a skewer and tried to feed the chicks. He was right—he was not their parent. The chicks would not open their beaks.

My dad tried to convince me, I guess, it would never work by giving me an actual demonstration of the futility. He even gave them a military-like command, but the chicks would still not open their beaks.

Imitating him, I also gave them a military command,

"Open beaks! Open!"

To everyone's surprise, the chicks opened their beaks wide all at once. Dad found it extremely amusing and told me to do it again. Then, it became clear that those chicks opened their beaks without fail upon my command, but no one else's. Not only that, they even ate the food gladly on my command. Dad started larking around like a kid, while I remained totally serious.

Dad gave up trying to talk me out of it and continued to help me raise the chicks. We put some warm water into tiny medicine bottles and made hot-water bottles for them to keep warm. At each mealtime, the chicks competed for food on my command. Dad and I paid special attention to protect them from cats.

As a result of the collaboration between Dad and me, the chicks seemed for awhile like they would grow up to be healthy birds. As more days passed by, however, they died one by one. Looking at the chicks cold and still, I was so overwhelmed with grief that I didn't know what to do with my emotions. Then I pledged to never catch wild animals and birds. Needless to say, I also learned the importance of life.

My father must have helped me raise those chicks in order to teach me all this. If your children don't (want to) understand, you have to let them experience life's lessons for themselves. Although there was a bit of a risk and sacrifice involved, Dad's teaching method was superbly effective.

Moko-suke's Strike

I started kindergarten, as mentioned, when I was only four years old—younger than most of my classmates and much smaller physically. This made me reserved. Although I became extremely animated when I found something amusing or funny, I was usually very quiet and rather shy. Nonetheless, I always stubbornly held firm to my convictions. I especially hated compromise.

I had a classmate named Yoko. This girl was very active and rather aggressive. She was the teacher's pet. She was physically bigger than my other classmates, and was bossy. She always wore a big ribbon in her long hair.

In my second year of kindergarten, Yoko brought from home her artwork, although it wasn't a homework assignment or class project. She boastfully showed it to all of us. Teachers praised her work. After getting her fill of the praise, Yoko placed her masterpiece on the floor.

During a break, without noticing her artwork on the floor (I swear!), I stepped on it. The artwork, made of paper, partially crumbled.

"Oh, I'm sorry, Yoko!" I immediately apologized.

Yoko's round cheeks turned bright red. She was really angry. But I hadn't done it on purpose. I hadn't realized her artwork was lying down there. No matter how much I explained and apologized to her, Yoko would not forgive me.

I finally got angry myself and said,

"I've told you I'm sorry!"

I decided then and there to give up on her and left the classroom. I walked into the hallway and sat down.

The teachers were astounded. No matter how many times they came to call me in, or even when the principal came to persuade me, I remained sitting in the hallway.

How can I be in the same classroom with a girl like her!

I went on a sit-down strike.

Starting the following day, as soon as I got out of my father's car, I went straight to the hallway and sat down.

My dad would return to the kindergarten after dropping me off to spy on me, I heard years later. I was on strike and so serious that I didn't even notice him scouting around.

Dad, peaking through the fence and through glass windows, saw his daughter sitting in the hallway.

"Oh no, Moko-suke is sitting there again. Who did she take after? She is so stubborn!" Dad talked to himself.

He neither treated me like a trouble-maker nor reproached me. On the contrary, he was rather proud of his young daughter for holding firm to her convictions.

The strike went on for several weeks. I continued it with much composure. Finally, Yoko was the one who gave in. One day, she came to me and said,

"I'm sorry, Tomoko."

I smiled and said, "Okay" and walked into the classroom with Yoko.

The case was closed. And I joined in again, after a while, the boring games and songs with my classmates.

Once the strike was over, my father seemed relieved and happy as though to say,

"Good job, Moko-suke!"

Parents' Open House

When I was in kindergarten, my mother used to attend our events. After I started elementary school, my father came to all the events including the entrance ceremony and graduation. Dad came neither because Mom was too sickly to attend, nor out of obligation. He really wanted to attend those events himself. He was very enthusiastic about his children's education. He was not only an affectionate parent, but also an "education papa."

At each open house, I so very much looked forward to my father's arrival. Dressed in a stylish suit with a tasteful necktie, he would walk into the classroom, and the atmosphere changed. That's how I always sensed his arrival.

Along with my classmates' mothers, Dad observed the class. I felt he looked shiny; I was so proud of his presence.

Speaking of the school's open house days, something interesting happened when I was in the fifth grade.

After the parent-teacher meeting following the class observation, my homeroom teacher, Mr. Takano, came back to the classroom. Then, he explained,

"The *kanji* [Chinese character] I wrote on the blackboard during the class earlier was incorrect. The correct one uses the *sanzui* [three water-strokes] on the left-hand side."

Embarrassed, he corrected the character he had written in front of the parents during the class observation time. I watched him make the correction and thought,

Even Mr. Takano makes a mistake in kanji . . .

He had tried to explain something earlier using this kanji that was so difficult that any adult might write it incorrectly. Naturally, we fifth-graders hadn't noticed the mistake at all. Parents wouldn't have noticed it either. It was a mistake made by a schoolteacher after all.

As soon as I got home, I reported the incident to my father,

"Hey, Dad, Mr. Takano told us that the kanji he had written in front of the parents today was incorrect. He realized his mistake, so he came back and corrected it. He was lucky because no one spotted it during the class observation."

Then Dad responded,

"Mr. Takano corrected his mistake . . . That's admirable. As the saying goes, even Kōbō [famous for his calligraphy skills] sometimes makes a calligraphy mistake.[7] And even experts like your teachers, too, sometimes make mistakes. Making a mistake is not bad in itself. All you need is to learn from your mistake. But it's not good if you don't correct it, or if you don't tell someone about the mistake even if you are aware of it."

He paused, and then added lightly,

"Actually, I spotted that mistake, so I told him about it."

Then Dad explained why the *sanzui* was used for that kanji by explaining the origin of the character to me much more clearly than the teacher had.

After discovering the truth, I said to myself, *I see!* I was a bit surprised, but soon thought, *Of course!* My father read newspapers from cover to cover every morning. He knew kanji shockingly well.

---

[7]   This is equivalent to a Western saying: "Even Homer sometimes nods."

His linguistic sense was very sharp too. I was convinced of that based on several incidents. He couldn't have missed the teacher's mistake, and he could not ignore it.

My dad would not, however, point out the mistake in front of other parents. That would disgrace the teacher's honor. Dad told the teacher about it in private after the class observation. Considering the teacher's feelings, I bet Dad tactfully used some humor to point it out.

If my father had been the kind of person who liked boasting about his extensive knowledge, he would have pointed out the teacher's mistake in front of everyone. But he was not that kind of person at all. As much as he was straightforward, he was also extremely considerate and unusually sensitive to others' feelings. Dad was a person of character.

My father also attended every sporting event at school. An enthusiastic parent, he got excited when it came to his children. At these sporting events, he stood out in the crowd. I felt so encouraged and said to myself,

Dad's watching. I won't let him down!

One year I was to be in a bottle-fishing race, a contest that involved picking up a bottle with a fishing rod. Since Dad loved fishing, I wanted to please him, so I practiced bottle fishing with great diligence. While practicing, I learned there was a technique in getting the nail into the bottle mouth—by having the nail on the string slightly tilted.

On the day of the event, as the fastest runner in class, I dashed out on the signal of the starting gun. I was the first one to get to a bottle. I carefully dropped the fish string. The technique I had learned worked beautifully. I hooked the bottle immediately.

"Nice!"

I heard a loud scream from afar. It was Dad, of course.

I slowly picked up the bottle hanging from the string and ran while carefully holding the fishing rod in order not to drop the bottle. I felt as if Dad were running with me. I broke the tape by a wide margin. Dad was ecstatic.

I can still hear my father's scream today urging me on.

Tomoko [author], Age 7, dressed up for the "Seven-Five-Three" celebration holding a delicate fan in her chapped hands
(November 1962)

Community Builder and High-Pressure Peddler

My father clearly viewed the community as an extension of his family. A strong and healthy community could only enhance the wellbeing of his family. He tried to do everything possible to contribute to the development of the town and the wellbeing of its residents. He was active in the Haraichi Shopping District Association and the neighborhood association. He also volunteered much time as a welfare commissioner to promote the welfare of the town residents.

In business, my father had a long-term outlook and rationally considered the future prospects of his enterprise. Early on, he foresaw that specialty retail stores would shortly be pressured by department stores and large supermarkets. Consequently, he proposed to other bedding retailers that they unite to cope with the coming changes—e.g., by jointly stocking up large amounts of merchandise and passing the savings on to the customers.

His proposal was to create a "voluntary chain" with fine specialty retailers within the prefecture—one store per town or city so that their business territories would not overlap. Dad thought this strategy would succeed if the stores united and advanced together.

As a result, he jointly started the Saitama Bedding Store Chain with twenty or so stores in Saitama Prefecture. The fellow retailers in the group all tried to be in friendly competition with one another and grow together.

As expected, the group members developed friendships with one another through their meetings and social gatherings. Dad seemed to be so energized at those gatherings that his keen sense of humor got even sharper, and he made everyone present laugh quite a bit. As a child, I remember how cheerful those adults were and how much they enjoyed themselves.

A decade or so later, the change predicted by my father became a serious problem for small retailers as large supermarkets and department stores extended their business territories.

In a letter I received from my father in the 1970s, when the business competition became fierce, there was mention of his visit to a large supermarket in a neighboring town.

Excerpts from my father's letter dated November 28, 1976

Consumers these days hunt only for cheap stuff and won't even consider buying high-quality goods. Naturally, the sections for the jewelers and expensive tailors were sparse. On the other hand, the grocery and household sections were so packed you could hardly move. As I pushed through the crowd, I happened to arrive at the bedding section. It would be embarrassing, I thought, if I ran into an acquaintance, but just to do a bit of research, I decided to look around.

> *The blankets, comforter covers, etc. that were displayed*
> *there looked like "cheap stuff" to me rather than just low-priced*
> *merchandise. We specialty retailers would feel too guilty to sell such*
> *low-quality goods. I saw a couple of customers shopping. I felt like*
> *telling them, "Excuse me, but those are very poor-quality." That*
> *would of course be awkward, so I didn't. Still, I was concerned*
> *and wondered if they would bring a complaint to this supermarket*
> *if their purchases were damaged or defective. I felt as if it were*
> *my own affair. Those customers, however, would never come visit*
> *specialty retail stores. I told myself not to even bother. So thinking,*
> *I looked around more.*

As I reread my father's letter, I felt appreciative—for his constant vigilance to keep his business going.

In addition to his efforts in the community focused on securing a healthy business environment, he was also an active volunteer in the PTA. It might have been due to his character that he always had some kind of educational influence on anyone he encountered—whether it was a stranger, a friend or a relative. It didn't matter. It could even be an *oshiuri* [high-pressure peddler].

You don't see oshiuri peddlers nowadays in Japan, but right after WWII until the end of the Shōwa era (1926–1989), they were still active. They would come to your house and peddle some unneeded goods like elastic strings and useless household items for outrageous prices in an aggressive and persistent manner. Normally, they would come to your house after the male head of the household had left for work, sit down at the entrance, and stay there until you bought the goods. It was a business exploit with great potential for cunning deceit.

One day, an oshiuri peddler came to my father's store. Usually, Dad would be there, so they would not come in, but on that particular day, Mom was the only one in the store. The young man with an intimidating demeanor thought it was his lucky day and entered the store to sell some elastic strings. Mom was in trouble.

Suddenly, with perfect timing, Dad came back to the store. The oshiuri guy was instantly flustered, but Dad didn't throw him out. On the contrary, he smiled and began having a one-on-one conversation with the young man.

"What have you got?

Oh, I see . . . elastic strings . . .

They are used for underpants, right?

Too bad . . .

Have you heard of the 'Genji's White Flag'?

I started wearing a string loincloth looking like that long white flag when I went into the army. And believe it or not, it's really comfortable—nice and airy. I still wear it. Once you try this 'Samurai underwear,' you can't switch to underpants.

So, I have no need for any elastic strings."

Dad spoke to him in a joking and friendly manner.

The oshiuri felt deflated. He had never met anyone who would converse with him like a friend, as his job was to corner and pressure people to buy those elastics at inflated prices. He started calling my dad "*Danna* [Master]" and began speaking intimately about his own life bit by bit.

Dad's advice was straightforward,

"Why are you still living with this post-war confusion in our new age?"

He sounded as if he were talking to a younger brother. He continued to persuade the oshiuri,

"Why don't you get a decent job?"

The oshiuri left without selling any elastic strings that day.

After some time had passed, the oshiuri guy came back to Dad's store—this time, not with elastics, but with a bicycle trailer. He proudly announced,

"Master, I started a respectable business. I'll take scrap iron if you've got any."

My father was elated. He immediately thought about the iron ties that were taken off of raw cotton bundles and simply discarded.

"I've got tons of iron wire used for raw cotton. It's piled up with old bicycles behind the factory. Go get them. They're all yours!"

The story of the oshiuri doesn't end there. His fate seems to have been intertwined with my dad's.

Sometime later, my father was in the downtown area of Ōmiya City, where he was being harassed by some gangsters. The oshiuri, who had once been a gangster himself, emerged out of nowhere and menacingly threatened,

"Don't you touch my Master!"

That was enough to cause the gang to move on, and Dad was saved.

One more connection . . .

A young man who worked for the wholesaler Dad did business with was in a traffic accident and hospitalized. Guess who was also in the hospital? Once the oshiuri found out that this young patient was "Master's acquaintance," he took great care of him.

My father had a genuinely kind and warm heart, not only as a father but as a human being. He had such charm and appeal that he could win anyone over.

6. Growing Together

Examination Hell

My siblings and I attended local public schools for elementary and junior high school education. Anyone could attend those public schools without taking an entrance exam. For high school and up, however, you must take an entrance exam to gain admission, whether it be public or private. For most Japanese children, therefore, "examination hell" begins in junior high school, as they must start preparing for high school entrance exams.

My brother, Hiromi, was such a bright student that he got into one of the top high schools in Saitama Prefecture, named Urawa High School, known as "Ura-Kō." He looked so cool in his high school uniform with shiny buttons that had the school emblem depicting ginkgo leaves. I thought I would love to attend the same school, but it was only for boys.

Instead, I decided to aim for one of the best girls' high schools in Saitama, called Urawa Dai-Ichi [First] High School, known as "Ura-Ichi." In addition to its reputation, I chose this school because my favorite cousin had gone there and she was my role model.

When I told Dad about my wish, he said,

"Right! It's good to aim high!"

He encouraged me to study hard. When I was in the sixth grade, he took me to show me the Ura-Ichi campus. My dream ballooned.

I was a good student, but not as good as my brother, who was famous in town for being so bright. Quite athletic, I preferred sports to studies. I played basketball and competed in track and field in junior high school. In the classroom I concentrated on each class and tried to absorb everything from it. Outside the class, however, I didn't study much except for doing some homework.

When I had to prepare for high school entrance exams, I didn't know how to study for them. I gradually realized that what I had learned in class was not enough. Preparing for entrance exams meant a lot of memorization work, which really turned me off. I didn't want to go to a cram school to get extra help. As a result, I just idled around feeling anxious.

Despite the lack of preparation, however, based on my prep test scores, I managed to get permission from my homeroom teacher to apply to Ura-Ichi. I also decided to apply to a private school called "Akenohoshi" just in case I didn't get into my first choice.

Entrance exams for private schools took place before those for public schools. My father drove me (of course!) to Akenohoshi for the entrance exam. The campus was new, and the room temperature was just right and comfortable. Everyone there was very kind, and I was quite impressed by the school. I finished the exam with no problem.

With my father, who had waited for me during the exam, I walked to the parking lot.

And then, what did we find? Dad's car had a flat tire!

No way! I thought.

How could such a bad thing happen to me at such an important time?

I soon realized, however, I was lucky that we discovered it *after* the exam.

Dad immediately started changing tires without fussing. My fellow examinees were passing by while casting a side-glance at us. There weren't too many students who came with a parent *and* by car, so that made me feel embarrassed. And I became overly conscious of their gaze.

As soon as Dad finished changing tires, I silently got in the car thinking,

This is my unlucky day. What a bad omen!

Dad must have sensed my feelings. He tried to sound cheerful and said to me,

"Now I remember . . . There was a piece of plywood lying on the road on our way here. I must have run over it. That was my fault. I should have been more careful."

Despite his cheerfulness, I was still feeling down.

As I look back now, I am overwhelmed by my father's thoughtfulness. How sweet he was! If he had taken me there unwillingly, he would have reluctantly changed tires, feeling rather annoyed. He wouldn't have had to take the blame either. But he was too kind. He was not just a doting, attentive parent, but was filled with gentleness as a human being and had incredible thoughtfulness for others.

When my father as a young student went to take an entrance exam for Yokohama Kō-Shō (see Chapter 2), he went there by himself. He had always lived an independent life with no one really cheering him on. He had yearned for a family with parents who warmly watched over him. That understandably became his wish for his own children. He tried so hard to give us what he had always wanted as a child himself.

"I didn't grow up in a warm family, so I am bound and determined to make sure my children are happy," said Dad once.

Unquestionably, it was because of my father's misfortune that I was lucky enough to grow up in a warm and loving family. He was indeed the best father in the world.

Better to Be a Chicken Head than an Ox Tail

The results of the entrance exam for Akenohoshi were to be sent to each applicant via express mail. I waited for the letter nervously. So did my parents.

Dad simply could not wait for the letter to be delivered. Early in the morning of the day of delivery, he called the main post office to see if the letter had already arrived there. As he found out that it had, he dashed to the post office. He showed his driver's license, signed the receipt slip, grabbed the letter, and hurried home.

As soon as he got home, he opened the letter and read it for me. "Admitted."

When I heard this word, I was in heaven.

"I did it!" I exclaimed and shared the joy with my parents.

After we had all calmed down from the excitement, the three of us burst into laughter. In unison, we had all noticed the tiny pieces of paper on the floor. Those were the pieces torn off the envelope by Dad. Wanting to read the letter so badly, he had ripped the envelope to shreds—all in the shape of his index finger.

That night, my father gave me those "finger-shaped" pieces of paper in a small envelope, on which he wrote,

"Don't forget the excitement you felt today. Don't lose your enthusiasm."

Since I had already secured admission to Akenohoshi, I felt relaxed when I took the entrance exam for Ura-Ichi, my first choice. It was extremely cold, however, when I went to the school for the exam. Because the buildings were old, it was freezing inside. I got a chill. I felt sick and went to the restroom a few times during the exam. It was impossible to concentrate on the exam.

I'm done for. It's all over for me . . . I said to myself and almost gave up, but as I thought what it would be like if I failed, I became very uneasy.

I wonder how people will look at me . . . Such trifling thoughts entered my mind.

In retrospect, I think this entrance-examination system in Japan is too cruel. No wonder it's called "examination hell." How could they make fifteen-year-olds face such hardship and overwhelming anxiety! It is unfortunate that there have been a number of teenagers who have committed suicide because of this entrance-exam system. If they feel pressured from their parents as well, they have no place to go. Fortunately, my parents didn't pressure me. Instead, they shared the agonizing experience with me, for which I am forever grateful.

The day had come—public schools announced the admission results all at once on the same day. A friend who was attending Ura-Ichi went to check the bulletin board at her school and then called me with the results. Unfortunately, I didn't get admitted.

Actually, I didn't mind having been rejected too much. I was just shocked to find out that my classmates who had applied for Ura-Ichi had all been admitted. I felt left out.

Everyone in my family was very sensitive toward my feelings and very considerate. My brother, a college student then, sat on the second-floor balcony with me and tried to cheer me up.

"Those entrance exams take place during the winter, you know. I've experienced them several times too, so I know how stressful and depressing they are. They make you feel like the cold winter weather. But when spring comes, it gets warm, and flowers bloom, you know. Then, we all feel like spring again. Winter always turns to spring. So, cheer up!"

As I sat in the sun with Hiromi that day, feeling the warm sunshine, I felt he was right.

Although I had wanted to go to Ura-Ichi so badly, the shock from not having been admitted gradually faded. At the same time, I was able to examine myself closer and realized that Akenohoshi might be a much better fit for me. I wasn't just trying to deceive myself in order to cover up my disappointment. I truly began to think it was the school for me.

I realized later that it was only because of a sense of competition with my classmates that I had ever wanted to get into the top school. Clearly, this ego-driven competition was a source of suffering.

Looking back over the past, I see a number of problems with the "examination hell" in Japan, which stirs up a spirit of jealous rivalry among children and creates an unnecessary, destructive level of anxiety.

My father said to me,

"Better to be a chicken head than an ox tail."[8]

---

[8] This is equivalent to a Western saying: "Better to be a big fish in a small pond than a small fish in a big pond." In Western culture, however, it might be used as a putdown for the big fish in the small pond. In Eastern culture, on the other hand, being the head of a group is considered better than being just another "fish" in any group, big or small.

His remark clinched my decision.

"You're right, Dad! All I need is to become number-one at Akenohoshi!"

With that determination and hope, I entered the school.

English Speech Contest

Akenohoshi was opened in 1967, and I became a member of its fourth entering class in 1970. Although the school was new, it had set admission standards very high and had already become famous for its high-quality English education.

In those days, it was rare to find a school with even one English native speaker. A Catholic mission school, my high school had English teachers who were Canadians and Americans. Not just one or two, but five or six native speakers of English. Even the school principal was a Canadian. It was quite international. Having many native-speaker teachers had made Akenohoshi already quite famous, especially for its English education.

I had never spoken English with native speakers before entering high school. Consequently, I came to realize how horrible my English was and felt quite embarrassed. I had thought I was good at English, but what I had learned at junior high school was not good enough.

At Akenohoshi there was a modern language lab set up, and teachers used the so-called "Audio-Lingual" method to teach English, in which a lot of drills were used. We were told, for example, to replace nouns or change the third-person singular into the plural according to different pictures, etc. I always became confused while doing those drills and got a headache by the time I finished the lesson.

In English conversation classes, I often became frustrated because I could not understand what the teacher was saying. Understandably, I gradually developed a dislike for English.

On the other hand, I loved math. I was good at it and was always competing to be number-one on math exams. In math you can reach concrete, unequivocal solutions. I found it quite satisfying. Naturally, I decided to concentrate on math rather than English.

One day, at the beginning of my second year of high school, I was studying for an English exam on my way to school; I reviewed the textbook on the train and bus. Perhaps I was getting a lot of good alpha brain waves that day; my brain was working so well that I was able to absorb everything from the sections in the textbook that the exam covered. I took the exam and got a perfect score. It was hard to believe.

Later that afternoon, it was announced that one school representative would be chosen to compete in the upcoming Saitama Prefecture Senior High School English Speech Contest. Also announced was the criterion for the selection process. To my surprise, we were told that it would be based on the English exam held that day—more specifically, the top student from each of the five classes would be writing an essay.

As a result, I was asked to write an essay although I had never thought English was my forte. I wrote and submitted an essay including thoughts and opinions about my school life. The title of my essay was "Why Do We Study?" In it I argued that we should not be studying simply to get good grades or to get into a good university, but to build a foundation for life-long learning and to become a better person who could contribute to the world.

Several days later, after I had already forgotten about the speech contest, there was an announcement: I would be competing in the contest as the school's representative.

"Dad, an unbelievable thing happened. I'm in trouble." I explained to my father about the contest.

"That's great! It's good to challenge yourself at your weakest points. Compete fair and square just as you are. Do your best not to have any regrets later. Plus, for the sake of your school you are obligated to try your best. So, *gambare gambare* [strive, strive]!" said my dad, patting on my back.

This expression "gambare gambare" was Dad's stock phrase.

An American teacher named Mr. Mercier soon started giving me English lessons. He corrected my pronunciation and even taught me about gestures. I had to memorize the entire speech because notes were not allowed at the contest. I practiced my speech every day.

It must have been Dad's idea; the dinner on the day before the speech contest was a *ton-katsu* [breaded fried pork cutlet]—*ton* [pork] + *katsu* [cutlet]. I could easily guess the reason for this menu choice—I had several nicknames other than Moko, such as Ton-chan or Tonko.

After the dinner, just as I had predicted, Dad said,

"Tonko will win [*katsu* in Japanese] tomorrow now that we had *Ton-katsu!*" (Of course, Dad had punned *katsu* [cutlet] and *katsu* [win].)

A bit nervous because of the contest scheduled for the following day, I told him,

"Dad, it's no time to be joking around like this."

I continued to practice my speech.

"Hey, that's pretty good!" said Dad with big smiles.

I know he was as nervous as I was, but he was trying to hide it with jokes and puns.

He then quickly moved from discussing my speech to something much more profound.

"Well, when I was your age, English was banned as the enemy's language. So, we were not allowed to learn it. If you had used any foreign words during the war, you would have been accused of being unpatriotic. Just unbelievable! For instance, a baseball umpire would call a strike '*yoshi* [good]' and a foul '*dame* [no good].' It was just laughable.

But I believe that we should have learned English *because* it was the enemy's language. Japan banned it for emotional reasons. That's against the principle of 'knowing your enemy.'

America, on the other hand, was totally the opposite. What a great country!"

He was quite right. The United States stood in contrast with Japan during WWII. It let the linguistically talented master its enemies' languages. Moreover, the foreign language teaching in the US Army and Navy was so effective, its approach became known as the "Army Method" later on.

After the war, among those who had been trained to master Japanese, for instance, were Donald Keene and Edward Seidensticker, both of whom developed distinguished reputations as Japanese literary critics. They also both taught at Columbia University.

Additionally, in the field of Japanese cultural studies, Columbia-trained anthropologist Ruth Benedict became quite influential. Her research papers compiled during WWII were published in 1946 under the title *The Chrysanthemum and the Sword*. Margaret Mead, one of Benedict's students, also taught at Columbia University with Keene and Seidensticker.

As Dad was saying, I agreed that America was rational for having tried to know its enemies. At the same time, in the peaceful era after the war, I felt lucky to be taught English by a teacher from the United States, Japan's former enemy.

On the following day, Dad took me to the nearby station, and I headed for the speech contest venue in Urawa City.

At the contest, I thought I did fine; I neither got nervous nor made any mistakes. We then waited for the results. The champion's name was to be called at the very last. They called the names of the award recipients one by one—from honorable mentions to third place, and so on. My name was not called for any of those. I soon realized that I had a good chance of winning first place.

"And the champion is . . . Miss Tomoko Takahashi from Urawa Akenohoshi High School."

When I heard this announcement, I looked to Mr. Mercier, my English teacher. He was on top of the world. I was relieved and proud that I was able to honor my school by providing proof of its good English education.

I wanted to let my father know right away, so I called him from Urawa Station. He was elated. As soon as I got home, he took photos of me holding the certificate and trophy.

The next morning, my father found an article in the newspaper about the speech contest. When I came to join him for breakfast still feeling sleepy, he pointed out my name with a huge smile.

Relatives and friends who had read the newspaper article started calling Dad, who looked extremely proud. I didn't think winning the contest was such a big deal; I only felt relieved. As I looked at my beaming father, however, the sheer joy of being the champion gradually began to sink in.

Sharing Joy and Pain

My high school days were spent joyfully and meaningfully. I was truly happy that I had entered Akenohoshi. In my studies as well as extracurricular activities, I gained valuable experience. And, of all things, I came to love English, thanks to the speech contest and to Mr. Mercier.

Of course, not every day in high school was perfect. I came home one day feeling like crying because of some problems I had encountered during the student council activities earlier that day.

In simple terms, I threw a minor tantrum in front of my parents. I let off steam kicking and shoving whatever inanimate object was in reach, all the while screaming my displeasure. It didn't really make me feel any better, so I just shut myself up in my room.

Dad followed me before too long. I thought he was going to scold me for displaying my frustration in such a manner. To my surprise, he didn't say anything. He just sat down on my bed and remained silent as if he were trying to feel my pain and ease it. Like a mirror, his face reflected my bitter feelings.

After a while, I don't know how it happened, but I felt light again as my pain evaporated. And I said to my father, who was sitting there looking sad,

"Dad, I'm sorry."

I was able to straighten myself out because I could feel his deep understanding and affection for me.

If my father had scolded me when he followed me into my room that day, I would have resisted.

Certainly, there may be times when it is best to reprimand a child; embracing him or her may not always be appropriate. The real art of parenting is knowing when to show disappointment and when to show understanding. And that knowledge, to some extent, is dependent on a parent's intuition. I would say my father had really good intuition.

He sometimes expressed his feelings without words at all, as in the episode above. When he verbally expressed them, I remember he would use "I" as the subject of the sentence. That is, instead of saying, "You made a mistake" or "You are wrong," he would say, "If I were you, I would . . ." or "I feel sad." In other words, he was always trying to stick to "I" messages instead of "You" messages.

My father didn't say to us, "Do this" "Do that" in general (except in the instructions he gave us out of concern for our health and safety), nor did he nag or complain. Rather, he always kept the door open to us. And he always happily gave us advice on any matter.

There is no one recipe for parenting. Parents need to grow with their children while learning and struggling with them. In Japanese, "education" is 教育, which is pronounced *kyōiku* [literally meaning "teach" and "raise"]. I would suggest *kyōiku* be written 共育 [literally meaning "together" and "grow"].

I am today filled with appreciation for my father for his willingness to share in both my joy and pain. His attitude towards his children was always:

"When you are in pain, I'm in pain. When you are happy, I'm happy."

Some experiences bring both joy and pain at the same time. The end of my high school years was such an occasion.

Great joy was brought to me in the form of high school graduation. As I had promised my father, I graduated at the top of the class. With this accomplishment came two humbling honors: I gave a commencement speech representing the entire graduating class, and I received the Principal's Award. In addition, I received a Perfect-Attendance Award, which of course I considered to be given to "me and my dad" as I owed it to him and all those rides he gave me to the near-by train station.

I looked forward to my father's arrival at the graduation ceremony and could not wait for him to open the program, in which my name was printed as the recipient of the Principal's Award.

After the ceremony, I proudly said to my father,

"Dad, I was able to become the 'chicken head.'"
Then he said,
"No. You became the 'ox head'?" Saying so, he looked beyond happy.

Right before graduation, I experienced great pain. I was rejected by the university of my dreams. This was the second big failure in my life. The first was not getting into the high school that was my number-one choice and now the same thing at the university level. And this time, I was rejected by my second-choice university as well.

In Japan you must choose a major before entering college and apply to the program in the major of your choice. I had originally aimed at getting into a math and science program, but since the English speech contest, I had decided to major in English at college. Unfortunately, I had come to this decision rather late—in the final year of high school. As the exam requirements varied for different majors, my switching from math and science to English disadvantaged me. And yet, I was overly optimistic about the exams and didn't really pay attention to prepping for them.

When I found out that I had been rejected by my second choice as well, I felt no hope for the future. I decided to wait and try again the following year.[9] When I told my father of my plans, he said to me,

"If I were you, I would probably try to get into any college that's still accepting applications instead of spending a whole year just studying for entrance exams."

I was shocked to hear his words. The universities I wanted to attend were prestigious schools. His words made me realize that prestige didn't matter to him. If it did, he would have encouraged me to try again the following year.

---

9   It is common in Japan for students to wait until the following spring to take entrance examinations again—a large number of students choose this option. These students, called "*ronin* [masterless samurai]," spend an entire year, and sometimes longer, studying for another attempt at the entrance examinations.

I had mixed feelings. I was just about to graduate with an excellent academic record from a good high school. Not being accepted by a prestigious university made me feel afraid of how people might look at me. My father was trying to teach me to not make important life decisions on the basis of my cheap pride and ego.

Around the time when I was struggling to decide what to do, I heard an announcement made by the junior college affiliated with my high school. It would be starting a new scholarship program for studying in the United States. I jumped and said, "This is it!"

Studying in America had always been my dream since kindergarten. I gave up on it once when I developed a dislike for English, but after I won the English speech contest, I had revived the dream and been thinking about studying in the United States.

My high school also had a study abroad program, in which a couple of selected students were sent to a high school in the States on a full scholarship each year. I once told my father that I wanted to try that program. He said,

"I would think it's better to wait until you become twenty or so."

Remembering those words, I said to my dad this time,

"In this program, I would be going to America after graduating from junior college at age twenty. It's perfect. I'm going to try it!"

I applied to the junior college, took the exam, and got accepted. In April 1973, I entered the college.

The study abroad program I aimed for was such that it would allow one graduate of the junior college to transfer to a four-year college called Albertus Magnus College in New Haven, Connecticut, for which all the tuition would be waived and all the living expenses paid.

At that time in the early 1970s, one US dollar equaled more than 300 yen ($1 = ¥300). Today (2011) $1 is much less than ¥100. That is, it used to cost more than three times as much to study in the United States then than now. It was also still rare to even travel overseas. This study abroad program sounded like a dream.

Because of that, competition was fierce. There were a number of students who enrolled in the college to apply for this scholarship program. I studied like a crazy person. I don't know where my energy came from. I still cannot believe how focused and determined I was. That experience taught me one thing for sure: once you are convinced a hundred percent about something and set your mind on it, you can bring your ability into full play.

When the second year of college began, the school's final decision for the study abroad program was announced. Absolutely convinced that this program had been created for me, I had no doubt that I would be selected. *It's impossible not to be selected*, I thought. And as the result of my strong determination and hard work, I was able to grab the chance to study in America!

Life is serendipitous. If I had gotten into the university of my dreams, I would have lived an entirely different life. I wouldn't have gone to study in the United States. Or, maybe, that was my destiny. I felt that I was pulled into the direction of studying in America no matter what. Why did I win the English speech contest, which triggered all this? It's just incomprehensible.

As a Japanese saying goes, "A horse comes out of a *hyōtan* [bottle made out of a hardened gourd]," meaning "An unexpected thing happens." Or, "Defeat sometimes means victory." I had experienced a defeat, but there was something unexpected and positive hidden under the surface. You never know what might bring you fortune.

I also learned that what you believe is good for yourself might not necessarily be best for you. You may sometimes fail to achieve particular dreams, but it's important not to give up. The key to victory is to turn your failure or disappointment into something positive with a forward-looking attitude and great effort. It was, of course, my father who taught me all this.

Family Alcohol Ordinance

I turned twenty years old when I was in the second year of junior college. I was so happy to become legally allowed to drink alcohol. It's important here that I'm saying "legally."

My father had a drink with his dinner every evening. He always exercised moderation in drinking, but I heard that he could drink quite a bit if he wanted to. On the other hand, my mother could not constitutionally accept alcohol at all. She would only happily watch Dad enjoy his drinks, sitting right next to him.

Dad had a large capacity for alcohol, and Mom had none. This is a big secret, but we children found out which parent we took after in terms of alcohol capacity when we were still very young. I was in kindergarten and only five or so.

Dad liked drinking saké warm even in the summer, but when it got extremely hot, he would switch to ice-cold beer. At dinner, then, he would drink beer, and we children would drink soda.

Since both beer and soda had bubbles, Dad didn't think we would notice any difference.

One day, his youngest, Moko-suke (author), attacked him,

"Daddy, how come yours has some color, but mine doesn't?"

A bit tipsy, Dad responded to my protest, by saying,

"Okay, then, I will add some color to your glass," and he poured a little bit of beer into my glass.

Dad was thinking,

Moko-suke is not going to listen to me even if I tell her that kids can't drink beer, but she will give it up once she tastes the bitterness of beer.

To his surprise, he heard,

"Daddy, this tastes delicious!"

He was dumbfounded.

Even though I was a young child, I really thought it was tasty, especially liking the harmonious mixture of the bitterness of the beer and the sweetness of the soda.

Then, my sister asked for some beer to be added to her glass. It was too late for Dad to make any excuses. From that time on, whenever we saw him drinking beer, we always asked him to share a little bit of his beer with us to add to our soda. This is how we learned the taste of "beer and soda."

Even though we were kids, we never got drunk no matter how many glasses of beer and soda we had. It's a bit frightening. Dad felt guilty but was rather happy, asking,

"Whom did they take after?"

Mom would get tipsy with just a lick of *ama-saké* [sweet saké]. In contrast, we, her children, would be drinking cup after cup of the same sweet saké. We indeed were able to drink. (*Ama-saké* had a small percentage of alcohol, but it was enjoyed by adults as well as children. In my family, it was made with the fresh saké lees [yeast deposits] bought from a local brewer, which had a lot more alcohol content than the lees sold at grocery stores.)

"In Europe, I hear, children drink wine with their meals. So, why not!" Dad made excuses.

When I became a high school student, I volunteered to prepare hot saké for my father before dinner. Why did I do that? Because it was to my benefit.

Dad would take an evening bath and come to the dinner table. I would always time his arrival and prepare his hot saké.

"Dad, here's your hot saké," said I as soon as he was seated at the dinner table. And Dad was always happy to receive it.

"Then, you should have a cup too," said Dad and poured some saké in my cup.

After repeating this routine, I had fully mastered the taste of Japanese saké well before I became twenty years old, the legal drinking age in Japan.

Dad, however, never allowed us to drink alcohol outside our home.

"As long as you stay home, you may drink."

This was the Takahashi family alcohol ordinance. And, as long as we kept it, we were safe.

Dad gave us several other rules:

- Exercise moderation in drinking.
- Never drink to excess.
- Never drink on an empty stomach.
- Parents' words and cold saké both have a delayed effect on you—i.e., "Be careful with cold saké."

And the list went on.

We also had other rules. As for smoking, "absolutely no." Dad kept us from smoking despite (or maybe *because of*) the fact that he himself was a heavy smoker. He started smoking when he was in the army during the war, and he was unable to quit even though he earnestly wanted to.

At the time when I became an adult, people did not look kindly on women's smoking in Japan. And I myself never had any interest in smoking. Today I feel fortunate I never started.

We had another rule—pierced ears were not allowed. I never had any interest in having my ears pierced either.

In the late 1970s, piercing ears was still rare but was gradually becoming popular in Japan, especially among singers and actresses. One day, as we were watching TV, my sister pointed out a singer and said,

"Look, she has her ears pierced."

As soon as Dad heard this, he responded,

"Confucius said, 'We received our body, hair, and skin from our parents and dare not harm them. This is the beginning of filiality.' That means: it is unfilial to harm your precious body received from your parents or to have it altered artificially or unnaturally."

Oh my, Mr. Confucius again, I thought to myself. There was nothing we could do when Dad quoted from *The Analects of Confucius*. I refrained from arguing.

Those words by my father have never left me, so I have never had my ears pierced and have always worn clip-on earrings.

When my brother, Hiromi, was in college, he started bringing his friends home, where they could happily drink together. They were sometimes his former classmates from high school or his friends from the yacht club at Hitotsubashi University, which he was attending. They all seemed to be having so much fun drinking together at our house. They particularly enjoyed drinking with my father, who was great fun to talk to.

My brother's friends were all very unique. Their university majors were different too, so the topics of interest and conversations were very diverse. I always had much fun listening to them and often joined their conversations. It seemed, however, my father was the one who was enjoying their company most.

Dad liked giving a nickname to Hiromi's friends. For instance, he would say,

"Hoshino reminds me of Hiram."

Then, it became this particular friend's nickname. We didn't use it in front of him, but reserved it as a secret code among ourselves.

Incidentally, this name "Hiram" came from the main character in *The Adventures of Hiram Holiday*, the TV program imported from the States we used to watch.

Intelligent looking and wearing glasses, Hoshino indeed looked like Hiram. His voice and demeanor were also reminiscent of the TV character.

"Yeah, Dad, if he carried an umbrella, he would be Hiram's twin!" I said, truly impressed by my father's talent for nicknaming.

I never drank alcohol outside home even after I celebrated the Adult Day ceremony, only because I loved having a few drinks with my dad at home more than anything.

Speaking of Adult Day, I asked my father for cash instead of a kimono to celebrate my coming-of-age. It's traditional in Japan for girls to wear expensive kimonos to go to the Adult Day ceremony, but I didn't think it made sense to spend so much money on something that you would wear only once or twice in your life time. I didn't think I would wear a kimono to the college graduation reception either.

"Dad, I'd rather buy books and phonograph records. So, would you give me cash instead?" I negotiated with my father.

"You are so mercenary!" said Dad, and accepted my request with a smile. I was given a large sum of cash!

I never wore a kimono. Nor did I go to the Adult Day ceremony. I was stumped, however, when my relatives showed up unexpectedly, wanting to see me dressed up for the occasion. Well, perhaps, they were the ones who were stumped because my Sunday best for that day was my pajamas!

Not only that, they heard me say,

"I had a bit too much to drink last night and have such a hangover."

They were utterly appalled. And I thought,

How annoying for them to just show up like that!

I made such a striking contrast with my sister, who had pleased everyone by looking magnificent in her beautiful kimono two years before. I'm sure my relatives were shocked and troubled by my behavior.

A year later, I wrote in my diary about my coming-of-age.

Excerpts from Tomoko's diary
dated January 15, 1976

Today is Adult Day in Japan. [. . .] A year ago today, I had such a hangover. I goofed around in my pajamas all morning and didn't even go to the ceremony at the civil hall. My relatives must have expected me to look gorgeous dressed up in a kimono, but I let them down. They looked appalled because it was obvious I had just gotten out of bed. In a fluster, I went to change, not into a kimono, but into jeans and a T-shirt. [. . .] When my sis had celebrated her coming-of-age, she was gorgeous. Mom and Dad were so content with her Sunday best! Why am I so different from her? Aren't we sisters? [. . .] I preferred cash to a kimono and received a large sum of money, but it disappeared quickly and instantly, spent on a camera, lenses, a tape-recorder, books, phonograph records, etc. I wonder if I'm a bad daughter? Rather than pleasing my parents, I wanted to spend money on myself. But I bet Mom and Dad like me for my eccentricity. If I were the same as my sis, then it would be so boring.

As I was chosen to be the recipient of the special scholarship for the study-abroad program in college, I was rather a good student. And yet, in other areas, I wasn't such a good daughter—I drank alcohol under age, I disappointed my relatives, etc. Despite all that, I think I have grown up to be a decent adult. I owe it, of course, all to my parents.

7. Dad's Dream, My Dream

I'll Gather Your Bones

In my second year of junior college, I kept myself busy studying and preparing for my study abroad.

One day, I was told that in order to study at an American college, I would have to take an English examination called "Toe-full." I had no idea what kind of exam it was. In those days, information about study abroad was almost nonexistent and very difficult to find.

The name of the exam was, actually, "TOEFL," an abbreviation for the "Test of English as a Foreign Language." It's an English proficiency exam taken by non-native speakers of English wishing to study in the United States or Canada. Today it has become a household name in Japan; the test has been taken by a large number of students wishing to study abroad as well as those who would like to simply prove their English proficiency.

Back in the early 1970s, the number of TOEFL test-takers in Japan was only 10% of that today. Also, around that time, the number of Japanese students studying in the United States was said to be about 5,000. After that, the number increased steadily and reached a peak in 1997 with about 47,000 Japanese students studying in the United States. Although the number slightly decreased after that peak, today it's still going strong with an average of 40,000 Japanese students studying at American colleges and universities each year. In addition, a large number of Japanese students visit the States to learn English in non-degree programs. Especially compared to the popularity of studying abroad today, one can appreciate how uncommon it was in the 1970s.

Besides, in the 70s, the Internet didn't exist. The amount of information you could find was extremely limited or almost nonexistent compared to what we can find on the Internet today. It was not an age when we could simply type on a computer keyboard to find information.

I struggled to find information about the TOEFL, but with some advice from a junior college teacher, I was able to find an English language school in Tokyo that was administering the test. I went to take the exam there.

Unfortunately, however, it turned out that it was just a mock exam for the TOEFL, not a real one. How disappointing it was! At the same school, I registered for the real TOEFL exam on a later date. Basically, I was in the dark. I didn't even know that there were textbooks you could study from as well as cram schools you could attend to prepare for the TOEFL. I took the exam without any special preparation.

Upon seeing my test score, I was devastated. It was far from a perfect score. And yet, it was good enough to get me into an American college. That much was a big relief. Nonetheless, never having received such a bad score, I felt shattered. (Later I found out that even native speakers of English would not be able to get a perfect score on the TOEFL. And, actually, my score wasn't really that bad, but it was a long time before I realized that.)

In March 1975, I graduated from junior college. Relieved, I was going to relax and enjoy myself for several months; my plans were to leave Japan in late August to enter Albertus Magnus College in early September. Soon, however, I learned that there was an English as a second language (ESL) program being offered at Yale University in New Haven, where Albertus was located. Since I was a bit worried about becoming a junior at an American college and majoring in English, I decided to attend this Yale summer program to prepare myself for college.

The Yale program was to begin in late June of 1975; I had to depart Japan earlier than planned. As a result, my anticipated summer of relaxation abruptly turned into a chaotic scramble. I ran around and rushed to make arrangements to travel to America. Until then, I had never left Japan, so I had to get a passport first.

Then, after receiving a document called "I-20" from Yale, I was instructed to go to the US Embassy to receive a student visa.

Because of the dearth of information available about studying abroad at that time, I had to figure out everything on my own and make arrangements all by myself. Since a lot of the details had to be dealt with in English, my father was unable to help me. Totally excited, however, that I was going to the country of my dreams, I did whatever was necessary to prepare for my departure.

I went to the US Embassy in Tokyo with my newly acquired passport and the required documents in hand. As soon as I stepped into the embassy building, I remember, I trembled with excitement. English was spoken there, and the whole atmosphere was America itself; it was my first experience of being in "America."

I sometimes felt anxious and worried about going abroad. But my father said to me,

"I will gather your bones.[10]

So, go to America and study hard with no worries!"

He meant that he would take care of me if anything happened to me in America. He would even find and pick up my corpse if I dropped dead! I appreciated the intention implied by this rather rough expression. I felt trusted. No matter what hardships I might encounter, my dad knew that I was determined and would face down any obstacles in the way of my success. Besides, it was my own choice to go to America. How could I retreat?

My father often encouraged me orally like this, but he also wrote down his words of encouragement and advice on pieces of paper and gave them to me. For instance, he wrote on a small price tag used at his store:

---

[10] This expression in Japanese 骨を拾う [pick up or gather bones] means that someone will be at your funeral (cremation of your corpse) to gather your bones into an urn. In other words, he or she will survive you and take care of your corpse after you die, so that you won't have to worry about your death and can challenge yourself to the utmost even until your death.

"Go your own way but avoid becoming arrogant."

On the card he gave me on Father's Day, a week before my departure, he wrote:

"Each time you overcome pain and suffering, your heart becomes bigger and richer."

This was followed by more encouragement and advice. For instance, he cautioned me to pay attention to my valuables—indicative of how worried he was about me. He obviously felt as though he, too, was going to America. I could feel his kind heart from the way he shared his wisdom to help me prepare for my study abroad.

My father undoubtedly had in his mind: *My daughter has the opportunity to live my dream.* Helping me cling to my highest aspirations, he cheered me on. He didn't get to go to the college of his dreams, Yokohama Kō-Shō, a gateway to America, but he was transforming his own regrets into making my dreams possible. How lucky and grateful I am!

My father used to call me his "clone." Letting his clone go to America meant that he was also going to America to chase his own dreams. To America . . . the country he had yearned for as a young man . . .

He also used to call me a "palanquin-bearing partner."[11] Because he always gave me a ride to school, he thought we were like two palanquin bearers, without one of which the other could not function. The legacy went all the way back to my kindergarten years, so we had a long history of "palanquin bearing." Just about to lose his palanquin pal, my father was indeed at a loss. He continued to mentally prepare himself, trying to repress his sentimental feelings, while his pal was busily preparing to leave home for America.

Dad gave me more advice. For instance, he counseled me, "If you want to change something about your personality, it's up to you."

---

[11] A Japanese palanquin called "*kago*" was like a sedan chair or a litter, suspended by a single crossbeam, carried by two bearers, usually used to transport one person at a time.

Because no one in America knew me, he suggested I could work on whatever I found wanting in myself and become a new and better person.

That makes sense, I thought. I would be freed from the images and perceptions other people had always had about me in Japan. I would freely be able to change myself to fit my ideals. I was totally excited about the possibilities.

My great-great-grandfather Kisuke became a "new person" in Kawagoe after shedding his samurai identity. My father, too, became a new person and fought as an army officer during the war. He became a new person again when he sang in front of hundreds of soldiers, when he threw his sword into the Yangtze River, and when he began working as a salaried worker in Tokyo . . .

I pledged to myself to become a global citizen, shedding my old self to become my true self.

There was a lot more behind my father's words "I'll gather your bones." He began it by saying,

"I was twenty years old when I left home to go to Manchuria. You, too, are leaving home at age twenty to go to America . . ." And he continued,

"When I visited home during the war, I found out my father had died some time before and everything was a big mess at home."

Upon hearing those words, I looked at him with alarm. Sensing it immediately, Dad said to me,

"Oh, don't worry! I'm in perfect health. I'm not going to die. Are you kidding? Actually, I will gather *your* bones. So, go to America and study hard with no worries!"

America Awaits Me!

On June 22, 1975, my adventure began. With my entire family, I left home for Haneda Airport. (Narita Airport had not yet opened.)

June is the rainy season in Japan. As expected, on the day of my departure, it was raining. Despite the bad weather, many friends and teachers from my high school and junior college came to see me off, as well as my relatives and even my sister's friends. Some of those who were gracious enough to come even brought me flowers.

Surrounded by a big crowd, I kept thanking them, feeling a bit self-conscious. My father also thanked and bowed to my friends and teachers much more politely than I did. My mother, although she was the sentimental type, was enduring the event without crying. My sister, in contrast, was in tears the whole time.

My father projected his typical calmness, but he must have been feeling unbearable heartache inside. He typically endured heat and coldness by saying, "Clear your mind of all mundane thoughts, and you will find even fire cool." I can only imagine that Dad endured his sentimental feelings by clearing his mind. As one might expect, he tempered his own emotions so that I would not feel any reluctance to leave.

It soon became the time for me to get ready for boarding. Not too good at dealing with emotions, I quickly said goodbye to everyone and walked toward the security gate.

America awaits me! I felt so excited that I walked lightly. I couldn't afford to be feeling sentimental; I had to be sure to get on board the right plane. I went through security, and headed for my aircraft on a bus.

Once I left the terminal and went outside, it was rainy and chilly. On the bus, all of a sudden, I felt lonely. Then I happened to look up in the direction of the terminal. And in the rain, I saw my family, teachers, and friends waving their hands on the deck.

Oh, I see . . . Those tickets Dad had bought and distributed to my friends and teachers were for them to get into the special spectator deck! I realized.

I could see my father drenched in the rain and frantically waving his hand . . . along with my mother, brother, and sister. I felt my heart tighten.

Up until that point, I had been dashing toward my dream to study in America, and it hadn't even occurred to me how sad it would be to say goodbye to my beloved family and friends.

I got off the bus and looked at the spectator deck far away. I saw my family and friends still waving their hands without pause.

I tore myself from the image of my loved ones and went up the boarding ramp.

As soon as I was seated, I felt like crying.

Ah . . . I'm really going to America, leaving my wonderful family . . .

Soon I told myself,

Yes! I am going because I want to! No matter how painful it is. To America!

Raindrops on the small windows looked like my family's tears. My plane started to move and the spectator deck was growing farther and farther away. Suddenly I was overwhelmed with loneliness. I never even realized when the plane took off.

An American passenger next to me was looking at me, seemingly concerned. I explained to him,

"I'm going to college in America. I'm sad because I won't be able to see my family until I graduate."

I watched the vast ocean of clouds outside the windows throughout my flight.

Airfares were unbelievably expensive; I remember an economy-class one-way ticket from Tokyo to New York was 200,000 yen in 1975. It was about $666 according to the exchange rate in the 1970s, but it would actually be over $2,600 today (2011) with inflation.

Considering the cost of traveling, I was determined not to come home until I had graduated. (The situation back then was so different from that of today. Japanese students studying in the United States today often go home for a summer vacation, Christmas, and sometimes, even for spring break!)

Furthermore, there was no direct flight from Tokyo to New York. My flight, JAL 06, stopped in Anchorage, Alaska, for refueling. It was night. I looked outside the windows to see if I could see an aurora, but it was just pitch dark.

I went through immigration to be admitted into the country.

I'm really in America . . . I reminded myself repeatedly.

Although I did still feel a bit lonely, I knew this was what I had chosen to do.

How can I complain about loneliness? Adventures await me! I told myself and went back onboard the plane, which flew to the JFK airport in New York.

My family remained anxious and worried about me until finally hearing from me that I had safely arrived in New Haven.

In the letter my father wrote after receiving a collect call from me, he described the day of my departure as follows:

Excerpts from my father's letter dated June 24, 1975

Thanks for your call this morning (night for you). My accumulated worries evaporated at once. [. . .] I knew you would safely make it, but I was still worried. Whenever I had a moment, I pictured you waving vigorously from the bus—the scene is imprinted on my mind.

On the day of your departure, so many of your friends and teachers came to see you off. They waved with me from the spectator deck. I was so appreciative that I didn't know how to thank them.

During the 40 minutes saying goodbye in the airport lobby, I felt my heart tighten so many times. It was really painful to endure that overwhelming sentiment. But the more painful it got, I thought, the more joy we would experience when we welcomed you back home. I reminded myself of this repeatedly.

After you left, we went to a coffee shop in the airport along with eleven or so friends of yours as well as teachers, including Sister Lavina, who spoke so highly of you and showed so much confidence in you. [. . .]

After saying goodbye to the teachers, we decided to have lunch at the Trade Center in Hamamatsu. The eight of us, including your cousin Hitoshi, Reiko's friend Mako, and your classmate Akiko, wandered around to find a good place to eat. Then we came across a Chinese restaurant called "Sha-Hō-Den." Because the Chinese characters in its name [謝朋殿] sounded like "Thank you, Lord Tomoko," we decided to go in there.

> *After that, we took Hitoshi home and gave the report of your*
> *departure to your grandparents.*
> *In the evening, we had dinner at home, thinking about and*
> *imagining you on the plane.*
> *At 2 a.m. (when you were scheduled to land in New York),*
> *your mother and I got up, burned incense, and prayed for your safe*
> *landing. [. . .]*

Arriving in New Haven

What a long journey it was! I finally made it to the JFK. Although I had had no sleep since I left home, I was full of energy and excitement. At the same time, I could almost hear my father's voice telling me to calm down. Following his advice, I paid attention to my belongings.

"Passport? Check.

Suitcase? Check.

Shoulder bag and typewriter? Check."

I talked to myself. I then got in a limousine bus bound for New Haven.

Finally feeling relieved, I looked outside of the window. In front of my eyes, I found the "America" I had always dreamed of.

Is this a dream? I felt like pinching myself. Normally, whenever I pinched myself, it turned out to be a dream and I woke up, leaving me feeling terribly disappointed. This time, however, I didn't. It was not a dream!

I was overwhelmed by the magnificent view of the elegant, yet mighty, Whitestone Bridge that crossed through Queens into the Bronx. Seen from the giant suspension bridge was the island of Manhattan . . . and the brilliant glitter of the East River's surface . . . Again, I pinched myself.

My limousine bus soon got on a highway called "Interstate 95 (I-95)," the main highway on the East Coast of the United States, paralleling the Atlantic Ocean from Maine to Florida. We were now on a direct route to New Haven.

Big sedans were driving serenely. They were actually going fast, but on the wide highway the speed was not easily sensed. It didn't even strike me as strange that the cars were going on the right side of the highway, unlike in Japan, where they drove on the left side.

There were rock walls on both sides of the highway. Behind the big rocks were lush trees. I could not believe there was so much nature just a bit north of Manhattan.

After about two hours of this scenic journey of eighty miles from the JFK, I arrived in New Haven. I got in a taxi at the limousine bus stop.

"To Yale University, please." I told the cab driver.

Then he smiled and responded,

"It's all Yale here. Where do you wanna go?"

I realized for the first time that almost the entire town of New Haven was the Yale campus.

"To Helen Hadley Hall, please," I told him.

The driver understood and took me there right away.

The Yale campus reminded me of Oxford University, whose photos I had seen before. There were reddish brick buildings as well as castle-like ones. As the name "Ivy-League" suggested, there were buildings and walls covered with ivy everywhere.

I saw students riding bikes on the streets . . . and those with their backpacks hurriedly walking. They all looked smart. I simply could not believe I would be joining them soon as a Yale student. I felt as if I were in a dream again.

I soon arrived at Helen Hadley Hall (HHH). As I entered the building, I found a reception desk, where a student was working as a receptionist. I introduced myself, checked in, and received my room key.

The student working at the reception desk was named James. His straight brown hair and mustache were quite distinctive. As I looked at the desk, I realized he had been studying. There were piles of books.

When I was just about to leave the desk, James stopped me and asked,

"Glad you're here. Do you know what this means?"

He showed me the book he was reading in Japanese. I was astonished and said to myself,

I can't believe he can read such a difficult book written in archaic Japanese!

He ignored my surprise and continued,

"What does this mean—*usagi-ni tsuno* [horns to a rabbit]?"

I almost burst into laughter. Then I read it slowly,

"*To-ni-ka-ku* [believe it or not]."[12]

James immediately got it and said,

"Oh, I see. It's *tonikaku!*"

Then, we both burst into laughter. In any case, what a difficult and archaic Japanese book he was reading!

James was a doctoral student majoring in Japanese Buddhism. I was lucky to have met him on the day I arrived in New Haven. I continued to cherish my friendship with him after I transferred to Albertus at the end of that summer. We often went to a bar called "Gypsy," where Yale graduate students drank, and we used to dance with the step called the "Bus Stop."

Most of James's close friends were also graduate students in East Asian studies. For instance, his girlfriend, Suzanne, was studying Japanese history and was fluent in Japanese; she even spoke a Kansai dialect like a native speaker, as she had studied in Kyoto. Mike, a Chinese history major, was proficient in Chinese, as he had studied in Taiwan.

After having a good laugh with James about "horns to a rabbit," I finally reached my room in HHH. It was already past 4 p.m. And almost twenty-four hours had passed since I left home in Japan. Although I had not slept at all during that time, I was still full of

---

12   *Tonikaku* is an idiomatic expression in Japanese meaning "believe it or not," "regardless" or "anyway," and the traditional way of writing this expression is 兎に角, which literally means "horns to a rabbit." The Chinese character 兎 [rabbit] could be read "usagi" or "to," and 角 [horn] could be read "tsuno" or "kaku."

energy. As soon as I put my luggage down in my room, I went to visit the campus of Albertus Magnus College.

Going up Prospect Street about a mile, one finds Albertus. Lush trees everywhere and very peaceful, it felt like a different world.

I will never forget how moved I felt when I stood in front of the main gate of the Albertus campus. Then, I saw the white building. It was Rosary Hall, whose photo I had looked at so many times before. Here it was in reality and it was beautiful!

Is this a dream? I asked again.

I met the nuns there and introduced myself. One of them, Sister Fidelis, was especially kind, asking me if I needed anything. And she, thoughtfully, continued,

"There is a concert on the green this evening. Why don't you come with me? I'll come pick you up later."

I said goodbye to the nuns and went back to my dorm.

After a while, Sister Fidelis came to pick me up.

The concert was supposed to start at 7:30 p.m., but I was surprised to see how bright it still was outside even after 7.

I wrote about the concert in a letter to my family.

Excerpts from Tomoko's letter
dated June 24, 1975

I had such a taxing schedule on the day of arrival, June 22.

I went to a concert with the sister I told you about on the phone. It was held on the lawn in a big park, which was only a 5-minute walk or so from my dorm. And admission was free, of course. Carrying blankets, people gathered on the green to listen to the orchestra—old folks, children, young couples, etc. They all looked happy. I thought it was much better than a concert in Tokyo that costs you thousands of yen and requires you to travel afar. It was informal and friendly. It's so comforting to your heart (and to your wallet too). Some read books or chatted on the green. I could see they were all enjoying the music with their minds and bodies.

This concert series was a great discovery for me, a classical-music lover. There were also concerts frequently held at the Yale concert hall. For the two years I lived in New Haven, I enjoyed a number of concerts. For instance, the conductor Seiji Ozawa came to New Haven a couple of times. I was such a big fan of his that I had even brought a copy of his book with me to America. After the concert, I went back stage to find Mr. Ozawa and asked him to autograph the book. I also traveled to Tanglewood to listen to the Boston Symphony Orchestra conducted by him. Those are truly golden memories.

By the time the concert on the green was over, it was already past 9 p.m. Sister Fidelis suggested that we go have some ice cream. So we went to an ice cream parlor called "Clark's" near my dorm.

As soon as we stepped into the place, I was shocked. First, I was astonished by the gigantic size of the dishes used for serving ice cream and banana splits. What's more, I saw huge piles of whipped cream on top of them, which made me sick to my stomach.

I was even more shocked to see middle-aged men about my father's age enjoying ice cream. My father didn't eat any sweets. Besides, in Japan, ice cream parlors were always thought of as places where young schoolgirls gathered; you would never find middle-aged men there eating ice cream.

That was my first culture shock. And yet, I recovered from it quickly, determined to be flexible enough to challenge my prior expectations. I picked one out of the thirty or so flavors, one that didn't look too sweet, and ordered it to indulge myself. It was a taste of America I experienced for the first time.

That night, after I went back to my dorm room, I unpacked my suitcase, which my sister Reiko had neatly packed for me before my departure. When I went to bed, it was close to midnight. I could hardly believe that it was still June 22nd, the day I had departed Haneda. That was truly the longest day in my entire life.

I wonder how everyone at home is doing . . . I thought about my emotional departure in the rain, while looking down at the streetlights on Temple Street. I released a deep sigh. It was my first night alone in America, but instead of feeling lonely, I felt content.

I'm training myself. When I look back to this time in the future, I'm sure I'll be impressed and say, "What a great adventure that was!" I pondered so and slept tight that night.

Play Fair and Be Courageous

The next morning I woke up refreshed. I didn't even feel jet-lagged after a good night's sleep. The first thing I had to do that morning was to register for the ESL program. I went to take care of it immediately. After receiving my meal card, I went to the dining hall named Commons for breakfast.

The dining room had high ceilings and was grandiose. It was so big and beautiful that it could easily be mistaken, I thought, for a museum or something of that sort. Its appearance was far from that of a university cafeteria in Japan.

The food wasn't too bad. Once I got used to eating there, I tried to taste everything, especially what I had never eaten before. I wanted to be adventurous. I also wanted to become like my fellow American students and assimilate into American culture.

After dinner, I picked up a couple of oranges. I then went outside and sat on the lawn to eat them, watching students playing Frisbee.

What a peaceful evening . . . I indulged myself.

Classes began. I found out that I had been placed in one of the upper-level classes; I must have scored high on the placement exam. Although that seemed hard to believe, I went on to class.

My class consisted of students mostly from Japan and South America. Japanese students were good at English grammar and composition, whereas South Americans were better at speaking English. It was a great advantage to be able to speak English well as those South Americans did. Whenever they argued in class, we Japanese students were overwhelmed and simply gave in. And yet, where English grammar and compositions were concerned, model presentations always came from Japanese students.

Tomoko T. Takahashi

Excerpts from Tomoko's letter dated July 11, 1975

Thank you for your letter. I'm happy today is Friday. After class, I went shopping leisurely. And I came back to the dorm to find a letter from home just as expected. I was surprised to see a big postage of 220 yen on the letter. I imagined the content as I went upstairs in the elevator and read it in my room.

I have finished the first three weeks of the program. Four more weeks to go! Classes start at 8 a.m. and finish at 3 or 4 p.m. The first class is Composition, where we study how to write academic papers and essays. We get a lot of homework every day. And believe it or not, I have been diligently doing all of it! I think I have improved my writing skills quite a bit. It's an interesting class; we analyze sentences, read books (one book per two days), etc. We are often given themes to write essays for homework. My compositions are always praised and marked "excellent" and I often get asked to read my essays as model presentations in class. [. . .] It seems that we Japanese students are good at reading and writing. When it comes to speaking, however, we are no match for the South Americans and Europeans. [. . .]

Speaking of speaking English, I have many opportunities to talk to students from various countries (and states)—of course, in English. It's really motivating. But they ask such difficult questions that I often break into a cold sweat! I'm desperate and trying very hard!

A struggle related to the difficult questions mentioned above was entered into my diary as follows:

Excerpts from Tomoko's diary dated June 28, 1975

Got up at 10 a.m. Slept very well. This is the first time I slept so late in many days. Went to the dining hall to have brunch. I was sitting alone, but soon an American student came to join me.

He started talking to me in a friendly manner. His English was difficult to understand, but I managed to converse with him.

He asked me questions about the Vietnam War:

"What do the Japanese think about American operations in South Vietnam?"

I could not answer his question. Not only did I not have enough English proficiency to answer him, I didn't have my own opinions to begin with. I felt keenly how difficult it was to discuss socio-political topics. I must study harder . . .

In another letter to my family, I wrote more about my English classes.

Excerpts from Tomoko's letter dated July 26, 1975

Everything is good in my daily life. But classes are tough. Some are utterly boring, and others are extremely stressful. For instance, conversation classes make me tense the entire time. Probably because I did well on the placement exam, I was placed in an upper-level class with really smart folks. This class has, for instance, two from the Japanese Ministry of Foreign Affairs (both are going to Harvard), a 30-some-year-old guy from Mitsubishi Corporation, and so forth. They are graduates of Tokyo University, Kyoto University, etc. I guess I shouldn't feel hung up on it, but I'm only 20 years old, you know, while those guys are pretty old. When we hold discussions in class, we just can't talk about the same topics. I'm the only one as young as twenty in this upper-level class. But don't worry. I'm trying to be as bold as brass.

By the way, this conversation class consists of Japanese students only. It was explained that it's more effective to have students from the same country in order to correct their pronunciation problems. Other classes have students from France, Spain, Portugal, Puerto Rico, etc. Due to their accents, their English is different and quite interesting.

In retrospect, I am puzzled by the English conversation class I was in. Conversation classes are different in nature from pronunciation classes. I have no idea why Japanese students were bunched together in those conversation classes. It's more effective, I would think, to have students from various countries and backgrounds discuss a wide range of topics, placing value on diversity.

In my conversation class, one day, the teacher suggested that we discuss "prostitution," of all things. I found the topic surprisingly inappropriate and objectionable. Could he think of no other topics for his students? How could he make me, a young woman brought up with tender care and the only female student in class, discuss such a topic with middle-aged men?! (When the summer course ended, I gave this instructor my feedback detailing everything I had found deficient about his instruction.)

As described above, there were a good number of Japanese students in my classes. Naturally, even though we tried not to, we often started speaking Japanese among ourselves.

One day, we were caught speaking Japanese by one of the ESL teachers. He said,

"Hey, why are you speaking Japanese? If you speak Japanese again, you'll be fined five cents."

I described this incident in my diary: "Ouch! Ouch!" I guess I was struggling with English every day. (Incidentally, you may think a penalty of "five cents" is really nothing. But if you take an inflation rate into consideration, it's about twenty cents today [2011]. You may still think it's a small amount of money, but the Japanese yen was not as strong as today back then. To us, it seemed like a steep fine and good motivation.)

Some teachers seemed to show favor to students going to prestigious schools like Harvard. I could tell from their attitudes. I'm certain it was not due to my jealousy or inferiority complex.

There was a teacher, however, who was never swayed by such concerns. Her name was Mrs. Hortas. Intelligent and embracing, she praised each and every one of her students for his or her efforts and tried to help them improve their English as much as possible. It didn't matter to her which countries we were from, which university we would be attending, or which famous company or school we were sent from. She had no prejudice, I could tell.

This ESL experience I had at Yale later became of great value. Needless to say, it prepared me for studies at Albertus. I never thought, however, it would become helpful in the future in a different way—when I became a teacher trainer. (I never even imagined that I would be involved in English education many years later.)

Facing two years of studying in America, I had to become fully independent. As my father encouraged me to "play fair and be courageous," I challenged myself in every aspect of my daily life.

I had to take care of things that I had never even done in Japan—such as opening a bank account. Even though I was on a full scholarship, I had to have some pocket money for personal expenses. I needed a bank account in order to receive money from my father.

Early on, I went to a bank. In the lobby, I looked around. Without knowing where to go, I spoke to a man who seemed appropriate to talk to.

"I would like to open a checking account," I told him.

Although I was twenty years old, I'm sure I looked quite young especially to Americans. It's possible that I could have been mistaken for a high school student or even a junior high school student. And yet, this gentleman responded to me courteously. Soon I found out that he was the bank's general manager.

"In order to open a bank account, you must have a social security number," he told me.

"What's that? Where can I get one?" I asked.

He kindly instructed me where to go. So I went to the social security office and took care of all the paperwork there. Then I returned to the bank with my own social security number. The bank manager welcomed me back with a big smile and took care of my application for a checking account.

That day, I got my social security number and my own checking account! I felt extremely satisfied.

Good for you! You can do anything if you're not too afraid to try, I told myself.

Letters and Comfort Bags

While studying in America, I was fortunate enough to receive a number of letters and packages from my family and friends. My mailbox was regularly stuffed with letters and package slips.

A letter from my father and family arrived every Friday without fail. Dad would write details about each of the seven days by excerpting from his diary. Then he mailed it out every Monday, which was delivered to me on Friday of the same week. He continued to do so throughout the time I studied in New Haven. He never missed a single week even once.

My father, Kiyoshi, Age 54 (1975)
One of the many photos received via airmail

His letters were always full of information about my family, his business, plants in the backyard, my pet dog Charlie, news about Japan and the world, results of ball games and *sumo* tournaments, his fishing trips, neighborhood association meetings, stories about the old days, etc. He often enclosed newspaper clippings too.

Since it was quite expensive to send letters overseas via airmail, letters were written on lightweight onionskin paper. Dad always used a fountain pen and wrote on each sheet of thin airmail paper with his meticulous handwriting. Every week I received abundant courage and energy from him through his letters.

The Internet was not available back then, and international phone calls were dreadfully expensive. The only regular means of communication we had was airmail. Letters received overseas back then were quite special and are not the same today.

My family looked forward to my letters from America and received them with an air of excitement. Each time my letter arrived, the entire family was thrown into an uproar. You can witness how excited my parents were from the way my father described his reaction to my first letter.

Excerpts from my father's letter dated July 7, 1975

6/28—Your long-awaited letter was delivered! Your mother came tumbling down from the back of the house as soon as she heard my voice announcing the delivery. I read the first page in one breath and gave it to her. And the second page again in one breath . . . Then, I perused all the pages again and again in order to digest the content 100% as though I were absorbing it into my flesh and blood. [. . .]

Reading your letter, I could imagine everything in my mind—at the JFK airport, riding in a limousine bus . . . I can picture it as if it's right in front of me. And your dormitory, the kind face of the heavy server in the dining hall, your conversation with him . . . I can picture it all.

I'm so glad, and your mother and I are both so relieved.

Speaking of the "summer time [daylight saving time]," I experienced it too when Japan had tried it around the time when I was still working in Tokyo right after the war. But I remember it was discontinued after two years or so because people tended to lose sleep due to longer daylight. Please have a good balance of sleep each day without staying up too late.

We are all well. I've been in high spirits since your phone call. We are having a summer sale at the store from June 26 until July 1. The weather cooperated on the 26th and 27th. It drizzled today, but overall, it's been going quite well. Today is the third day of the sale, and since we've been so busy lately, I was even praying for rain so we could rest a bit. (Is it too extravagant?) Then your letter arrived and gave us a lot of energy. Taka-chan [store clerk] laughed and said, "It's more effective than a camphor injection."

You must have received a letter from us by now and must be reading it and thinking of us.

By the way, is your dorm room a single? Your brother showed me the postcard from you. So, that's the dining hall. What a great building it is! You have meals three times there, I heard. There must be certain hours for breakfast, lunch, and dinner. I hope you won't oversleep and miss your breakfast. [. . .]

7/2—We closed the store today because we had the sale until yesterday. I gave a ride to your sister to Higashi-Ōmiya Station. After having lunch, I'm alone with your mother. We offered a cup of tea for you, and the three of us (including you) had tea together. We then took out your letter and read it again. [. . .]

This morning, Reiko was saying we should write another letter soon. But I told her that I've been writing every day like a diary, so I can mail mine out anytime. You can see it from the way this letter is written, can't you?

My father gave me a series of instructions and advice as seen in this letter. He was thinking about me all the time, my mother later told me.

"As soon as he got up in the morning, he would say, 'I wonder how Moko-suke [my childhood nickname] is doing?' and at night

136

he would say, 'I wonder if Moko-suke has woken up?' He couldn't stop thinking about you."

Excerpts from my father's letter dated July 20, 1975

Thanks for your letter. I'm happy to have read that you are healthy and well. I never stop thinking about you, picturing you all the time, saying to myself: "Tomoko must be in class now," "I wonder if she's having dinner now," "She must have gone to bed by now," etc. After reading your letter, I confirmed that your life there is just as I have been imagining, which delights me so much. [. . .]

7/17 (Thu) Fair—It's been two days since the end of the rainy season was officially announced. And then, it got hot soon after. I realized it had been a long time since I last had a haircut, which was before we saw you off. I decided to go to the barbershop for the first time in 40 days. As I was just about to leave home, your letter arrived. And it's 7 pages long!! Your letter gives a full impression of how strong you have grown. You have been making decisions on your own and carefully managing everything by yourself. I can feel it and am so touched by it.

At the barber, I told everyone how you're doing. Your friend Chieko's mother [the barber—my childhood friend's mother] was really impressed by your courage.

I came home and read your letter again. You have really grown strong in 3 weeks. So, you bought a poster of a lion cub. You must be striving like a lion cub pushed down into a valley. Is that why you have it on your wall? (I learned many years ago that lions would push their cubs into a valley and raise only those that are strong enough to climb up the valley.) In any case, it really sounds like you.

You wrote you're trying to save money, but please don't try to save to the extent that you would spiritually starve. Your mom and I have no intention of making you suffer like that. Do you understand? [. . .]

> *7/16 (Wed) Fair—When I woke up and washed my face this morning, I thought about you. You used to have nosebleeds in the morning. I wondered how you are now. Cold water might be a bit too harsh on your face and make your nose bleed, so how about using lukewarm water? How are your teeth? [. . .]*
>
> *I got up at 6:30 this morning. It's 5:30 in the evening your time. I wondered if you're in the dorm after finishing classes. And before 9:20 p.m. here (8:20 a.m. your time), I am telling you, "Hey, Tomoko, wake up!" I wonder if you could hear me. It's really hard to believe, but it's true. When we are having a late dinner, you would be having breakfast. When you are having dinner around 7 p.m., we would be having breakfast around 8 a.m.*
>
> *Since we set out a meal for you here at home, you are having a total of 6 meals a day including the real meals there and the home meals with us. And you have meals with us around the same time twice a day. I've figured this out after looking at two sets of hours for the Japanese and American time zones. I have those time-zone tables posted in front of my desk. Parents are such silly beings, aren't they?*
>
> *I've rambled a lot, writing some silly stuff. I just hope you know how we're doing.*
>
> *In any case, please use good judgment to determine what to do after the summer program ends on August 9. We have sent you a few items including something Reiko knitted for you, ramen noodles, Asada lozenges (I thought it might be good for your throat in the dry weather), etc. Okay, be careful and take good care of yourself.*

As you see here, my father sent me care packages frequently. He called them *"imon-bukuro* [comfort bags]." This term was used during the war. He also called meals set out for me *"kagezen,"* another wartime term. Dad must have felt as if he had sent me to the battleground.

He once told my brother about his experience with comfort bags during the war—that all he received from his stepmother was *furikake* [a dried seasoning for sprinkling over cooked rice], while noticing, out of the corner of his eye, that other relatives of his had received canned meat and much better stuff from her. Since then, my father had developed a dislike for *furikake*.

In contrast, my comfort bags were like Santa's bag and made me feel as if I were celebrating Christmas every week.

Letters from my father arrived every Friday without fail. I tried to write every week, but I didn't mail them out regularly like my dad did. When my letter didn't arrive as expected, I could tell Dad was extremely disappointed.

Excerpts from my father's letter dated July 27, 1975

7/13 (Wed) Fair—Whenever I get bored dealing with customers, I go water the garden plants (of course, including your shiso *plants) and take care of them in about 10 minutes. [. . .]*

Hydrangea and gardenia cuttings have rooted well and started showing green buds. Charlie [my pet dog] had a nice shampoo the other day and is so clean he's looking quite handsome. The goldfish in the pond is getting big and round although he's in solitude. (How about you? Are you getting big too?) He seems happier because two frogs (large and small) have now joined him in the pond. I don't see that familiar creature, Mr. Lizard; maybe he's away, knowing you are too. Around 11 a.m. the oak tree next-door started shedding leaves like in the fall. I believe the smog is to blame. But I'm not afraid of smog! I'm so healthy and strong! [. . .]

7/25 (Fri) Fair—Every Friday, your mother becomes restless. She's waiting for the letter carrier. But he didn't bring your letter today. I told her, "Tomoko is fine. Don't worry. The letter will arrive tomorrow." I also added, "She went to America to study, not to write letters." Maybe I was telling that to myself. What do you think? But don't feel pressured. We will write even if you can't.

7/26 (Sat) Fair—The letter came as expected. I'm happy to read that you are well without catching a cold. I know I've already told you this over and over again, but I ask you earnestly to please take care of your throat.

Today I'm alone with your mother as your sister is gone for a short trip. We read your letter together again. Also happy to know how excited you are each time you receive a letter from home. Your letters arrive almost every Friday. That means our letters cross each other in the sky. I wonder if they greet each other in the sky! What a silly thought . . .

You must have received and opened the package by now. I imagine you are enjoying listening to the cassette tape; Reiko had secretly taped our conversation after watching a TV show together. Can you tell whose voices they are? [. . .]

I thought you were making tea with a strainer. But what a surprise! You want us to send you a teapot? You are a real gourmet! You are a pro! Well, you always grabbed my cup to steal my tea. You really love tea.

By the way, have I told you that we offer a cup of saké for you every evening? Since your sister is out of town now, we have two cups set aside for the two of you. What a silly dad, aren't I?

Once you settle down at AMC [Albertus Magnus College], I will be sending you more comfort bags [care packages] regularly and whenever we find something you might like. Please look forward to them. [. . .]

My father waited restlessly for the letter carrier on the day he thought my letter might be delivered. He wrote it was my mother who got restless, but clearly he did as well.

If the letter carrier passed by without delivering a letter from me, I heard from my mother, Dad would be standing there staring at the back of the letter carrier with a rueful look. And he murmured,

"Stupid postman . . . he's gone . . ."

After the summer course ended in mid-August, I went traveling with friends to famous places such as the Niagara Falls. When I ran out of funds, I went back to New Haven and found a comfort bag waiting for me. I also found that my father had wired money to my bank account. I wrote to my family with much appreciation and excitement.

Excerpts from Tomoko's letter
dated August 19, 1975

How is everyone? You must be surprised to see the postcard I sent from the Niagara Falls! Imagining your surprise, I am writing this letter. Sorry I keep surprising you . . . and making you worry. I'm also sorry for making so many requests like "Send money," "Send contact lenses," etc.

I returned to New Haven today and went to the bank to find out that the money had been wired as promised. Dad, I trusted you, but it was a big relief to find it there and I am truly appreciative. Until I left for America, I had never even lived on my own, so I have realized the importance of money for the first time. When I lived at home, I would ask for extra allowances by making excuses that they were for "books." But now, I have to write a letter and scream: "Send money!" What a tough life! Seriously though, I am grateful. I'm counting on you for more. [. . .]

I enjoyed with friends the Japanese pastries and tea you sent. They were delicious! Perhaps due to the kagezen *[meals set out for me], I guess?*

8. College Junior

My Parents' New Daughter

After finishing the summer program, I enjoyed a short vacation, traveling around with friends I had met at Yale. I also experienced a homestay with an American host family. And in early September, I finally began my long-awaited college life at Albertus Magnus College.

Tomoko [author] as a college junior
(September 1975)

Most of the students at Albertus were Irish Americans, and I was the only Japanese. It was an ideal environment for me to improve my English as there was no one else who spoke Japanese. Besides, it was a women's college,[13] so I was able to live a carefree life and to concentrate on studying without worrying about the opposite sex.

In many ways, campus life at Albertus was quite comfortable. Its cafeteria often served New-England-style dishes, which I truly enjoyed. The servers were all cheerful and friendly. They quickly learned my name and treated me like their own daughter. I can still picture the smiling faces of those kind women.

The campus was surrounded by a beautiful natural setting, full of the New England fragrance and exotic atmosphere. In the fall foliage season, the streets were aflame with autumn tints of maple leaves. The reddish orange leaves made a sharp contrast with the blue sky, which was simply breathtaking. In the winter, the campus was enveloped in glittering snow. It was so beautiful that even the snowstorms were exciting and the stinging coldness struck me as pleasant. In the spring, daffodils sprang up and bloomed a symphony of yellow and white flowers. Lilies of the valley were sweet and fragrant, creating a dreamland.

At Albertus, old mansions on and around the campus were (and some still are) used as student dormitories. The rooms were all different in size and design. Larger rooms usually housed three or four freshmen per room. Small rooms were used as singles or doubles by upperclassmen. This dorm situation was rather unique and created a family atmosphere.

When I arrived at Albertus as a transfer student, I was placed in a room on the first floor of a dorm named McAuliffe Hall. This room was most likely used as a parlor or something by the family that used to own this mansion. With its walls covered with old-fashioned wallpaper, the room was very antiquated. Since it was not intended as a bedroom, there was no built-in closet. Instead, antique chests of drawers and wardrobes were placed there. With a

---

[13]   Albertus Magnus College became coeducational in 1985.

powder room and cloakroom adjacent, my accommodations were quite comfortable and convenient.

Rosary Hall, Albertus Magnus College

Originally, I was supposed to be occupying the room by myself. Upon arrival, however, I found out that I would be sharing it with a roommate, who decided at the last minute to live on campus. The moment I met her, I liked her, and we immediately hit it off. Her name was Meg.

Excerpts from Tomoko's letter
dated September 2, 1975

I moved into a dormitory at AMC [Albertus Magnus College] yesterday. The room is a double; I have a roommate. Her name is Meg. She's a senior. And an English major like me. She's really nice and pleasant. I first thought I would feel more carefree living in a single room, but I now feel lucky to have a roommate who's so kind and helpful. [. . .]

I am enclosing postcards. The brown building is my dormitory. I live on the first floor of this building. The white building [on the other postcard] is the library. Beautiful buildings like these are

found here and there on campus. It's such a peaceful and quiet
campus.

Oh, I almost forgot to write . . . I have received all the boxes
sent by ship. I said to the packages, "You came all the way to
America without being damaged!" I praised them while picturing
in my mind Dad and Bro packing them up. It was good timing;
I was just thinking I would soon need sweaters, etc. I found three
cushions, so I gave one to Meg. Another one is on the rocking chair
she has brought. Meg's home is in New Haven, so she doesn't
have a lot of belongings. But she's got a lot of plants, and they
are all lined up and hung in front of the windows. Most of the
stuff in the room is mine. It's such a big room (about the size of
a 12~13 tatami-mat room, I guess); it's so spacious I can walk
around freely.

The cushion handmade by my mother fit the desk chair
perfectly. I had never thought those cushions stuffed with cotton
to be anything special—just another thing I had taken for granted.
I felt, however, much appreciation for the first time to my parents
as I watched Meg excited to have received a soft cushion suited for
the hard wooden chair.

My roommate, Meg, was a bright student with a beautiful
aristocratic face and a warm personality. An English major like
me, she was a senior and about half a year older. Since she was
from New Haven, she could have commuted to school from home
but decided to live on campus, she told me. I soon learned that
her parents were divorced. I imagined she had a complex family
situation.

In those days, divorce was still rare in Japan, especially compared
to the situation in the States. That was my first experience with the
state of American social affairs in regard to the increasing divorce
rate. How naïve I was! I was fortunate, however, to be naïve in this
regard.

My parents continued to send me letters and comfort bags filled
with love, which were delivered weekly without fail.

Tomoko T. Takahashi

Excerpts from my father's letter
dated September 8, 1975

PS—I thought of mailing out the letter yesterday, but I waited for one more day because I had a hunch your letter might arrive today. And, sure enough, my intuition was right! Today is the day when the mail delivery was scheduled to start from this side of the town, so we received your letter at 11:30 a.m.

We read your letter, while picturing you living comfortably in the dormitory. After learning that everything was going smoothly for you, your mom and I were absolutely elated. We read your letter again and again. We didn't know what to do as our reading glasses got foggy . . .

Even before you left home, I was already thinking we would not have to worry once you started your college life at AMC. But until then, I was so anxious because you had to move from place to place. Now I'm really relieved! We can also send you packages regularly and as we please.

I was also anxious to find out about your dorm life and rooming situation, but I'm very happy to hear that you have a nice roommate. I am grateful to AMC for its kind consideration and arrangement for you.

So, you have received the packages sent by ship. You must have received an airmail package too by now (9/8). As such, you should have received everything you need for now. We'll send you lots of "comfort bags" (army terminology). Now, study hard and be well!

Your mom is telling me she's so happy that she feels like screaming "Banzai [Hurray]!"

Once again, I'm relieved and happy for you. Please send our best regards to your roommate, Meg. When we send you packages from now on, we'll include something she might like too.

Take care,
Your happy parents

As seen in the expression "I am grateful to AMC for its kind consideration," my father always taught me the importance of "appreciation" and "gratitude" by setting a personal example. Reading those letters several decades later, I am deeply moved by and grateful for my parents' profound love. Back then, however, I didn't understand their hearts and took everything for granted. Today I regret that I didn't express even more gratitude for the care they took of me even from such a distance.

Following my letter describing my settling down on the Albertus campus, the photos of me taken on campus had finally reached my family. My parents knew pure happiness.

Excerpts from my father's letter dated September 21, 1975

We have received your photos! We are really relieved to see your face looking truly content. We still have mid-summer weather here, but I see some fallen leaves in your photos. Please don't catch cold.

Your roommate, Meg, has a handsome face; she looks very bright. I'm really happy that she seems like a nice person with a warm personality.

While you were traveling during the summer, we asked you to write more often because we were anxious. But we are no longer worried, so please write when you can. I don't want letter writing to become a burden to you.

So, you often go out for shopping and other things with Meg. You seem to have put on some weight too, looking really healthy. It's more than we could have hoped for. Take care of yourself and stay healthy both mentally and physically. You may try to put on some more weight to be on an equal footing with the Americans.

Your mom is so excited and happy that she can't stop showing the photos to everyone. This is more than we had hoped for. I'm so happy that I can only come up with ordinary expressions, but I hope you understand how we feel.

Tomoko T. Takahashi

I'll write again.

Dad

PS—I am now placing those photos in a new photo album dedicated to you. I also have a special filing book to keep your letters.

Back then, it used to take at least a total of two to three weeks to have film developed and photos made, and then to have them sent and received by airmail from the States to Japan. How much has changed with the Internet! It's almost mindboggling to think about how easy it is now to take digital photos and send them anywhere in the world instantly via the Internet. We were forced to be very patient in those days.

Not only in terms of sending photos, but with communication in general, the times were extremely inconvenient. It's almost beyond the imagination of those who haven't grown up without modern technology or even those of us who've grown so accustomed to its conveniences. My parents could do nothing but wait for my letters to arrive. If they didn't hear from me, they tended to worry. Looking back today, I'm grateful that they were willing to let me go abroad even though they knew how distant we would truly be.

I used to watch *Star Trek* on TV in the college dorm. I wished I could go anywhere anytime and communicate with anyone freely like they did on that program. And yet, because I could not easily see or talk to my family and friends in Japan, I was able to experience the true "exoticism" of my new world. Also, the airmail letters I received from my family offered great insight into my family, greater than I would have gained had I continued to live with or near them. Today, I truly appreciate the distance that was forced upon us.

Excerpts from Tomoko's letter
dated November 1, 1975

I received your letter filled with love on Friday, as always. I'm extremely happy that a huge "comfort bag" has also arrived.

Meg was really touched by Dad's words: "I feel as though I now have two daughters at AMC." I will share with her the sweets you sent. By the way, Meg loved the chitose-ame *[sticks of red and white candy for a November festival for children] so much that a half of it is gone. I look forward to more goodies you said you'd be sending. Thank you in advance!*

Once they learned about my roommate, as the earlier letter from my dad indicated, my parents would always add to their letters, for instance, "How's Meg?" "Hi to Meg," etc. They even wrote that they felt Meg was like a new daughter to them. And, treating the two "sisters" equally, they always included in the comfort bags something for Meg as well. My parents were so considerate of her that they made sure I was not the only one benefiting from the care packages. Touched by my parents' consideration for her, Meg often asked me to enclose her thank-you note in my letter to them.

Meg was a great roommate. First of all, we got along extremely well. She also taught me about American culture and tradition. At the same time, she tried to learn about Japan and Japanese culture from me. It was such a marvel that we could talk about anything.

I went to visit "her mother's house" several times. And I gradually learned about her family circumstances. I used to think that my parents' house was my house too, so I thought it was rather strange when I heard Meg call her home "my mother's house." Since she was already a grown-up, I thought she was using such an expression out of a sense of independence. Perhaps, she was trying to distinguish her mother's home from her father's since her parents were divorced.

Excerpts from Tomoko's letter
dated November 27, 1975

Today is Thanksgiving, and turkeys are tormented everywhere in the nation. The school is in recess from yesterday until this Sunday. During the holidays I'm staying at Meg's; everyone goes home during the Thanksgiving holidays. [. . .]

We've been cooking since yesterday evening—baking pies, preparing the stuffing for the turkey, etc. It's been a riot! And I'm learning a lot!

This morning we started roasting the turkey. Once the meal was ready, we ate everything really fast including three different kinds of pies. I'm now so full; I'm lying on a bed and writing this letter. [. . .]

I gave Meg's mom a furoshiki *[Japanese scarf-like cloth for wrapping and carrying items], and she loved it. Meg has a younger brother, and I gave him a* kendama *[Japanese cup-and-ball toy]. He was very welcoming and friendly, so I told him about Japan. Meg's mom is a schoolteacher. Because she's interested in so many things, it's really fun to talk to her.*

By the way, Meg's parents are divorced. But her dad came to the dinner this evening. Then, to my surprise, I found out that he had been to Japan! I probed a little more and found out that he was a member of the Occupation Army!

I, a daughter of a man who had fought in China during WWII, was eating turkey with Meg, whose father had been in the Occupation Army sent to Japan right after the war. This was taking place in America, once an enemy to Japan . . . It was such an inexplicable feeling.

I was also pleasantly surprised to see Meg's parents having dinner with their children on such an occasion. At the same time, I had a hard time understanding how a divorced couple could sit at the same dinner table on Thanksgiving. Not having any friends whose parents were divorced in Japan, I had no idea. I just imagined that a couple would not want to see each other after their divorce.

Throughout my college life, I made many discoveries like this one. Sometimes these differences made me realize how naïve I was. One could say that I was learning as much about myself as about the broader cultural differences between Japan and America.

Cigarettes, Booze, and Poetry

My parents were happily married, which is evident from the letters I received from them.

Excerpts from my father's letter dated December 14, 1975

To change the subject, the bill supporting a price hike for alcohol and tobacco was passed late last night. It took the third time for the bill to become law; the bill had been rejected twice. What's more, it will take effect on December 18—such short notice. When the bill was sent up the last time in June, I went around to buy cigarettes before it was voted on. But it got rejected. It didn't happen the second time either. Although I was worried about it, I didn't take it seriously this time because I was too busy. Then, I got outwitted.

As for alcohol, it was such a relief that my favorite second-grade saké was excluded from the price-hike items. But the 50% raise for tobacco hurts. Today, somewhat belatedly, I decided to stock up on cigarettes. After I took your mom to a physical exam at Iwatsuki Hospital, I went to Hanabishi Shopping Center to start off from there to look for cigarette vending machines and empty them out, as I knew I wouldn't run into any acquaintances there. I still felt guilty and embarrassed since it was such a petty thing to do. But if you buy a pack of cigarettes for 50 yen now, you'll make 25 yen per pack as an extra profit (what a calculation!). I brought with me 5,000-yen worth of 100-yen coins in Reiko's money pouch as well as a shopping bag, which was really a good idea. Just imagine. After I got home, I counted my booty. To my surprise, I got a whopping 62 packs! Then, I called Yasuzawa [wholesaler and Dad's fishing buddy] and told him to buy more cigarettes for me in his area. He said, "Certainly, it's an easy task" and promised me to buy as many packs as possible. His reply came so easily that it made me wonder how he would pull it off. We'll see!!

I'm just enjoying a thrill like this. I've written some silly stuff; please have a good laugh. I also wanted to tell you we are all doing well as usual.

But come to think of it, people may cut back on their smoking after the price hike and become healthier. I guess the government folks are thinking hard. Starting this year, the government has been collecting reduced taxes from corporations, so they are conceivably trying to depend more on indirect taxes.

Okay, I'll stop now, and I'll write from my diary as usual. [. . .]

12/10 (Wed) Fair—The weather has finally improved. We were blessed with fine weather all day today. I worked in the store while imagining how cheerful the Tōkamachi Festival in Ōmiya might be. Today is the anniversary of my mother's (your grandmother's) passing [see Chapter 1]. Last year I had her kaimyō *[posthumous Buddhist name] upgraded to be at the same rank as my father's [Kiichi's].[14] And I decided to erect a new tombstone for them. I asked the priest for permission to do so and hired a stonemason. It's been one year since then. We had a*

---

14   *Kaimyō* refers to a posthumous honorific name given to one whose death is commemorated in certain Buddhist tradition in Japan such as the Pure-Land-Sect tradition. Posthumous names are categorized into hierarchical rankings, which are determined according to the social status of the deceased as well as the amount of money paid to the priest—the name is not free and there is no fixed price for the service. The ranking of the name can be changed/upgraded when the family of the deceased pays extra money to the priest.

Buddhist service for my parents, and you visited their grave before your departure. I'm convinced my mother must be very happy.

The statute of limitations on the 300-Million-Yen Robbery [the single largest heist in Japanese history that took place on December 10, 1968] passed without an arrest, and its investigation team was dismissed today. The Chief Commissioner of the Metropolitan Police, Mr. Tsuchida, thanked the investigators for their hard work. I was struck by the way the investigators clenched their fists and looked so vexed—now that all their efforts and hard work for 7 years have come to nothing. And yet, as we think about all the staff involved in and the 900 million yen spent on the 7-year investigation, this entire affair has certainly left us, taxpayers, quite unsatisfied. [. . .]

You haven't mentioned the weather there in your recent letters, but I assume it must be getting cold there. That reminds me . . . When I went to China (Qinhuangdao) as a member of the North China Detail Troops in 1941, I received letters from home that kept asking, "Is it cold? Is it freezing?" As the saying goes, "When in Rome, do as the Romans do," so you must be managing by adapting just fine to the weather there. That's what I keep telling myself. [. . .]

I have just packaged the hagoita *[Japanese badminton rackets made of wood] and decorative fans that your mom had bought in Iwatsuki. I made a large envelope out of a cardboard box and turned it into a small parcel package. She forgot to buy shuttlecocks, so I'll go buy some tomorrow and enclose them in the package. Please use them on New Year's Day.[15] I guess you'll have to explain this custom to Americans. That'll be a task for you again!*

In any case, while I was frantically collecting cigarettes, your mom was looking for gifts for you. How great mothers are! I'm totally struck with admiration for mothers! You must never forget your mom's unconditional love. Well, I'm getting carried away here . . . But she really is so thoughtful. I'm no match for her. I feel

---

[15] Children in Japan used to play badminton on New Year's Day.

153

like running off barefoot and hiding. Thanks to her, our family
has been kept together. For 28 years!?

   I've written silly stuff, but please understand I wanted to
tell you we are all doing well and you don't need to worry about
anything in regard to us.

   I'll write again. Hi to Meg.

Dad

This is a long quote, but it's just a small fraction of the entire letter. As seen here, my father's letters were, at turns, serious and hilarious. They were also full of information about the good old days and news about current affairs in Japan and the world as well as the family's everyday life. His writing was so descriptive that I could picture it all quite vividly in my mind. How much time he must have devoted to these letters!

My father's letters, each page methodically written with a fountain pen, were five to six pages long, including daily excerpts from his diary. His letters were always accompanied by shorter letters from my mother, which were studded with gem-like words of maternal gentleness.

   When I included a maple leaf in my letter, Mom sent me the following *waka* [31-syllable Japanese poem]:

   One leaf of maple
   Found in the airmail . . .
   To my daughter's heart
   I press my cheek.[16]

When I wrote about the way dandelions were being mowed away in the spring, my mother sent me the following:

---

[16]   一葉の紅葉（もみじ）に託す航空便（エアメール）
吾が子の心にほほすり寄せる

When young and innocent,
I picked dandelions in the fields.
Their fragrance I still remember.
The thirtieth wedding anniversary is near.[17]

Mom loved composing *waka* [31-syllable poems]. Dad, too, sometimes wrote a *haiku* [17-syllable poem].

Excerpts from my father's letter dated September 21, 1975

I saw the harvest moon (August 15 on the lunar calendar) yesterday. It's rare to see it since it's always rainy or cloudy on this day every year.

I'll write from my diary starting from yesterday going backwards—20th, 19th, 18th, 17th, and 16th.

9/20 (Sat) Fair—Taka-chan [store clerk] has been down with a cold and off since yesterday. [. . .] It's been as hot as ever. Whenever I move, sweat pours off me. In the evening, I watched a sumo tournament—3 matches including Takanohana v. Kongō. After seeing Takanohana win—6 victories and 1 defeat now—I happily went out to deliver three futon mats to Haraichi Danchi [housing development]. I made three round trips up and down on the stairs. To the 5th floor! But I considered it good exercise and didn't find it too tough. After finishing the delivery, I was relieved and looked up in the sky to find the full moon of the 15th night [in a lunar month] rising in the east. It was quite pleasing to admire the harvest moon from the 5th floor of the housing development. I wondered if you would be watching the same moon and composed a haiku poem:

The harvest moon shines.
Looking up in the sky,

---

[17]　幼きは野辺にて摘みしタンポポの
　　香もなつかしく象牙婚かな

155

I think about my scion.

—*Kijirushi* [18]

*I saw people carrying Japanese pampas grass [one of the
decorative items used for a moon-viewing festival] at Kitaguchi
Shopping Mall. They seemed to be enjoying the fall festival in a
modest way. After getting home, I wrote down my haiku poem with
a brush and ink and posted it under my New Year's calligraphy.*

My father signed his haiku here as *Kijirushi*. He evidently came
up with this name using one character from his first name—i.e., the
喜 [Ki] of 喜儀 [Kiyoshi]. And he playfully added *jirushi/shirushi* [印
"mark"] to make it to resemble *kijirushi* [crazy].

In my response (dated September 30, 1975), I wrote: "Your
haiku is very nice, Dad, but people here don't regard watching the
moon as a good thing. There is even a word in English 'lunatic,'
which is derived from 'moon.'"

Later I wondered if my father was aware of the English word's
etymology and that's why he came up with the name *Kijirushi* [crazy/
lunatic].

In the same month, I received another haiku from Dad.

*On the world map
Where my daughter lives
I paste a Jizō talisman.*[19]

Right before this poem arrived, I had received a letter from
my father telling me: "We received a *Jizō* talisman from the Temple
today. I have posted it on the map where New Haven is and prayed
for your safety from far away. I especially hope that you will take
care of your throat and won't catch a cold."

My father composed haiku poems occasionally, and perhaps
it was around that time that he gave himself the haiku pen name

---

18 　中秋の月を仰ぎて吾子（あご）思い—喜印
19 　吾が子住む地図のところへ地蔵札

"Genkai." This name must have come from the Genkai Sea, which he had crossed several times to travel from the Kyushu Island through Pusan to China during the war.

Working "My Ass Off"

Luckily, I didn't experience too much culture shock at Albertus. Having been able to adjust to my new lifestyle there rather easily, I found my life quite comfortable. And yet, I was a foreign student from Japan who became a college junior without having studied all the subjects in English prior to coming to the States. Unsurprisingly, I experienced a lot of frustration academically in the first semester. I often felt vexed, telling myself: *If I were studying in Japanese, I wouldn't have to feel so frustrated. I would be unbeatable . . .*

Excerpts from Tomoko's letter dated September 10, 1975

In class I try to keep my eyes and ears open and concentrate on the professor and my fellow students' discussions. I have gotten used to it pretty much. Studying itself is not that hard. But it's really difficult to participate in class discussion. Even when I want to say something, I can't find the right time to join in. And when I do contribute to the discussion, I don't often feel afterwards that I was able to express what I wanted to say well enough. Whenever I feel dissatisfied, I go see the professor after class (during the office hours) and tell him or her my opinions. Without doing so, I would never be satisfied. When that's not enough, I write down my opinions on 3~4 pages of report paper, and ask the teacher to read them. Professors often tell me to present those opinions to class after reading them. As you can see here, I'm trying really hard! Since I'm linguistically handicapped, I've got to work two or three times as hard as the others.

By the way, I made an interesting discovery in one of the classes. I am more knowledgeable of English grammar than the American students! My professor and classmates were surprised

> *to find out that I know what even American students don't know*
> *about English grammar.*

In Japanese education, students are generally not encouraged to express their opinions in class. Instead, they listen to teachers' lectures passively. Having received that type of educational training, I had a hard time growing accustomed to expressing my opinions in class in the American educational setting.

Being far better at writing than at speaking English, I always tried to express in writing what I wanted to say if I could not express it orally. At the same time, since I had learned English by studying its grammar, I was better at grammar than American students, who grew up speaking English without consciously learning its grammar. This gave me an advantage in a class that involved a bit of grammar and linguistics.

Even though I was good at grammatical analysis or linguistics, I was still handicapped when it came to actually using the language. I often became frustrated.

Excerpts from Tomoko's letter
dated October 3, 1975

> *I took the first exam on the history of the English language a few days ago, which I got back yesterday. I was disappointed to see a B on it. Actually, I got all the 25 questions right in terms of content. Other students made terrible mistakes, but they also received a B. I received the same grade because I had points taken off for making errors in the use of prepositions and spelling in my writing. When I asked the professor why, she told me, "The content of your exam was excellent, but you made a spelling error here, and you forgot a preposition here" and so on. She was so picky. But those are typical errors made by non-native speakers of English. I wrote everything in a hurry because I had to finish the exam within the same period of time as other native-speaker students. I have never been so disappointed in my life. Then, the professor said to me, "You are not a native speaker. If you can*

get a grade as good as American students, that's great." But think about it. She thinks the spelling error like "declention" for "declension" should cost you the same points as the mistake like "Anglo-Saxon Conquest" for "Norman Conquest."

I took another exam for a different class. The professor for this class was overly conscious about me being a non-native speaker. For instance, she thought I might need 2 hours to finish the exam while other students would finish it in an hour. She even told me I might use a Japanese-English dictionary. This time I felt upset because she was too conscious of my second-language status. In the end, I didn't use a dictionary and finished the exam before other students did. [. . .] This is only the beginning. I guess I must grin and bear it. I keep telling myself, "Once I overcome this linguistic handicap, I'll ace everything!"

The History of English professor said to me, "No one has ever received an A on this exam," to comfort me. That's ridiculous! I am now really fired up. Well, I am determined to become perfectly proficient in English—even better than in Japanese! Watch me push myself to the limit!

Grammatical and spelling errors are considered minor (local), while content-related mistakes are major (global). When those two types of errors are contrasted, it's reasonable to assume that the latter type has more negative weight. My professors, not used to having foreign students in their classes, were at a loss and didn't know how to deal with me. I was often frustrated.

Since my parents were relieved to find out I was doing well, they included in their letters lighthearted topics. For instance, they wrote about my sister (twenty-three years old at the time) being of "marriageable age."

Tomoko T. Takahashi

Excerpts from my father's letter
dated October 5, 1975

Today, on Sunday, October 5, we've had rain all day, and occasionally some strong showers, since the morning. Because we didn't have too many customers due to the bad weather, your mom started cleaning here and there. I also started organizing my office and taking care of some paperwork. When we finished, it was already past 3 o'clock. Because of the rainy sky, it's dark like in the evening. The autumn rain brings a tinge of melancholy.

It's been a month since you started in the mainstream (college). How did you do on the exams? How are you doing with Meg? Getting along well? [...]

Your sister has been actively involved in the upcoming junior-high-school reunion as one of the organizers, along with other former classmates. She's out today again to plan for the reunion. Since many of her former classmates from junior college have gotten married one after another, she seems a bit pensive these days. As her father, I'm feeling somewhat responsible.

In those days, Japanese parents would in general begin worrying about their daughter's marriage once she grew older than twenty years of age. Generally in America, marriage is considered the business of the adult child, not his or her parent's.

Decades ago, Japanese would use the expression "marriageable age" quite often. There was also an expression: "Age twenty-five is the crossroads for your skin." Even worse: "You are left on the shelf [unmarketable] after turning twenty-five." Women were constantly judged according to their age and some rather disrespectful expectations and standards.

My father was relatively liberal, so I was surprised at the new discovery that he was worried about my sister being of marriageable age.

As for me, such traditions and expectations were something to be ignored. Considering marriage entirely irrelevant, I openly enjoyed my college life and continued to study hard with all I had.

A little more than a month after I started the fall semester, I began feeling gradually relieved of the frustration I experienced in the academic sphere. I was finally able to relax a bit. Each day became such a joy. I even felt as if I were acting the role of a heroine in a novel—like Judy in *Daddy Long-Legs* by Jean Webster.

As those of us who went to college then know, things were much more labor-intensive and time-consuming compared to today. For instance, neither word processors nor personal computers were available, so we had to type academic papers on a typewriter. Since electric typewriters were still rare and extremely expensive, I used a manual typewriter I had brought from Japan. This typewriter made a lot of noise, so after Meg went to bed, I used to go to the laundry room in the basement to type my papers. I also often studied in the library until closing time. I didn't feel, however, it was arduous because I was filled with the joy of living my own dreams.

Excerpts from Tomoko's letter dated October 27, 1975

I got some of the recent exams back. I received B+'s and A's, which are about 85 to 90 points. When I was in Japan, I never received grades lower than 90, so I'm upset with grades like a B or a B+ (80~ 85 points). But I was told that they were better than what other students were getting. Well, if I ever master English, I will probably become an honor student (?!). Ha ha ha!

It's true I felt very competitive with American students. At the same time, my affection for America and Americans got stronger as time went by. The rivalry I felt was sublimated into a positive sense of competition.

Excerpts from Tomoko's letter
dated November 6, 1975

*By the way, when I wrote to you right after moving into
the dorm, I wrote about Meg and said, "I feel lucky to have a
roommate who's so helpful." But so far I haven't asked her for
help in my studies. And yet, she is still a teacher to me. That is so
because she is teaching me a lot of new expressions in English. I've
learned a lot of slang, which you cannot even find in a dictionary.
In that sense, I think I'm learning English to the extreme.*

I had fun learning new slang terms and phrases. Meg in turn
would get such a kick out of hearing me, a foreigner, use those
vulgar expressions. She was kind enough (?) to continue teaching
me more. And, she often suggested, "Why don't you use those
expressions in front of the nuns?" smiling with impish eyes.

One day, I said to Meg,

"I just saw Sister Joan. I told her 'I'll work my ass off.'"

"Did you really say that?" Meg asked, astonished.

"Yeah. And I told her that I had learned this expression from
my roommate Meg." I said with a straight face.

"No way! You must be kidding!" She was instantly flustered.

"Yep! Kidding!"

We both laughed.

Winter Holidays

I was able to finish the first semester with grades I found satisfactory.
Then, the winter break began. I went to stay with a friend named
Jane, whom I had become friends with in Japan while she was
working as an English teacher's assistant at my high school. She was
from Massachusetts.

Jane's mother had passed away several years before. Her father
and brother lived at home by themselves. Jane was coming home
from a college in Boston for a winter break, and she invited me to
spend some time at her home.

Excerpts from my father's letter dated January 4, 1976

I trust that you are doing well at Jane's home. I deeply appreciate her family's hospitality and kindness. Please tell them again that I prayed for their happiness on New Year's Day.

Three days have past since New Year's, and today is Sunday, the 4ᵗʰ. It rained late last night, and I was concerned the rain might inconvenience some people today. But it turned out to be a fine weather all day today.

As you can see from the excerpts from my diary, we've been having good weather. I heard someone say on TV, "With the good weather, we made a good start this year. This is a good omen for the economy too." Since the government has set a budget with a larger public investment, I also think business will pick up, but I don't think it'll get as prosperous as it was in 1972~73. I'm now sounding like a news commentator. Let's change the subject . . .

It's 12:30 now. I'm writing in my office, getting some warm sunlight. Can you picture me? I'm wearing a V-neck sweater that Reiko knitted for me. I think I look pretty good in this sweater with white patterns, which matches your mom's sweater. [. . .]

I'm checking all of the merchandise in the spacious store by myself. Punching in the price, tallying up totals . . . As I touch each item, I feel as though it's saying, "Thank you for your hard work at the beginning of the New Year!" Thinking about the business after the holidays, organizing the store, and so on . . . I find it really fun.

Around 11 o'clock this morning, your mom and sister left for Shima to make a round of New Year's calls. As of 5 p.m., they still haven't come home. And I'm now getting really hungry. It's "the first hunger of the year."

1/1 (Thu) Fair—A peaceful opening of the New Year. As I do each year, I took a morning bath to purify myself, offered New Year's rice cakes with a votive light to the Inari shrine in the backyard, and prayed for the wellbeing of my family, your health and academic success, and Jane and her family's happiness and prosperity. I also offered the first water of the year to the ancestors and gave the same prayers. Then, I offered you some cold saké and celebrated New Year's Day with the family (including you) with the festive food including dried anchovies and mashed sweet potatoes with chestnuts. But, to be honest, it's quite boring to not do any work. [. . .]

My first calligraphy of the year . . .

和気扶合 *[Peaceful Sprit and Cooperation]*

This year's resolution is to keep my spirit [気] *peaceful* [和] *and live the year in a spirit of cooperation* [扶合].

Please write and share with us your discoveries about American families, especially the positive aspects of their daily lives and relationships. I would like to learn from their approach and incorporate anything constructive into my own family.

Please send my best regards to Jane and her family. Also, I know you are getting well acclimated to your new environment, but please don't become lax in taking care of your health.

I will write again.

Dad

Having sacrificed his dreams, my father had rebuilt the family business (see Chapter 3). And on a New Year's holiday, he was working in the store. As I read his letters today, I reconfirm that my parents, in addition to being devoted to us, were also working equally hard at their business. I grow overwhelmed with a sense of appreciation. I simply cannot thank them enough, and my appreciation for my parents increases as time goes by.

In this particular letter, my father wrote: "Please write and share with us your discoveries about American families, especially the positive aspects of their daily lives and relationships." He was forever willing to learn.

Incidentally, the Inari shrine mentioned in the letter was our family shrine that stood on a fenced lot the size of three *tatami* mats [about 65 Sq. Ft.] in the backyard of our house. It had been kept as a place of worship by my ancestors from generation to generation.

Excerpts from Tomoko's letter dated January 1, 1976

Sorry I haven't been able to write for a long time. I've been busy having fun with Jane. I'm doing well as always—healthy and vigorous just like the Alinamin-A [Japanese vitamin drink] commercial.

On December 19, after finishing all the exams, I went to thank my teachers for their help this past semester. They all told me I had done a great job even though it was my first semester in America. I was happy to receive such praise. Then, I left the dorm on the 20th. It snowed a lot that day! We literally had a White Christmas in Southbridge, where Jane's family lives.

The houses here [in Southbridge] look a bit different from those in New Haven. Most of the houses stand on the hills high above the streets, looking like the imagined houses in fairy tales.

Jane's Papa is doing a lot better than expected. I heard he'd be getting remarried before long. Jane's brother, David, is 12 years old, but he's taller than Jane (he's skinny, though). Having feet bigger than Papa's, David reminds me of Mickey Mouse. He's growing so fast that he grows out of his clothes very quickly. He does everything he's asked to do without complaining. He's such a good kid. David has a pet dog. And, believe it or not, the pet's name is Charlie! (How's my Charlie at home?) I became good friends with Charlie here too.

We celebrated Christmas in serene surroundings. On Christmas Eve, Jane and I prepared a Japanese dinner. I brought with me some canned food sent from home, so we could even make some appetizers using Pacific sauries as well as dessert made of azuki-bean soup. Plus, we had green tea. The main dish was "Tempura." I think it turned out pretty good. The white rice was delicious too. We also enjoyed the heated Gekkeikan saké.

In those days, it was difficult to find any Japanese food in America, so I always depended on the "comfort bags." When I found Japanese saké in a liquor store in New Haven, I was excited. I told my dad on the phone that I had bought a bottle of Gekkeikan. He said, "So, you are drinking the first-grade saké, and I'm drinking my usual second-grade Kenbishi." And he laughed.

When I told American friends about *sushi*, they showed their disgust and asked, "You mean, Japanese really eat raw fish?" Considering that sushi is universally enjoyed today, it's hard to believe.

On the other hand, *tempura* was accepted easily because it was originally a European cuisine. Even in the 70s, most Americans were already familiar with *tempura*.

Excerpts from my father's letter dated January 18, 1976

Yesterday we received your joyous letter. By the time my letter arrives, you will be into the second week of the spring semester. I'm sure you will have switched gears from vacation mode (you probably didn't even allow your brain to relax even during the break, however) and must be concentrating now on your studies. I trust that Meg, too, started the new semester in high spirits. I feel as though I have not written to you for a long time. [. . .]

1/17 (Sat) Fair—Today was another cold and hectic day. I was thinking earlier today your letter might arrive. And it certainly did, just as I expected!! Your letter energized me at once. It also made me feel a bit envious. But knowing that you're doing what I couldn't do, I feel so much joy and find myself fully enjoying my life. It's just marvelous.

I read newspapers thoroughly, and when I find anything relating to America, I always put a red circle around it. Yesterday, I found a news article about the Polish consulate in New York having some damage caused by terrorists' bombing.

The more I read and learn from your letters, the more deeply I understand how great and big America is. Once younger generations rule Japan, the insular mentality will be overcome, and we'll perhaps have a better and bigger-hearted country.

Today, January 17, is the day when Kan'ichi of The
Golden Demon *[a novel by the author Ozaki Kōyō] "kicked"
O-miya [his former lover, who betrayed him] on the Atami beach.
He then declared he'd make the moon cloudy with his tears on the
same day the next year and 10 years later again. It was just a
coincidence, but on January 17 of the following year and 10 years
later, it really did turn out to be a cloudy night, which I heard on
the radio. Plum blossoms are beginning to bloom in Atami, I also
heard on the radio. The Kōyō Festival (also known as the "Plum
Festival") will start today and go until mid-February. It's still too
cold in our area for plums, however.*

*1/16 (Fri) Fair—Today is traditionally called "yabuiri
[servants' holiday]," which you probably don't know. In the old
days, apprentices working for a store would go home twice a year
(January 16~17 for New Year's holidays, and July 16~17 for
Bon holidays [holidays honoring the deceased]). The apprentices
at our store each received 5 yen as pocket money. Wearing an outfit
provided by the store—a kimono with striped or splashed patterns
and a flat cap—they tied their wallets tightly to their* obi *[sash
belt], and left the store joyfully. As I remembered such a scene, and
compared today with that time, I'm amazed by the development
Japan has made since the war. If Japan had won the war, we
wouldn't have such a good era now. So, you never know what may
bring you good fortune. Even though you don't know about those
old times, you may be saying, "I see" and find it interesting.*

As reflected in his words, ". . . knowing that you're doing what
I couldn't do, I feel so much joy and find myself fully enjoying my
life," my dreams were my father's dreams, just as I had guessed. In
other letters too, he mentioned several times that his "clone" was
doing what he couldn't do.

Being far away in America and reading about the Japanese
apprentices in the old days, I found it nostalgically delightful. My
father was talking about the time in which his great-grandfather
Kisuke was still alive. As an elementary school child, Dad must have

167

witnessed those scenes where apprentices went home wearing a flat cap, which was popular among merchants at that time.

I could also see that my father wanted me to not forget about Japanese culture and history and to shoulder the future of the world with youngsters of the same generation from around the world.

Defense on the Home Front

In January 1976, I celebrated my twenty-first birthday while enjoying a fulfilling college life in America. Lots of friends celebrated it with me. I also learned that my family did so in Japan despite my absence.

Excerpts from my father's letter dated January 25, 1976

Tomoko and Meg, how are you? We didn't receive a letter from you this week, but I trust that you are doing well. Have you received the birthday card we sent you on the 19th? Today is January 25. Happy birthday!

It's cold but quiet today and it's a bright Sunday. As Reiko had to leave home early to go to her flower-arrangement class, we got up early this morning. To prepare for your birthday, your mom got up extra-early to make sushi rolls (authentic ones with sweetened gourd shavings). We offered them as kagezen *for you, and the four of us (including you) enjoyed the special meal together. And, we are now preparing a festive red-rice meal for the evening. (Earlier we had gone to a supermarket and bought some red beams.) The rice is from Sendai [the best kind]. By the time we are ready to enjoy the special meal, your brother and his wife will be here to join us in the celebration of your birthday. How is your celebration going there? [. . .]*

It's been cold here in Japan, but it appears much colder in New York and Boston. I have enclosed a newspaper clipping about the weather there. Please don't touch metal with your bare hands. You don't want to get frostbitten. I've also heard that there's a flu going around. Please don't catch cold. You ought to gargle often. [. . .]

I received an electric foot-warmer as a gift this winter from one of the wholesalers. It keeps my feet warm in my office. It's comfortable as I can keep my feet warm while keeping [the room temperature low and] my head cool. You should keep your feet warm too. [. . .]

By the way, Wajima and Kitanoumi [both sumo champions] have just had a match. Both had 12 wins and 2 defeats. This was the final match to determine who would be number one. Kitanoumi won and became the tournament champion for this season. This is his fifth championship win.

We are now preparing for your birthday celebration. We will joyfully celebrate your birthday, praying that our wishes will reach America. We pray for your successful year and more health and accomplishment.

My father's detailed instructions made me wonder how he could come up with so many things to tell me. His advice regarding my health came without pause. I sometimes felt like saying, "Gee, Dad, trust me!" but I understood his intention, took it to heart, and told him, "Sure, Dad. I know. I will." And I appreciated his consideration for me.

My father's birthday came two weeks after mine, on February 11th. He was an Aquarian, like me. He loved the birthday card I had sent from the States. His appreciation of the card reflected not only the almost childlike exuberance he unselfconsciously expressed but also his willingness to share his joy with those around him.

Excerpts from my father's letter dated February 15, 1976

2/10 (Tue) Fair—The birthday card has arrived! Despite your busy life, you didn't forget my birthday and sent the perfect card for me . . . from the other side of the globe! A huge fan of fishing, I am always thrilled to see anything to do with my favorite pastime—e.g., pictures of fish and fishing rods and tools. What a great selection! Nicely crafted! Thank you, Tomoko! [. . .]

2/11 (Wed) Fair—It's my birthday. I'm 38! [55 in actuality, but he was responding to my card congratulating him by pretending it was his 38th birthday]. And I have the greatest card. I'm so happy that I decided to give a paid day-off to all the employees at the store and the factory. People might think I'm treating my own birthday like ○○○○'s [probably meant "the Emperor's"], but so what? It seems that a celebration dinner is being prepared now, although it's not as grandiose as that for your birthday.

When I was in the army, we had a hinomaru bentō *[a lunch box stuffed with white rice with a pickled red plum in the center depicting a Japanese flag] and a baked fish served whole (we had this special meal because my birthday happened to be on the National Foundation Day). As I reminisced about my youthful days, I even pulled out and read the lyrics of the song of the 27th military regiment, to which I had belonged during the war. I felt somewhat younger and more energetic.*

My father's birthday, February 11th, used to be called "*Kigen-setsu* [Imperial Epoch Celebration]" in the old days. It's the present-day National Foundation Day. It became a national holiday some time ago, but his store was normally open on the holiday at the time of this birthday in 1976. For that particular year, he decided to close the store that day. I guess he was that happy about receiving the card from me.

My father spoke about the war whenever he was reminded of it. His youthful days were spent in the war, and my youthful experience in America must have triggered the memories of his war experience.

I found another letter that mentioned something quite interesting.

Excerpts from my father's letter dated March 28, 1976

I feel strongly that there is an invisible string connecting us all—between you striving with all your might and the family supporting you. Allow me to talk about the old days again. I just thought about the "defense on the home front"—family members protecting the home front while their loved one was away as a soldier, in order not to worry him. And the beautiful human bond between the soldier and his family—family members kept sending comfort bags to the soldier on the battlefield. Although I don't like wars, it was as if a beautiful flower blossomed during the war. That is not limited to the war situation. As in our case, I feel blessed to see us connected with such beautiful family bonds, helping each other. I feel no pain from being apart because of that. So, please don't worry about anything. Just take care of your health and concentrate on your studies. And, absorb the great America.

My father didn't lose his sense of appreciation for his family although (or I should rather say *because*) he had not been blessed with a warm family as a child himself. Instead of becoming soured by the notion of family that he experienced in his own abysmally deficient childhood, he built a warm family for us. He looked at life so positively that he was genuinely able to call family bonds "beautiful." As a consequence, he was able to declare, "I am blessed." He truly lived a life with no regrets.

Because of the strong, united family he helped create, I felt blessed. My sister would hand-knit sweaters or use her good taste to select nice clothes and send them to me. My brother would send me books and any information I asked for. Not just tangible items, but their heartfelt support was the best encouragement for me.

I sometimes asked myself where my good fortune could have come from. I was so appreciative of my blessings that I couldn't help but secretly fear losing them. I honestly felt both thankful and apprehensive.

9. Farewell, Albertus!

Bicentennial and Hamburgers

I finished the second semester in good academic standing. Then, it was summer vacation. Before that, there was a graduation ceremony. It was the first American college commencement I witnessed.

Excerpts from Tomoko's letter dated May 25, 1976

The commencement ceremony was held on the lawn in front of the white building (library) called "Rosary Hall." Everything was wrapped in the early-summer fresh green, against which the white building was beautifully silhouetted. The graduating students came marching solemnly, clothed in black caps and gowns. The professors followed the graduates' processional, wearing the academic gowns of their alma maters. (Their gowns varied in color and style as they were from different universities. Some were navy blue, some burgundy, etc.) They certainly looked cool.

I felt excited to see the processional and to think that I would be marching like that next year. Those with good academic records received honors. [. . .]

Before getting ready to leave for the ceremony, Meg had had a hard time finding her cap and gown and had been fussing around. But during the ceremony, she looked calm and collected. Afterwards, we celebrated Meg's graduation at her home, where I stayed for dinner.

Meg's mother and brother as well as her father came to the commencement. Just as had happened at Thanksgiving, we all had a special celebration dinner at Meg's mother's house.

After the commencement came a summer recess. For me, as an international student who could not easily return home, it was a big problem to figure out how to spend the three months of a summer recess.

My parents wanted me to come home during the summer, but I had already decided to take a summer course at Georgetown University in Washington, DC and then to travel around the States.

Instead of returning to her mother's house, my roommate, Meg, who graduated in May, decided to live in an apartment and concentrate on job hunting. She asked me to live with her. It was an offer too good to be true.

Excerpts from Tomoko's letter dated May 18, 1976

We've already moved into the apartment. Meg and I struggled quite a bit to move all our stuff here. My belongings have multiplied over the past year. The apartment is right next to the campus; it's on the same street where some of the college dorms also stand. It has 2 bedrooms, a kitchen, a dining room, and a living room. It's a very nice apartment. It's furnished too. Two Albertus students who live in the apartment went home for the summer, so Meg and I are subletting it while they are away. It's very cheap. It's almost impossible to find such a nice apartment in this location for such low rent. Everything has worked out. [. . .]

For security reasons, Meg has borrowed a dog, named Sweet Pea, from her friend. I'm not too fond of keeping a dog (especially a big one) inside the house, but I do feel safer with Sweet Pea living with us. It's a bit of a hassle to take him out to go to the bathroom, though. In any case, we are doing quite well.

A year prior to that, I had experienced living in a dormitory for the first time. I never even imagined I would have a chance to live in an apartment. It allowed me to experience what I normally would not have been able to. I finally had time to do more than study.

I practiced driving in Meg's car and got a driver's license during the summer. I also enjoyed spending a lot of time with Meg, playing tennis, cooking, going to the beach, and so forth.

Before coming to the States, I had never done very many chores at home. My father seemed to have found it rather amusing to hear that I was cooking with Meg.

Excerpts from my father's letter dated May 30, 1976

> *Tomoko, you must be enjoying living in an apartment with Meg. A week has passed, and my letter-writing day has arrived.*
>
> *So, how is your apartment life? Do you two cook and do laundry together? I'm imagining you and Meg cooking with your world-class skills (?). I wonder what it's like to live just the three of you (including the dog). It must be such a chore to feed the dog. I bet you are already missing your dorm life with all three meals provided . . .*
>
> *Let me say this for your own good . . . (I'm sure you two are very careful, but) please be very careful with fire and theft. And have a balanced diet. [. . .]*
>
> *5/24 (Mon) Cloudy—When I was just about to seal my letter, your letter arrived. We've waited for it for a long time. I read and reread it several times. Reiko left for Hokuriku feeling relieved after reading your letter. From your letter, I can picture how you are doing as though I were right there with you.*
>
> *After reading your letter, I felt so happy to know things are going well for you that I decided to go to Sumitomo Bank in Akabane to send you some money. And on the way home I bought some cream puffs for your mom. I also brought home something called a "hamburger"(?)—a ground-meat patty sandwiched between pieces of bread. We thought you, too, might be eating this*

in America and we enjoyed it. But you know, this is the very first
time that your mom and I have ever eaten this sandwich called
"hamburger." Don't laugh!

I was quite surprised to see the word "hamburger" in my father's letter.

Five years prior to that time, in July 1971, McDonald's opened its first store in Japan—on Ginza in Tokyo. McDonald's hamburgers soon became a sensation in Japan. Especially on Sundays, thanks to the pedestrian zone known as *hokōsha tengoku* [literally meaning "pedestrian heaven"] on Ginza Street, the McDonald's first store attracted 10,000 customers per day. Those eighty-yen (¥80) hamburgers sold like hotcakes. Many youngsters enjoyed eating hamburgers while walking around, which became the talk of the country. Soon, McDonald's stores mushroomed one after another all over Tokyo.

"It's preposterous to eat food while walking!" I remembered my father saying. And this same man bought hamburgers in Tokyo and brought them home to enjoy with Mom!

The industry that enjoyed the most growth in the 1970s in Japan was the automobile industry. Fortunately for me, the Japanese yen was beginning to become increasingly stronger around that time.

My brother worked for one of the major automobile manufacturers in Japan. Because of that, I personally enjoyed watching the rapid growth of the Japanese automobile industry overseas. I used to write to Hiromi how popular Japanese cars were in America.

Japan and America appeared to be having a give-and-take relationship. Japanese automobiles were massively exported to America, while the waves of fast food such as McDonald's and KFC were rushing to Japan.

And those fast-food waves were finally reaching my home in Japan too! With a bit of surprise, I imagined my parents eating McDonald's hamburgers.

In mid-June of 1976, I left for Washington, DC to attend summer school at Georgetown University. Why did I choose Georgetown? Because it was a Catholic institution like Albertus, and it was in Washington DC. Why DC? Because I thought it would be great to celebrate the Bicentennial in the capital of the nation that summer.

Excerpts from Tomoko's letter dated July 6, 1976

> *I went to see a parade this Saturday (7/3). It was incredibly crowded. Since we got there late, we couldn't see the parade itself. All we saw were spectators' heads. [. . .]*
>
> *It would have probably been wiser to stay home and watch the parade on TV. At the parade site, it was hot and simply exhausting. We couldn't see anything. Nothing good about it . . . Plus, I got sunburned. After coming back to my room, I found my nose burned red—totally spoiling my good looks.*
>
> *Also, the buses both ways were packed. Already overcrowded, they didn't even stop to pick us up. After seeing so many buses go by, we finally had one stop for us. And, on the way back, we were caught in an evening downpour and got soaking wet. And again, there were no buses . . . No good . . .*
>
> *The next day, July 4 (Independence Day), I felt tired all day. I went out to see fireworks in the evening.*
>
> *We waited for a bus, but again, several buses passed by without stopping for us. We finally were able to get on a crowded bus. It was like rush hour in Japan.*
>
> *Then, we finally got close to the Washington Monument area. And I just could not believe the sight . . . there were people everywhere. People, people, people, people . . . I have never seen so many people in one place. It was almost frightening to see so many in one big open place like that. [. . .] Then around 9 p.m., fireworks finally started. Unfortunately, our location was horrible. We couldn't see any of the fireworks that were shot low. Even so, the little bit of fireworks I was able to see were beautiful.*

My friends ignored the fireworks and got drunk. It was like a Japanese hanami *[cherry blossom viewing]. Americans seem to like drinking sprees too.*

It was dreadful again on the way back to the dorm. We realized that it was impossible to catch a bus, so we decided to walk back to Georgetown. It was late at night, but there were so many people walking that it was just like daytime. But please don't worry. I was very cautious in the crowds. Nothing was stolen.

After such a big hassle, I'm now asking "So what? What was that whole Bicentennial celebration about?" I know people were excited about it, but there was nothing as special as what everyone in Japan had expected. I feel bad for those foreign tourists who spent a lot of money to come all the way to see the celebration. They must have expected to see something incredible on Independence Day, but in reality, there wasn't much, except for fireworks and stuff. And in order to see those fireworks, they had to go through all the trouble that we did. On TV and the radio, they kept saying, "Happy Birthday, America!" That's all. Locals, it seemed, were enjoying their own private parties. But what about the tourists? I felt really sympathetic toward them.

I bought the July 4ᵗʰ issue of a newspaper and found a 10-page booklet in color entitled, "Greetings from Japan to America." It explained the US-Japan relationship and so forth and carried celebration messages from a number of prominent companies in Japan. I was so impressed, but I also felt Japan was sort of brown-nosing. [. . .]

By the way, thanks for the photos. Mom and Sis look alike. Having the same smile, as my friends pointed out, they look like sisters. So cute! Dad, you are young and handsome. Your azaleas are gorgeous too. I bet they are blossoming well thanks to all your care, getting rid of insects, fertilizing, etc. But more than that, it must be your love that keeps them so beautiful. I heard plants have feelings too. I would assume that whatever you are growing, if you nurture it with a lot of love, it will grow big and beautiful . . . just like us, your kids. Ha ha ha . . .

In my letter, I never wrote about the parade and fireworks themselves, but rather kept describing the crowds and the atmosphere. And the hassles I went through . . . What was I thinking? I wonder if I felt guilty that I was the only family member enjoying the Bicentennial in America while my family could not experience it.

Nevertheless, my father loved reading my letter, as strange as it was. He wrote to me that my letter had made him feel as if he were also there at the parade, which made me feel better.

Excerpts from my father's letter dated July 11, 1976

Thanks for the letter—really fun to read. So, you like my letters because they are so descriptive that you can see what's happening at home quite distinctly. Even if you're flattering me (?), I'm happy to hear it. Your letters are also well written and they help us imagine your activities quite distinctly. The one we have just received is especially so; we could picture everything quite distinctly. (Oops, I've used the expression "distinctly" three times. I flunked.)

You have described the parade, fireworks, and the surrounding situation as well as American culture so well that I feel as though I were watching them right there with you while reading your letter. I've just read it again.

We watched an American Bicentennial Special on TV, where a parade in DC and a parade of ships in New York were shown. When we saw the parade led by officers in decorated army uniforms begin, we grew excited, saying, "Maybe, Tomoko's there watching the parade!" But they showed only the parade itself, not the crowds of people watching it. If they had taken more time to show faces of the spectators, we might have spotted you and screamed . . . Too bad we didn't get to see that. [. . .]

This morning I went to attend a neighborhood association meeting to discuss the "ōmikoshi" [a festival where a portable shrine is carried around] to be held on the 14th and the 15th. Each block has a representative, and we had a meeting the other night at my house, but two of the block reps didn't make it. So, I asked those two to come to my house this morning. I gave them some details and spent time with them.

It's lunchtime, and I'm finally free. But it's raining outside. I don't feel like watching TV by myself. Thinking that it would be a lot more fun to have a chat with you, I took out your letter to read again.

And, as I was just about to read your letter, it started raining hard. My habit immediately kicked in; I ran upstairs. Just as I thought, one of the windows was open. The room almost got wet. Then, I went around to check each of the rooms, including yours. Everything was fine. I have such good intuition!!

Thanks for your compliments on my azaleas. As you wrote, I also think the fertilizer called "love" is most effective.

A mention of the traditional town festival in my father's letter made an interesting contrast with the American Bicentennial celebration I had described. Seeing the word *omikoshi* and picturing Dad going upstairs to close the window, I found the descriptions so "distinctive" that I missed home quite a bit.

Homesick

I made a lot of friends at Georgetown. When the summer course ended, to my pleasant surprise, Meg drove with her childhood friend Laurie to Washington, DC for a bit of sightseeing and to pick me up and drive me back to New Haven.

I returned to New Haven and became terribly homesick after having been away from home for more than a year. I spent days in great distress.

I thought I'd travel around, staying with host families in various places introduced by an association for international students. And yet, I was unable to make plans as I liked. The whole task seemed overwhelming and became daunting. I grew irritated. I became depressed. Since I had already told my parents that I would be going on a trip after the summer program, I felt awkward telling them the truth that I didn't get to go traveling.

Soon I lost energy to even write letters. I spent days with no sense of purpose. Having stopped hearing from me, my parents worried so much that they even lost their appetites. Until that time, they had always received a letter from me at least once a week. Not having heard from me for three weeks, they became gravely concerned. They couldn't call me because they thought I had gone off on a trip.

When my parents finally heard from me after a while, they were thoroughly elated. They never even scolded me saying, "You made us worry so much!" They were forever embracing.

Excerpts from my father's letter
dated August 16, 1976

P.S.—Really happy!! I can only express my joy in a simple way. After writing in my letter, "Let's get back to our regular correspondence," I left the desk, as if I were drawn by some force, and opened the front entrance door. Then, I found two letters from you delivered at once.

Your mom and I read them without taking a breath. So, you didn't go on a trip. I didn't feel it was a good idea either. I had even asked you to check the credibility of the student association.

We were so worried. We never stopped thinking about you day after day. We are just relieved and happy—so much more than feeling like scolding you—we kept saying, "Good, good . . ."

To tell you the truth, your mom has lost 3 kilograms [6.7 pounds], so her summer clothes are too baggy now.

Let's stay in touch. Let's keep our heart-to-heart string unbroken. It's for our own sake. I'm really happy!!

Dad

After this, I was finally able to get back to my usual correspondence and to enjoy reading the letters that arrived weekly without feeling guilty. Once they were relieved, my parents began sounding in their letters as though they had completely forgotten about the worries they had had.

Stories about the summer festival written by my father were heart-warming and so vivid that I could picture the faces of the neighbors and imagine the ambience of the town.

Excerpts from my father's letter dated August 22, 1976

Tomoko and Meg, I trust that you two are doing well. I'm happy and relieved that I could open my letter with my usual greetings.

It's extremely hot here—especially today. I'm writing in my office.

We had a Bon festival [festival honoring the deceased] for the town this week. Since I was in charge of it, I had such a busy and hard week. I think I did a good job; it turned out pretty nice although it was the first time I took charge. Everyone kept complimenting me on it, saying it was extremely well done. It made all my hard work worthwhile.

The festival site was cleaned up this morning. Each sponsoring store also made the rest of its final donation to the festival. The festival committee broke up around 11 a.m.

During the festival, I had to sit on a tiny bench (for elementary school children) in a tent for hours each of those 3 days. I'm really exhausted. I had to take care of so many things. I sometimes had to settle some small quarrels too. As the person in charge, I had to shoulder all the various duties and responsibilities by myself. No wonder I have such a backache today.

As I told you, the festival was from the 19th until the 21st. On each day of the festival, other committee members and I went to the festival site around 5 p.m. to light the andon lanterns, to decorate the stage with more branches with flowers and paper lanterns, and to get ready for the festival. Once searchlights were turned on, how bright it got! When the volume of the speakers was turned up, the music echoed all over town, and it created a splendid festive atmosphere.

Dancers and spectators came in small groups to the festival site, wearing summer kimonos and dresses, etc. Also among them were 2~3 women wearing Hawaiian muumuus in bright colors.

Dancing started at 7 p.m., and it peaked around 8 p.m. when about 200 people crowded the site dancing in circles, which was quite spectacular. During the intermission, as the committee chair, I gave a speech. Toward the end of the evening, I was starving, but there was no food left. All I had was soda and Calpico drinks; I really felt water-logged.

On the second day, since I learned a lesson from my starving experience the day before, I had two slices of toast and some milk before going to the festival site. The music, like "Chichibu Song" and "Tokyo Song," began blasting around 5 p.m., generating a festive mood. I could hear the loud music even in my store, which made me feel restless.

Later I heard some complaints from folks that their children, as soon as the music began, kept bugging them so much that they couldn't concentrate on getting chores done to get ready for the festival. I couldn't help laughing. If adults like me got antsy, I'm sure, children did more so.

On the stage were some experienced dancers like Mrs. Uchida (Komuroya Store), Mrs. Saito (Shintaku), Mrs. Saito (Granny Hina), Mrs. Hosono, and Mrs. Yagi dancing in a circle. Those much less confident watched the dance teachers and danced in a circle on the ground.

Young children were more interested in food than in dancing. They kept coming to the refreshment stand, asking for soft drinks and rice crackers. They seemed to be having a lot of fun. And no one was irritated (?).

Oh, by the way, this is unrelated to the festival, but I'll tell you what. I wrote to you in my last letter that we were relieved after finally receiving your letters on the last day of the Bon holidays after waiting so long. But it was such a hassle *afterwards. Your mom and I rushed to the main post office in Ōmiya to send out our letters, while thinking we might be able to have a nice feast on the way back home. So, we looked for a restaurant—preferably a nice sushi place. But unfortunately, most places were closed due to the Bon holidays. The one we found open wasn't that inviting. So, we detoured through Hongō Town on purpose, hoping we'd find a restaurant in that area. We had no luck and got to Higashi-Ōmiya, but we still couldn't find a desirable place. We then reached the Oyamadai and Haraichi Housing Developments. We finally got home without finding anything! We ended up having a simple chazuke meal at home—rice with furikake sprinkled on it and tea poured over that! But because we were so relieved about you, it was really delicious! Your mom and I had a good laugh together!*

As we returned to our usual letter-exchanging routine, I felt I had overcome my homesickness . . . and reached a state of "enlightenment." I was not even afraid of expressing my weakness candidly. Overcoming the mountain of homesickness, I felt I had become stronger.

Excerpts from Tomoko's letter dated August 25, 1976

I have made you all worry by not having written letters for such a long time. While I didn't (couldn't) write, I did feel very guilty thinking, "I bet they are really worried about me."

When school was in session, studying kept me busy, so I didn't have to think about anything else . . . But during the summer vacation, I felt frustrated. I kept thinking, "I should be doing something." I had planned to travel around, but the planning didn't go well. I said to myself, "I wish I could go home," but at the same time, I thought to myself, "No, I can't." So, I ended up staying in New Haven doing nothing. Then I gradually became so down and depressed that I couldn't even write letters. It really made me understand that there's no place like home. It's the only place where I could just hang around without thinking too much about accomplishing something. Well, I've overcome all that homesickness and loneliness, and I've started writing letters again in good spirits.

By the way, I went to Salem on the 20ᵗʰ of this month to see Sister Hilda [my former teacher at junior college in Japan]. I met her at a bus station in Boston and went to Salem with her. [. . .] She told me how the other nuns were doing back in Japan, and I told her about my college life. We had a great time together.

On the same day I was invited to dinner by the Spanios family. And believe it or not, they served Japanese noodles, bean sprouts, meat marinated in soy sauce, etc.; Mrs. Spanios is a Japanese native from Okinawa. I felt fully satisfied after having a Japanese meal. Then I stayed with the family until yesterday (the 24ᵗʰ). Sister Hilda left for Canada on the 20ᵗʰ. I would like to go visit her in Canada next time.

After receiving this letter from me, my father embraced me with his tender understanding, as always.

Excerpts from my father's letter dated August 29, 1976

I'm more than happy to learn that you are doing well although you experienced a lot of struggles and pain. You had started your long summer vacation with detailed plans to travel around, but those plans didn't materialize. You ended up changing your plans in the middle of the summer vacation. You must have had such a hard time adjusting your rhythm in daily life and shifting gears in your brain. I could definitely understand how you felt from reading your letters.

We, too, had often discussed, out of concern, various options as to how you should spend your long summer vacation. At one point, we had reached the conclusion that it would be best for you to come home for the summer, but then we learned about your plans to attend a summer school program. We didn't want to interfere with your plans, so we decided not to tell you about our desire to have you come home. We had also struggled while giving a lot of thought to this whole matter and considered various possibilities.

Anyway, what great timing it was that Sister Hilda came to see you! And, you got to know the Spanios family. I'm truly happy for you. When you are homesick, missing your family, the best way to cure it is to be welcomed by a warm family with a Japanese meal! Thanks to their hospitality, you seem to have overcome your melancholy and regained your usual self. I will write a thank-you letter to the Spanios family and mail it out right away when I send this letter to you. [. . .]

It really sounds like you after all, Tomoko. You seem to have gotten even more strong-minded after finding enlightenment in the midst of suffering. I guess it's true that "Those who don't suffer never become enlightened."

You wrote that you had had to cancel your traveling plans but gained a lot more than you would have from traveling. I cried when I read that. I pay respect to you for enduring all the pain and reaching an unexpected conclusion and learning from it. [. . .]

I've become a bit sentimental, but don't worry. I'm fine. By the time this letter reaches you, it'll be 3~4 days before school starts again, I guess? I bet you are filled with a fighting spirit and lots of new expectations for the coming new semester. Please thrive even more during the remaining year.

I understand that you have been working out by playing tennis every day. But how about finding a stick and practicing kendo strokes too? I do it all the time. I can't afford to go playing golf, so I keep my bamboo sword in my car and go to the garage in the evening to practice kendo. I often practice about 200 strokes. But when I'm hungry, I stop before doing that many. Kendo practice is a great way for me to clear my mind and come up with good ideas when I have a decision to make.

Even though we are far away, I feel our hearts are connected. Let's take care of ourselves and strive even more. Please send our best regards to Meg and everyone else. I wish you all my best.
Dad

I remember, when I was in elementary school and junior high school, I used to (be told to) practice kendo. When I got restless with too much energy, my father would tell me to "go out and do 100 strokes!" and I would go to the backyard and cut air with a bamboo sword. Then, I always felt my mind was cleared and refreshed. For my dad and me, kendo practice was, in a way, a method of meditation.

First Scholar from the Takahashi Family

The fall semester started in my second year at Albertus. Blessed again with a nice roommate, I was able to get back into the campus-life mode.

Excerpts from Tomoko's letter
dated September 7, 1976

The summer ended. I've moved many times: in May after the final exams, Meg and I moved to the apartment; in June, I moved to Georgetown; then I moved back to the apartment; and in late August, I moved all my belongings to a new dorm, and stayed at Meg's home for some time. And today I finally finished moving into Marian Hall.

As I wrote before, my room for this year is much better than the one I had last year. Because it's on the second floor, it's quiet. The walls are painted a light cream. The big window adds a nice touch. In addition, it has a lot of shelves installed on the walls, which make it easy to keep things in order. [. . .] Last year I started growing some plants from cuttings of Meg's plants. Those starters have grown into full plants now. Meg is no longer with me, but I have the offspring of her plants. My window is now beautifully decorated with those plants potted in colorful planters. [. . .]

My new roommate, Roni, is close to Meg too. So, when Meg comes to visit me, I bet the three of us will have a great time together. [. . .]

This summer, I learned the value of my parents and family
soooooo much. I used to be ungrateful about a lot of things and
took them for granted.
Thank you for the comfort bag, as always.

Like with Meg, I got along well with my new roommate, Roni. Because she was my age and in the same class, I felt as if I had grown mature. Since Meg was a bit older, I often felt as if she were like a big sister. Actually, Roni was half a year or so younger, which made me feel even more grown up.

Roni's family and mine had a lot in common. Her parents were happily married with three children—Roni and her older and younger brothers. I visited her house several times and found it comfortable and homey.

Roni's parents used to stop by the campus unexpectedly and sometimes took Roni and me out for dinner. They also often brought homemade pies and cookies for us. I remember going to see a football game and a skate show with Roni's family, who really treated me as one of them. I have so many memories of them. I told my parents they are "my American family."

Excerpts from my father's letter
dated September 12, 1976

We have received your letter of September 7. I'm very happy to
hear you're doing well. It must have been difficult to move so many
times during the summer. Each time you moved, your environment
changed and exhausted you mentally and physically. I'm grateful
that you overcame all the hardships without ruining your health. I
admire your spiritual resilience. You endured it all well.

During the war, I received spiritual and mental training on
the Chinese soil. I was, however, just a part of the collective force
driven by authorities. In your case, you had to overcome everything
all on your own. So, you experienced different types of trials and

tribulations. I'm sure that's why you have gained and learned a great deal.

With all the experience you've gained over the past year as well as more to come, you will never be defeated by any obstacles you will encounter in the future. Just think of what you have already overcome. Weigh it, compare it, and think: "This is nothing compared to those struggles."

As much as you have gained from your valuable experience, we have also learned a great deal. We all have experienced such a good summer, haven't we?!

Unequivocally, my father's wartime experience was much worse than any struggles I had at school. This again shows his unceasing thoughtfulness and the connection he felt to my life. He encouraged me by humbly saying, "I was just a part of the collective force driven by authorities." Even then, I was mature enough to realize that my struggles were nothing compared to his, and I was determined to grow strong to overcome any hardships.

Excerpts from Tomoko's letter dated October 23, 1976

I'm doing well, getting along well and having fun with friends, especially with my roommate, Roni. [. . .]

Roni is a math major. She's good at Spanish too and is taking Spanish classes. The other day she was working on a paper for her Spanish class, which was about comparative studies of Spanish and American literature. She said she was stuck and had run out of ideas. I asked her what her paper was about. I thought I might be able to help her because I'm an English major. I suggested a few ideas. Then, Roni got inspired. She and I had a really fruitful discussion for a couple of hours. We both learned a lot. We talked about literature, sociology, American culture, art, and music . . . Isn't it great that I can talk about such a variety of topics with her? [. . .] We joke around a lot too. We are helping each other grow this way.

Everything was new last year and I was extremely busy with so many things. But now I feel that I'm well accustomed to the way of life here in America. I feel that I have both American and Japanese cultures coexisting nicely in myself. I think I now have my own opinions about a variety of topics too.

I've gotten used to studying in English. I don't find anything awkward or perplexing anymore. I'm really content because I can now bear down and compete with American students.

When the fall semester of my senior year started, I was able to enjoy my college life much more fully than in the previous year. At the same time, I began pondering my future after graduation.

Right after finishing the first year at Albertus, I thought about going to graduate school. When my father saw "graduate school" in my letter sent during the summer, he wrote back: "I feel a bit sad because I'm afraid you might not be coming home at all." I soon told him I was thinking of attending a graduate school in Japan. My father was relieved to hear it.

I gradually felt, however, I would rather stay in the States and study further. Boldly, I began preparing myself for that goal without telling my parents. My roommate, Roni, supported me in every way possible—e.g., by giving me a ride to the exam site for the GRE (Graduate Record Examination), etc.

Then, I finally revealed my wish to my parents.

Excerpts from Tomoko's letter dated November 22, 1976

I briefly mentioned this in my letter during the summer vacation, but I'm now seriously considering going to graduate school to continue my studies in America. I really want to give it a try and am now preparing the application documents. I've kept it to myself until today, but the more I thought about it, the stronger my desire for graduate school study became, so I began the application process. I would feel terribly lonely if I didn't get to come home at all because of graduate school. If it's financially possible, I would

*like to come home whenever I could. I would love it if that's possible
and I could continue studying in America. [. . .]*

*I apologize for having begun the process without asking for
Dad's opinion. I miss my family so much that I wish I could come
home and stay. But if I don't do what I can now, I know I'll have
regrets for the rest of my life. I promise I will come home whenever
I can if that's all possible. Please allow me to go to graduate school
if I get admitted. Please . . .*

To this letter, my father immediately responded by calling me
on the phone and encouraging me to pursue my dream of going to
graduate school by saying, "Try your best. Work hard!" My mother
also gave me her permission, as seen in the following letter.

Excerpts from my mother's letter dated December 5, 1976

*First of all, thank you for the heart-warming birthday card.
In the photos you sent, I see it's snowing in New Haven. I also see
that Venus-like ladies live in your castle [dormitory]. Everyone
looks bright and beautiful. You look great too, especially with
a nice tan. You are tall, so you never suffer by comparison with
Americans. I think the body and mind you were born with are
suited to your present environment. You don't need to worry about
us. You should advance on the path you have chosen. Your father
says, "I want our children to grow up without too many constraints.
That's the way parents should be. As the character 親 [parent]
is made up of 立 [standing] 木 [tree], and 見 [watch], parents
should be watching their children forever like trees standing next
to them." [. . .]*

*I'm sure you will become even busier, but please take good
care of yourself. Do what you must do so that you have no regrets.
And become a person who can contribute to society. Keep your own
pace and do your best without worrying about anything else.*

Having received permission from my parents, I still didn't know if I could even get into graduate school. I just decided to wait for the results.

Excerpts from Tomoko's letter
dated December 2, 1976

Mom and Dad—As I told you on the phone, I am really happy to have received your permission to go to graduate school. After hearing your voices, I became a bit faint-hearted, thinking, "I'd rather go back home than go to grad school in the States . . ." But I soon started telling myself it's more valuable to choose a challenging path and overcome all the hardships I face than choosing a comfortable path. If I didn't go for it now, I would have regrets later on . . . Even though I'm far away, you two always feel very close to me. I can almost hear Dad's encouraging voice: "Try your best. Work hard!" It's definitely having a good effect on me.

I'm majoring in English now at college, but in graduate school I would like to study linguistics. All I can do at this point is to send applications for admission. If I get accepted and can go to grad school for a master's degree or even a PhD, I'll perhaps be able to teach at a university after returning to Japan. [. . .] As a university professor, I will be able to continue doing research and write books. I'd also like to translate books . . .

Linguistics was the subject in which I had become extremely interested since taking an introductory course in linguistics at junior college in Japan. At Albertus too, I had an independent study course in linguistics and became even more interested in the field.

As is evident by the career plans I told my parents about, my dreams for the future were becoming bigger and more concrete. And my father truly appreciated my dreams. After the news had sunk in that I would be gone for several years more, he sent me the utmost encouragement as if he were trying to toss away his loneliness.

Excerpts from my father's letter dated December 12, 1976

Tomoko and Roni—I'm more than happy to hear about your strenuous efforts as always. Yesterday, we received the photos and the stuffed doll. Your mom looked perfectly content looking at the photos while hugging the doll.

Since your brother had a day off yesterday, I called and told him to stop by. I gave him one of your photos. As soon as he saw them, he said, "Wow, she has grown up!" His words "grown up," I thought, implied a number of things. It is the face of a person who has made all the important decisions by herself over the past 20 months. It is also the face of a mature adult who has become independent while being away from her parents. I have a photo of myself that was taken when I visited home during the war when I returned to Japan to attend the army chemistry school. I find a lot of resemblance between my face in that photo and yours in the photos you have sent. Your photos reveal that you have endured a lot of hardships and have experienced all the joy and sadness. I'm sure this experience will add a lot to your confidence in the future.

I remembered seeing the photo of my father in an army uniform mentioned in this letter. I learned for the first time the context of that photo (see page 38, Chapter 2).

Having sent out my grad school applications and finished the fall semester with much satisfaction, I went to Roni's house to spend Christmas and New Year's. Then I visited Florida with Roni and a few other classmates and enjoyed the winter break to the fullest.

My letter dated January 11, 1977, in which the Florida trip was described in a very amusing way, was concluded: "I finally got to travel. And I'm fully content."

When the spring semester began, we, graduating seniors, started preparing for our May graduation. The preparatory work for our yearbook had already begun in the previous semester. I gave a lot of thought as to what to write on my page in the yearbook. In the end, I decided to write a haiku poem in Japanese.

Excerpts from Tomoko's letter
dated March 9, 1977

It might be the influence of my family. I've learned to compose haiku poems. And I've written one for the graduation yearbook. (I actually wrote it in December.)

How fast days go by!
Smiles of joy
Awaiting Satsuki to blossom in May.[20]

Interpretation: Time flies. May is just around the corner; May, of course, means my Commencement. The smiling faces of my friends and family waiting for me will blossom like flowers in the month of Satsuki *[azalea/May].*

The word 笑み *[smile], I found in a Japanese dictionary, is sometimes used to mean "bloom/blossom." I decided to use this word to go with the* Satsuki *[azalea] flowers. The season word in this haiku is, of course, "Satsuki." The important point here is that I used the word meaning both the beautiful azalea and the month of May; I avoided the use of the modern word 'Gogatsu [May]." By the former, I implied my sentiment for the colorful Satsuki flowers Dad is so proud of growing.*

As I saw the photos of my family smiling standing next to Dad's Satsuki flowers, I really felt that everyone at home was also waiting for my smiles to blossom at my graduation just like they were waiting for the beautiful azaleas to smile/bloom. What do you think?

---

[20] 日々早し笑みはさつきを待ちながら

Dad with his *Satsuki* flowers (1976)

My father calligraphed my poem with brush and ink and sent it to me with his return poem, which read:

> *As we embrace each other,*
> *In the sky of Haneda [Airport]*
> *Winds blow fragrantly.*[21]

Although it was only March, our hearts were already in the month of May.

---

[21]　肩をだく羽田の空に風薫る

In mid-March, I received letters from the graduate schools to which I had applied. To my surprise, I was admitted to my first choice, Columbia University, and to my second choice, Brown, as well.

In Japan, my entrance exams had barred me from the top schools at both the high school and college level. Given that, I felt passionate about what a great country America was in allowing me my first choice. In Japan, doing poorly on entrance exams was fatal even if your grades were excellent, whereas in the United States, academic records including both GPAs and standardized exam scores, such as the GRE, were taken into consideration for admission. I really thought the latter was fairer. (Of course, I did!)

The reason why I applied to Columbia and Brown was that I just didn't know any other schools; those schools were famous enough that even I knew of them. Their location was an important factor in my choice; I wanted to attend a school that was close to my favorite town New Haven. Columbia and Brown were both adjacent to Connecticut; Columbia is in the state of New York and Brown in Rhode Island. In other words, I chose the two famous schools that were closest to New Haven. (Actually, I wanted to attend Yale, but linguistics students had to fulfill language requirements in both French and German before enrollment. Never having studied German, I had to give up on Yale.)

The linguistics department at Columbia had a long history and had produced a number of famous linguists. What's more, the university had faculty members such as Donald Keene, a Japanese literature scholar famous in Japan, and Margaret Mead, a renowned anthropologist. (See Chapter 6.)

I immediately wrote to my parents about my admission to Columbia and Brown. After receiving my letter, my father gave me a telephone call and said,

"I asked your brother about those schools. I heard that they are members of the so-called 'Ivy-League Schools' and are very prestigious. What a great achievement!"

Dad could not hide his strong emotion. Then he mumbled in an undertone,

"The Takahashi family will have a scholar . . ."

I thought I would never forget those words of my father for the rest of my life. I made up my mind to go to graduate school and become a respected scholar, in place of my father, who could not attend college due to the war and his family circumstances.

Cherry Flowers in Full Bloom

Until that time, I had not told my brother and sister about applying to graduate school. I had even asked my parents to keep it to themselves. When my siblings found out about it, their surprise was inevitably beyond description.

To be honest, I had felt uneasy about it because I was the only one in my family given the opportunity to go to graduate school. But my brother and sister both were happy for me and wholeheartedly congratulated me. My brother, Hiromi, wrote to me with much excitement.

Excerpts from Hiromi's letter
dated March 31, 1977

Congratulations on your admission to Columbia and Brown. I say this to you from the bottom of my heart. Since you had never said anything about it, my surprise was profound. Just imagine. Because of the way you dealt with it, I could understand how determined you must have been.

Although Mom and Dad rarely call me at work, they immediately did so. When the phone rang, I was in a meeting. I answered the phone. They said, "It's about Tomoko . . ." and I said, "What happened to her? Tell me!" Those who heard my phone conversation probably thought it was a family emergency. I then heard the news. What great news it was! As soon as they told me, I screamed out of excitement, "She did it! She did it!" with no thought of my colleagues in the same room.

You should definitely try what you want to do while you're still young. I wish I could come to see you right now to congratulate you face to face. Dad is saying he'll fully support you. Mom is wholeheartedly in agreement.

Our parents are the best in the entire world. And, because you have been earnestly working hard, everyone is supportive of you. Please continue to thrive and expand your horizons. I will also try my best to keep up with you.

From that point on, my parents began generously expressing their happiness for my admission to grad schools in every letter they wrote.

Excerpts from my father's letter dated April 24, 1977

I received your letter and copies of the admission letters yesterday.

I tried to read the acceptance letters in English as much as possible although I couldn't understand much of it. Wanting to appreciate them to the fullest, I decided to use my English-Japanese dictionary. I keenly feel how important it is to study when one can. After reviewing the acceptance letters, which only a handful of people in the world have the thrill and honor of receiving, I appreciated them as proof of your efforts and the results of all the work you've done, while dealing with the additional language burden, leading to your victory today. [. . .]

4/20 (Wed) Fair—Today is the anniversary of the Founder's (your great-great-grandfather's) passing. To celebrate it, I went to buy some kashiwa-mochi *[rice cakes wrapped in oak leaves] and* kusa-mochi *[rice cakes with herbs]. I offered them for our ancestors as well as for you. I could sense that the ancestors were all happy for your brilliant achievement. [. . .]*

4/23 (Sat) Fair—We received the copies of the admission letters from Columbia and Brown. I was so busy when they arrived and was just about to go out for a business meeting scheduled for 2 p.m. Although I wanted to take a closer look at the letters, I skimmed them through and left for Kōnosu City. I got home around 6 p.m. I read the letters again. Even though I don't really understand English, with the dictionary in hand, I tried to digest the content as much as possible. And then, all of a sudden, I felt deep joy welling up in me from the bottom of my heart. It was so intense that I didn't know how to control it. At the same time, I promised myself again to take good care of my health to be able to fulfill my responsibility as your sponsor.

In reality, it cost a good deal of money to attend graduate school. That was my number-one headache. To attend Albertus, I was lucky enough to have been awarded a full scholarship covering both tuition and living expenses. It seemed, however, that I would have to spend personal funds to cover the two years—especially, the first year—of my graduate studies. It seemed almost impossible for international students—especially for Japanese students due to Japan's rapid economic growth at the time—to receive any financial aid for graduate studies.

My father told me to forget my concern,

"Leave it all to me!"

Around that time in 1977, luckily, the Japanese yen was getting stronger, and the exchange rate became about $1 = ¥200. This made me feel easier. Still, I continued to apply for scholarships, and, fortunately, I was able to secure one to cover my living expenses.

In April, one of my professors was going to New York City and asked me if I wanted to go with her to visit the Columbia campus. I did.

Excerpts from Tomoko's letter
dated April 18, 1977

I feel spring has finally arrived. Maple trees are budding new leaves. Tulips and daffodils are blossoming in all their glory everywhere in town. Today has been such a good day. [. . .]

My professor and I took a train called "Amtrak" from New Haven to New York City. We then changed to a subway and got off at "116th Street, Columbia University." We went up the stairs to find the magnificent gate to the main campus of Columbia University. Beyond that gate was a campus walk with cherry trees. While going down the walk, I saw two huge library buildings on both sides,[22] between which was a vast lawn, and students lounging around. They are quite different from the Yale buildings. Still, they are quite impressive! Columbia is in an urban area of New York, so its main campus is not as big as Yale's. But the buildings are tall—even student dorms are as high as eleven-stories. As I looked around, I became incredibly motivated.

So, the impression of Columbia was much better than expected. Unlike universities in Tokyo, the Columbia buildings are mostly Roman and Greek architecture. [. . .]

After our visit, we got on a 3-o'clock train and arrived in New Haven at 4:40 p.m. As I returned to the campus, I went to check my mailbox and found a letter from Sister Hilda. She told me her convent in Canada had decided to continue giving me a scholarship. Hurray!

In reality, my trip to Columbia from New Haven was full of adventures. For instance, as soon as we got on the subway, a homeless man approached us to beg for some money. My professor and I were very scared; we had never encountered someone begging in New Haven.

As soon as we went up the stairs at the subway station on 116th Street and went through Columbia's main gate, we saw an entirely different world. Cherry blossoms were in full bloom. The soft pink color made such a contrast against the blue sky.

It was so beautiful that I felt my heart was purified. Well, I should perhaps say it was almost intoxicating. Intoxicated by the beauty of the cherry blossoms, I decided to attend the Columbia

---

[22] The Lowe Library on the left side is no longer used as a library.

graduate school. My path was determined. All that was left now was to wait for my college graduation.

Magna Cum Laude

The final semester at Albertus was drawing to an end. I felt a touch of melancholy, but remained hopeful and continued to push myself every day, looking forward to visiting home after graduation.

My father wrote to me: "To use an analogy of climbing Mt. Fuji, you have reached the ninth uphill station [out of the ten] of the mountain as you have twelve more days to go. It might be the most challenging time as you face the summit. As I always tell you, please take care of your health and reach the goal."

Excerpts from Tomoko's letter dated May 15, 1977

I finished all the final exams on Friday. Since then, I've been feeling weird. Two years has past so fast that I simply cannot believe I will soon be leaving AMC. I'm happy that I will be graduating, but at the same time, I'm feeling sad about leaving. This bittersweet feeling means that I've been blessed with many good teachers and friends here.

As I walked on the campus green yesterday, struck by its beauty, I stopped to look around to appreciate the campus . . . I'm feeling a bit sentimental. In the past, I have experienced many farewells and have grown more mature each time I said goodbye. This time again, I will have to make a big jump. A new life at Columbia awaits me. I will start afresh today as if I had just arrived here in America for the first time.

Needless to say, my family in Japan was eagerly awaiting my homecoming. I could deeply feel how excited they were from their letters.

Excerpts from my father's letter
dated May 15, 1977

Tomoko, I trust that you're doing well.

After finishing all the exams on the 13ᵗʰ, without a moment to relax, you must be busy getting ready for graduation and for your trip back home.

5/15 (Sun) Rain—Feeling impatient, your mom is acting as if you'd be coming home tomorrow. We still have two more weeks, but she went with your sister to a beauty parlor. So, I'm alone again.

Watching the drizzling rain outside the window, I began thinking about you . . . "It's 10 p.m. in America. I wonder if Tomoko is finalizing her schedule, sorting out her belongings, or making a list of items to take home? Or, maybe she's at a party because it's a weekend, I wonder?" etc. etc. I'm using the TV monitor in my head to picture you.

With the long-awaited rain, I feel relaxed. Smoking a pipe, I'm driving a pen, which may sound as if I were writing without stopping. But I keep wondering about your graduation, your homecoming, and your stay here . . . I wonder if you'll spend time with us at home . . . Before you left for America, you were out so much that you spent little time at home . . . So many thoughts whirl around in my mind. Soon I realize I'm watching outside the windows, with a smoking pipe in my mouth. I keep stopping and am making little progress. [. . .]

Everyone at home is now busily preparing for your homecoming. We had the fusuma *[sliding doors] re-papered, rooms re-carpeted and cleaned, etc. to welcome you back. But everything in your room has been kept the same as before you left—the books in the bookcases, candies in the small jar on your desk, pencil shavings in the pencil sharpener . . . They are all waiting for their owner's return. Your stuffed dolls too, including Snoopy . . .*

Thank you for the invitation card to the May 22 graduation. We now have one more family treasure. We will cherish it. I will attend your graduation on the 23rd at 4 a.m. (Japan time), using the TV monitor in my head—picturing you wearing a cap and gown. You will be experiencing the excitement you tasted when you sent off your seniors last year. It's your turn now. How exciting! I'm sure the images in my head will be very accurate, which I will confirm as I look at your graduation photos.

I have so many thoughts that I cannot even express them with words. They are swirling around in my head. I'm just speechless . . .

Excerpts from my mother's letter dated May 15, 1977

Tomoko, congratulations on your graduation! The exciting day is just around the corner. You saw Meg graduate last year, which seems like just yesterday. It's your turn now. The azaleas are beginning to blossom. I'm sure they will be in full bloom by the time of your graduation and will be congratulating you. Of course, everyone in the family as well as every creature and every physical object around the house are all rejoicing. [. . .]

The store employees are also looking forward to seeing you. They even took the time to clean your room during their breaks. Whenever your sister goes to the supermarket, she thinks of you and buys stuff like a new toothbrush, etc. And, all we talk about now is: "What shall we have Tomoko eat when she comes home?" We are saying, "How about lots of sashimi *[raw fish] and baked eel?"[. . .]*

We will all attend your commencement in spirit. Please be assured. I'm grateful from the bottom of my heart that your American Papa-san and Mama-san [Roni's parents] as well as the many friends who have taken good care of you will be there on our behalf.

Excerpts from Hiromi's letter
dated May 21, 1977

*Congratulations on your graduation! You did it at last! You've
hung in there without giving up! I'm not surprised, however. I've
kept telling myself, "Of course! Tomoko would never fail," given
your typical, strong desire to improve yourself and your outstanding
adaptability (including the ability to make lots of good friends).
Looking back over the past two years, like you, we are all filled
with deep emotion.*

*The image of you departing from the Haneda airport in the
rain is engraved in my mind—carrying a bag hanging heavily on
your shoulder, you looked tiny mixed in among those tall travelers
(foreigners). [. . .]*

*You have always kept in touch with us to keep us from
worrying (except for a few times when we were really concerned).
I appreciate those efforts. I also realize that Mom and Dad's
support was so strong it kept you going.*

*I'm sure you have already been reflecting upon this experience
of yours. Let me just say, I am so happy for you that I feel as if it
were my own graduation. From the bottom of my heart, I express
my congratulations to you. Your stay in Japan will be short, but
let's talk to our hearts' content. I will be at Haneda no matter
what. See you there.*

I became quite busy before my graduation; there were a series of
celebrations and parties. My Yale friends, too, threw parties for me.
I was quite touched and especially moved by the party arranged by
my friend James, whom I had met right after arriving in New Haven
in 1975, and his close friends Mike and Aileen.

As soon as I arrived at Mike and Aileen's apartment, which I
had often visited, I found the three of them already waiting for
me with a big feast. As I entered the living room, two big volumes
of a dictionary sitting on the stereo caught my eye. A dictionary
lover, I was drawn to them. I immediately noticed they were a set
of the compact-edition volumes of the OED (Oxford English

Dictionary). Having used several volumes of the regular-sized OED in the Albertus library, I was excited to see the compact edition.

"Wow! It's the compact edition of the OED! I wish I had one of these. Whose is it?" I asked.

James said jokingly,

"Well then, you can have it."

Because I was dead serious, I felt upset with him for joking like that. I continued to admire the dictionary. I took out the accompanying magnifying glass for reading the small letters of the compact edition and started turning pages. I kept saying,

"I'm so jealous. I wish I had one of these . . ."

My eyes were firmly fixed on the pages. After a while, I realized James, Mike, and Aileen were watching me with big smiles. All of a sudden, it dawned on me, while still thinking, *No way!*

Smiling, the three of them said to me in unison,

"It's a gift for you, Tomoko!"

"This is for me!?" I screamed with huge surprise and even bigger joy.

I had never received such a great gift in my entire life. I was ecstatic. That night, totally excited, I read the OED in my bed and fell asleep with it by my side.

The commencement took place in front of the library building, Rosary Hall, blessed with the most beautiful May weather. The academic dean called each graduate's name, sometimes adding award titles to the names of those graduating with honors. Each graduating student went up to the stage and received her diploma from the president.

It was in alphabetical order, so I knew my name with the initial *T* would be called toward the end. In the meantime, I watched my classmates go up on the stage, sending them big cheers. Then, it was finally my turn.

I heard my name, and . . .

"Magna Cum Laude!"

I received loud cheers from the audience. My friends from Yale, aware of how hard I had worked, especially appreciated and applauded my achievement. Having studied abroad in Taiwan and Japan, they knew how difficult it was to study in a foreign country.

And, of course, I celebrated our graduation with my beloved roommate, Roni, and my classmates. Surrounded by Roni's family, Meg, and all those wonderful friends, I blossomed with big *Satsuki* smiles. My heart was already on the way back to Japan.

Tomoko [author] after receiving her BA (May 1977)

10. The Price We Pay for Love

Homecoming

On May 29, 1977, I flew back to Haneda Airport to be home after an absence of two years. On the day of my departure from Japan in June 1975, the sky had mimicked our tears in a ferocious downpour. On the day of my return in May, it again reflected our feelings, spreading out in a beautiful swath of radiant blue.

I flew from the JFK on a cheap flight to San Francisco and made connections in Hawaii. I was scheduled to arrive at Haneda early in the morning—at 7 a.m. Despite such an early arrival, it was simply unthinkable that my family would not be there to welcome me.

I grew restless while going through immigration for re-entry, picking up my luggage, and going through customs. Knowing that my family would be waiting for me in the lobby behind the doors right there, I impatiently anticipated our reunion.

My family was also anxiously awaiting me. As soon as the automatic doors opened, I found them right there. What a moment! I heard my mom scream, "Wow!" Having a big girlish smile on her face, Mom clapped her hands. I dashed toward her to give her a hug, and Dad watched us with a big smile, looking completely satisfied.

Two years prior to that, my father described my departure in his letter (dated June 24, 1975): "I felt my heart tighten so many times. It was really painful to endure that overwhelming sentiment. But the more painful it got, I thought, the more joy we would experience when we welcome you back home. I reminded myself of this repeatedly."

It was indeed a moment of the utmost joy, as my father had predicted.

(Top, center) Tomoko [author] hugging Mom; (top, left) Hiromi;
(bottom, from left) Dad, Mom, Tomoko [author], Reiko
(May 1977)

Dad had brought a hand-made banner saying, "Welcome home, Tomoko," but he felt too embarrassed to hold it up in the airport lobby, he said. Hearing his explanation, we all laughed.

The family car was loaded with food and drinks. On the way home, stuffing myself with rice balls, I kept talking. I had everyone's attention. I went on to describe the commencement,

"Then I heard the dean announce 'Magna Cum Laude!' And the crowd cheered like crazy. I was awarded a prize of honor. My friends from Yale were there too. They were all excited and happy for me!"

I pulled out my diploma from my backpack and showed it to my family in the car.

As we approached Ōmiya City, I suggested,

"Why don't we stop by to see Grandpa and Grandma in Shima?"

There was a bit of hesitation among the family members, but soon Dad said,

"You must be tired. Let's wait until tomorrow."

I learned shortly after we got home that my grandfather Shinsaku had passed away a year before in June 1976. My father explained that he had decided not to inform me of the news; he thought it would be too harsh for me to accept alone and so far away.

I was shocked to hear this painful news. My grandfather had been doing well when I went to see him before I left for America. How fragile human life could be . . .

I went to see Grandma Tema the following day. Having lost her beloved husband, she apparently was broken-hearted. She was bed stricken. Her frail body lying on the futon mat, she welcomed me and expressed her joy. Tears rolled down the laugh lines on her face.

When I showed her my college diploma, Grandma held it in her hands and looked at it as if it were a Japanese document written vertically. That scene made a striking impression on me. Without correcting her to hold it as a document written horizontally, I translated it into Japanese.

When I was about to leave, Grandma held my hands and started crying. It suddenly occurred to me,

This trip home could be the last time I see her . . .

I was so severely shaken that I began questioning,

Do I still want to go back to America even after this?
I repeatedly asked myself. Nonetheless, my answer was ultimately "yes."

I found my home extremely comfortable, especially after such a long absence. I felt as though my life in America over the past years was simply a dream.

It was heaven when I took a bath in the big deep Japanese-style bathtub. The bath was in a separate building annexed to the main house of my home. This bathhouse had a big tiled room with a fan-shaped bathtub, and a changing room next to it. On the other side of the changing room, there was another small room with a stove to heat the bathwater. It was all quite indulging. A gas water-heater was also installed there, but I still remember that water heated with logs in the stove felt different from gas-heated water.

Since I was a child, I had always looked at the patterns and designs of the tiles in the bathroom, so they were imprinted on me. When I saw those tiles after a long period of absence, I had a strange time-traveling experience.

For a Japanese house, my home was relatively large and had Western-style rooms as well. But every doorframe seemed shrunken and the bathroom-sink lower as though I had somehow grown taller.

In the evening, after a hot bath, I had saké with my father and enjoyed my mom and sister's home cooking. I cherished every moment at home, while asking myself,

Why am I leaving this wonderful family and warm home to go to America again?

My father must have already anticipated how I would feel after staying home for three weeks. He was worried that I might get homesick after becoming re-acclimated to the comforts of home. In other words, even though he wanted me to enjoy myself, he was worried that it would become a cause for my suffering later.

The three weeks at home went by all too soon. Although I was able to see many of my friends and indulge myself in my family's comfortable home, it was way too short.

Why did I stay home for only three weeks? It was because I had planned to attend a summer school at Yale to study French. The MA program at Columbia I was going to attend required reading proficiency either in French or German. The Yale summer school offered a special intensive program in reading French, geared toward graduate students.

Oh, how ambitious I was! (I can't believe it.) I had studied French for two years in college, so it would have been enough if I continued my study of the language after enrolling in the MA program. But I didn't want to take the risk of that not being sufficient to acquire reading proficiency. So, I went back to New Haven to study French in this intensive program before I began my graduate studies.

Back to New Haven with Reservations

In mid-June of 1977, the departure date arrived. I was leaving home for America again. Everyone, including myself, felt downcast. Dad and everyone else were thinking: *We waited for two long years. And she's already leaving us again* . . . I felt my heart torn apart.

When I had left the first time, my mind was set on my new adventure, so my hesitation to leave was easily overcome with anticipation. This time, I began to question whether I wanted to continue to put my family through the worry and sadness caused by my absence. The questions lingered. After all, my grandfather had died while I was gone.

It was raining, just as it had two years before. Drenched in the pouring rain, my friends and family again waved while seeing me off.

My father sounded a bit different from usual in the letter he wrote to me right after I left home this time.

Excerpts from my father's letter
dated June 19, 1977

It's a quiet, rainy Sunday—it's softly drizzling. After reading through the morning paper, I helped your mom with household chores, taking trash out, etc.

While I read the paper, when I took the trash out, and whatever I did, I kept asking: "How is Tomoko doing?" "How far has she gone?" "Has she arrived in San Francisco yet?" etc.

The sadness we have been experiencing since you left is no different from two years ago. I keep telling myself, "I should brace myself so that I can concentrate on my business." I'm sure you're going through the same experience; you unintentionally think about home even while studying or interacting with your friends. Well, that's natural—we are human. We might try to appear or sound tough, but it's impossible to deny our loneliness. Once we overcome this sadness, our joy will be doubled when we meet again. (I wonder if I'm just saying all this to myself?)

I have never been able to write like this before because I was afraid you might become fainthearted. So, I always tried to encourage you by sounding strong. But after confirming you have grown strong over the past two years, I feel assured that you would be fine. Now that I have openly written my thoughts, it feels rather encouraging and even empowering for us to express our honest feelings like this.

I sat down in my office and spent 20~30 minutes or so, gazing blankly at the rain through the windows while smoking a pipe. After thinking for a while about your short 20-day stay at home, from arrival to departure, I picked up my pen and began writing this letter.

By the time you receive it in the mail, your summer course will have started, and you will have enjoyed the reunions with your friends. And I'm sure you will have organized your environment well and adjusted to your new schedule. [. . .]

On the day of your departure, luckily, your brother took a day off from work and drove us to the airport. I was very much concerned about you because you looked dispirited in the car all the way to the airport. I tried to cheer you up, but I didn't know what to say. And after I could finally find something to say, I pitied myself because I couldn't maintain a conversation with you. As I mentioned, however, it's natural to feel sad. At the airport, I was happy to see you behave more like your normal self as you interacted with your friends and teachers who came to see you off. [. . .]

We had a slanting rain, just like two years ago. I followed your red jacket with my eyes. And your hand waving at us . . . I watched and followed attentively the bus you were on. But just as I felt annoyed by an umbrella next to me blocking my view, I lost sight of you. [. . .]

After spending time at home, you might have developed a bit of amae *[tendency to depend too easily on someone close, such as one's parent]. Here's what worries me and what I want you to think about. The first time we human beings face a new challenge, we go at it with vigor because we don't really know how difficult it is. But now, when you think about your life in New York and going through a hot summer and freezing winter again, you may feel overwhelming weariness and start saying to yourself, "I don't like this . . . I don't want to go through this again." We often quit at these junctures and choose an easier path. But we make no progress that way. [. . .]*

Writing something like this to you, after all, is like preaching to Shakyamuni Buddha, but I just ended up writing it anyway. [. . .]

You might find New York similar to Tokyo; I'm sure you'll find good people and bad people coexisting there. Wherever you go, please observe, investigate, and understand well human nature and the culture of the country. [. . .]

There is a saying: "Adversity makes one shine."[23]

---

[23] This expression in Japanese 艱難なんじを玉にす literally means, "Adversity makes you a gem."

The same applies to the growth of grain. If rice doesn't have a hot summer, there is no harvest in the autumn. If barley doesn't go through a freezing winter, the time of the barley harvest will never come.

I guess I'm saying all this to myself, rather than to you. Let's look forward to the day we reunite again and work hard while encouraging each other to grin and bear it. [. . .]

PS—It's the 20th [the day after the letter was written] at 8:30 a.m. I couldn't help picking up the pen again.

As your mom and I were just talking about you at dinner last night around 8:30 p.m., we looked at the clock and reminded ourselves, "Tomoko must have arrived in New York by now." Then, the phone rang.

Just as we thought, it was you calling. Such great telepathy! I was so excited that I don't even remember what I said on the phone. But I could understand what you were saying clearly. After traveling a long distance with continuous stress, you were exhausted—mentally and physically. Your mom and I, and your brother and sister too, are also experiencing a lot more sadness this time around. Why? Two years ago we were determinedly focused on helping you succeed no matter what. But this time it's different, because of what I described above.

This is your choice—you have already made up your mind, so please pull yourself together and do your best. And whenever you want, on a winter or summer vacation, come home again. You can then go back to America after refueling at home. That would be best. Don't you think so?

That way, you will be motivated by hope—counting days and telling yourself, "I'll be home soon"—and you will be able to joyfully work hard every day. Don't you agree?

Unlike what I wrote two years ago, my words now sound somewhat soft and indulgent. Actually, however, I feel much better now that I've written my true and honest feelings.

Let's do our best while hoping for a better tomorrow!

After arriving in New Haven, I, too, wrote a letter openly expressing my feelings.

Excerpts from Tomoko's letter
dated July 5, 1977

On the day I left Haneda . . .

Because of the friends and teachers there, I had to look cheerful. But inside my mind, I was screaming, "No! I don't want to go!" It was completely different from two years ago. I was devastated. After I left all of you, I kept asking myself, "Why am I going to America to face all those challenges again?" Whenever I remembered how sad you looked, I kept blaming myself for causing my own parents such pain. It was really agonizing . . . On the plane, I couldn't sleep. It took only 8 hours or so to get to San Francisco. The flight time was much shorter than I had expected, so despite my actual physical location, I felt as if I were still in Japan; the feeling of being home was fresh and lasting. It was strange—I felt out of place. [. . .]

That night I kept thinking: "I don't want to go to graduate school," "I'm too weak to make it," etc. (As Dad wrote) I imagined myself going through another long winter, walking alone on the snow carrying heavy books, feeling sleepy and tired . . . I couldn't help longing for my warm family. There I have Dad, whom I can totally depend on, Mom so sweet, and Sis, who's my best friend. I wished I had stayed at home. Why do I have to experience this much loneliness? Why don't I just live happily with my family who share the same blood? Why don't I stay with Mom and Dad forever?

But I can't go back. I'm the one who said, "I want to go to graduate school." I even requested and received a scholarship. My friends also supported me. "I can't go back." I literally felt [like a famous Japanese song title], "I want to go home, but I can't." I was torn in two different directions. It was painful.

I got onboard again to fly to New York. On the plane, I just kept reading, so I wouldn't have to think too much. Exhausted, I arrived in NY. Then, it occurred to me, "I should call Mom and Dad." And immediately I called you . . .

I became a weakling when I spoke with you. After finding out that you two and everyone else were experiencing the same loneliness, I felt so sorry that I just couldn't hang up the phone . . . I kept screaming, "Dad, you hang up for me, please!" After the phone call, I imagined you two having dinner alone, looking downcast and heavyhearted. That made it even more distressing.
[. . .]

Holding back tears, I got in a limousine bus. I wasn't happy at all even though I was on the way to my beloved New Haven. As I vacantly looked outside, I soon saw the familiar town emerge in front of my eyes.

"This same view appeared glorious to me just two years ago . . ." The magnificent Yale campus didn't even look appealing to me this time.

Then I arrived at my destination. The limo driver was kind enough to help me with my luggage. I almost left my bamboo sword behind, and the driver said to me, "You almost forgot your fishing rod." Funny he thought it was a fishing rod . . .

I immediately called Roni in Waterbury. Papa-san [her dad] answered the phone. It was a collect call, and I could hear the operator asking him, "This is a collect call from Tomoko. Will you accept the charges?" To that question, Papa-san answered, "Yes" clearly and crisply as if he were saying, "We've been waiting for this call! Connect to her immediately!" I was really touched by his sincerity. Then, Papa-san asked me, "Where are you now, Tomoko? We've been waiting for you!" After I told him where I was, he said, "Stay there. We'll come get you right away."

I was in the lobby of a big hotel. I sank into a sofa, and started thinking about my life again. I felt everything was growing dark. My head was getting fuzzy. After a short while, I heard someone running toward me. As soon as I saw Roni happily dashing toward me, I was so relieved that I hugged her tightly and said, "Ahh . . . I'm so happy to see you . . ."

Roni was beaming and said to me, "The moment Dad told me you were back, I raced over here!"

I got in her car. I told her about what I had experienced. She listened to me attentively. Then I gradually felt lighter and better...

We arrived at Roni's home. Papa-san must have been waiting at the front door looking outside all that time. He was standing there with the door open.

Luckily, I've got a great friend. Without Roni and her family, I would have just shriveled up in that hotel lobby.

It was still around noon when I arrived. The four of us—Papa-san, Mama-san, Roni, and I—went on a picnic at the nearby lake. The scenery outside was gorgeous. Inside the car, I felt the wind on my face without a troubling thought. I didn't have to say anything to Roni. I felt absolutely at ease. Then gradually, having been in Japan felt like a dream. At the same time, I was able to start telling Roni about the fun I had back home. She also began telling me, "While you were away, this happened, that happened..."

That evening, so relieved and thoroughly exhausted, I went to sleep around 8 p.m. after taking a shower.

The next day, Roni brought me here to the Yale campus; I had to register for the summer course. So, here I am, back at Yale... I told myself, "I've got to work hard."

As soon as I got here, I ran into James. He welcomed me back by saying, "Okaerinasai! ["Welcome home" in Japanese]. Glad you're back!"

My dorm is the same one as two years ago [Helen Hadley Hall]. I'm so familiar with the dorm that everything went smoothly. Roni helped me organize my room. After a short break, we went to see our classmate Sue, who's been working part-time at Albertus for the summer.

Everyone was waiting for my return. Just knowing that, I felt I was recovering from being homesick.

That evening, Mike, Aileen, and James invited me for dinner. They prepared an incredibly big feast for me, I guess, to cheer me up; they must have been concerned about me. (They probably could tell I wasn't really my usual self when they had seen me earlier that day.) I gave them souvenirs from Japan. Their happy faces were infectious. [. . .]

Soon, upon the news that I was back, many friends came to visit me or telephoned me. The intensive summer program has also begun; it's been keeping me busy every day.

A Broken Teacup

I returned to New Haven once again. My dorm room during the summer was in the same residential hall where I had stayed two summers ago. My Yale friends welcomed me back.

James was also taking a summer course to brush up on his reading skills in German. His girlfriend, Suzanne, happened to be in the same French class as I was. Happily, we struggled together learning a foreign language.

After about three weeks, I felt I had regained my usual self. At the same time, my sense of appreciation for my family had become even greater, surging toward me like tidal waves.

Excerpts from Tomoko's letter dated July 10, 1977

It's been only three weeks since I started the French class. It's so intensive that we have already been reading (forced to read) novels in French. We must translate everything into high-level English, so it's also a good exercise for me in writing English. Even American students are struggling in this course. Needless to say, it's a lot harder for me, a Japanese, whose native language is not English, which is at least similar in some respects to French. But I'm trying hard with an "indomitable spirit." [. . .]

Writing a letter home like this again as I used to, I feel as though my three-week stay in Japan was just a dream. While reading Dad's heart-warming letter, I'm reminding myself, "I'm really back in America again."

When I was home, I couldn't tell you how much I appreciate you. But being away from home, I really want to shout, "Thank you!" I should have done it when I was there with you. Now that I can't say it face to face, I write it in my letter, feeling frustrated . . .

But because of that, I am now able to feel and appreciate the warmth from each and every word expressed in Dad's letter more deeply than ever before.

I'm really glad I went home! Although I experienced a bit of loneliness, I find it more like a chapter I couldn't skip. I see it now better than before.

My father responded: "We are human. It's natural to feel all these emotions. But you become truly courageous when you don't allow them to drag you down but pull yourself together as quickly as you can."

He continued to encourage me as always with little thought for his own sadness.

I spent the summer enjoying myself with friends. Still, I couldn't help feeling a bit homesick whenever I thought about my short stay at home in Japan.

I had brought with me my father's favorite teacup. One day, I carelessly dropped it in the hallway of the dorm. It may be hard to believe, but I wasn't someone who cried easily. Maybe it was my culture, maybe it was just me, or maybe it was a combination of the two. Even during those times when I had felt horribly homesick, I had never cried. On that day, however, while picking up the broken pieces of the shattered teacup, I came close . . .

I also spent two days sick in bed. I had never even caught a cold when I was studying at Albertus. I realized that one could get sick easily when becoming weak in spirit.

When my father heard that I had gotten sick, he wrote to me about his experience during the war.

Excerpts from my father's letter dated August 14, 1977

I read your letter again in my office. You spent three weeks at home, went back to America in the hot weather, and readjusted to the lifestyle there. You were exhausted from traveling. On top of that, you began the intensive summer program. Imagining how hard you must be studying and how stressed you might be, I was concerned about your health. And just as I was thinking about it, I heard you had been sick in bed for two days. It must have been such a trying experience.

As I read your letter, I began reminiscing about the distant past. Although we are in different eras, I found it mystical that we, father and daughter, experienced something similar—becoming sick on foreign soil. [. . .] [See "The Battlefield" in Chapter 2 for the description of my father's experience contracting malaria during WWII.]

Two months after leaving home, you got sick just as I had when I was your age. I'm in grief over our mystic fate.

Tomoko, never say die! Keep at your own pace and hang in there. Don't feel that you have to push yourself beyond reasonable limits. I'll leave the rest to your good judgment.

Please take care of yourself, especially learning from this experience of becoming sick.

This was when my father wrote to me about his life-or-death experience with malaria (see Chapter 2). My experience was much less serious than his and far from being life-threatening. I was just exhausted. Being far away, however, my father was gravely concerned about me.

Reading his letter, I thought about my father as a young man. He had gone back to Japan from the battlefield in China in January 1944 to enter an army chemistry school after spending three years on the war's front lines, and soon left Japan alone to go back to Manchuria. His letter (dated August 14, 1977) read:

> *Two months had already passed since I left Japan. Due to the series of stressful experiences pursuing my corps all alone, even though I was young, I was exhausted. Then the corps was reorganized and went into combat. Not being able to rest even for a moment, I came down with malaria when we reached Changsha in Middle China.*

My father was contrasting his state of being when he again left for Manchuria and mine when I went back to America. We were actually about the same age—he was twenty-three and I was twenty-two. It was indeed mystical.

In my case, however, I was studying abroad, which was my choice—and a rather luxurious problem. My father, on the other hand, was drafted into the army during the war. His tribulations were incomparable to mine.

Moreover, in my father's case, he went back to the battlefield right after he had found out that his father, Kiichi, had died while being away from home. Then, he contracted malaria . . . What an atrocious scenario!

My father's words I had heard two years before came back to me: "At age twenty I left for Manchuria. When I visited home during the war, I found out my father had died some time before and everything was a big mess at home."

I felt myself blessed because my father was in good health. Nonetheless, I thought it was mystical, as Dad mentioned. My father left home at age twenty and went to a military prep school on a foreign land, while I had left home to study in America at the same age. He visited home after becoming an army officer, and I visited home after graduating from college . . . We each learned about the death of a beloved one that had taken place unbeknownst to us during our absence. While acknowledging and taking into account the significant differences in our relative circumstances, I simply could not help thinking how parallel our emotional lives were.

I studied French single-mindedly that summer as if I were trying to block the pain from being away from home.

In late August, I finished the summer program. And the day before Labor Day in September, I moved to the campus of Columbia University. James and another Yale student drove their own cars to help me move my belongings from New Haven to New York. I was grateful for my good friends.

Graduate School and Discontent

The gate to the main campus of Columbia University is located on Broadway and 116th Street. Beyond that gate you see a path called "College Walk" with cherry trees on either side. Having lost their flowers months ago, the cherry trees had deep green leaves instead when I arrived.

As you walk on the Campus Walk toward Amsterdam Avenue, you'll find the Roman-style building called "Lowe Library" on your left hand, and the Greek-style building "Butler Library" on your right. On the steps in front of Lowe Library is the university's symbol, the "Alma Mater" statue.

As you go farther toward the east, you'll find a building called "Kent Hall" that houses the East Asian Studies department. After crossing Amsterdam Avenue, there you find the "Law School" building. Behind that building is a dormitory called "Johnson Hall" (present-day "Wien Hall").

I moved into Johnson Hall. This dorm had been a women's dorm, but it had become coeducational two years before I moved there. It housed graduate students from various majors. Soon I realized it didn't have that family atmosphere I had experienced at Yale and Albertus. There wasn't a larger community atmosphere either.

Unlike the small and peaceful town of New Haven, the City of New York was so urban that I felt it lacked human tenderness.

My room was on the eighth floor, and from my window, I had a full view of Harlem. It was depressing rather than scenic. I constantly heard police cars and ambulances. I sometimes heard people screaming.

Since I didn't want to make my parents worry, I wrote to them: "The night view from my room is spectacular. I can go anywhere by subway. There are so many department stores, museums, and theaters that I feel there is no greater place than New York. Anywhere is home once you get used to it."

Classes began. And I soon became disappointed with linguistics. It was the subject that I had wanted to study badly, but I didn't find it as exciting as I had expected. There were different types of classes in the subfields of linguistics—some were extremely interesting and others utterly boring. Good at grammatical analysis, I came to like the syntax class that focused on Chomsky's transformational generative grammar. On the other hand, I thought phonetics was tedious.

What I hated even more was that I found my classmates unfriendly and rather cold. I also thought they were very competitive. (But of course, it's funny for me to say this because I was competitive during my college years at Albertus.) The atmosphere I experienced there was quite different from what I had felt from the Yale grad students I knew. I wondered whether my negative sentiments were due to the nature of the locality, or because I was spiritually defeated.

In that environment, I often wished to go back to Japan. Obviously, however, I knew I would disappoint my parents, so I checked myself and continued to study hard. But honestly, I would say, I was like a rudderless ship.

I continued to receive letters and comfort bags from home regularly as always. Needless to say, they were the best source of encouragement for me.

My father always tried to write funny stories in his letters. His story about handmade noodles was superb. I could tell he was trying hard to make me laugh. At the same time, he might have written it as a comical sequel to what he had regretfully written in his previous letter, probably thinking: *I shouldn't have written about Japanese noodles to my daughter far away in America because she might pine for them.*

Excerpts from my father's letter
dated November 6, 1977

I wrote in my last week's letter about the restaurant featuring handmade noodles that your mom and I had visited. Here's a sequel to it.

After lunch, we bought 5 orders each of soba *and* udon *noodles to take home, thinking of giving some to your brother too. But the next day, I found those noodles had mashed together in plastic bags and turned into big balls. Surprised, I tried to disentangle them carefully in water, but they were stuck together so well that the noodles simply broke into short sticks like matches. If I gave them to your brother, he would probably laugh, and yet I didn't want to waste the food. So, the three of us [my dad, mom, and sister] ended up eating them the following night again. It was really like that saying: "It's so hopeless that it's impossible to even pick up with chopsticks or sticks."[24] Instead of using chopsticks, we ate them with spoons like eating wanton soup. Our wish to have delicious handmade noodles shattered. The* udon *noodles became reminiscent of the wartime food* suiton *[flour dumplings boiled in soup]. Your mom even began talking about the wartime food shortage.*

A week later, we still have one more meal's worth of udon *noodles left. I think I'm going to eat it this evening and clean it up. This is literally like "being hit by a* soba *cane."[25]*

---

[24] This expression in Japanese 箸にも棒にもかからない [literally "cannot be picked up by chopsticks or sticks"] means, "good for nothing," "hopeless," etc.

[25] My father wrote this expression as ソバ杖を食う, which is normally written 側杖を食う [literally "to get a blow from a nearby cane"]. He changed 側 [nearby] to ソバ [*soba* noodles] in his letter. Since the "*soba* [nearby]" of 側杖 ["soba-zue"] is homophonous with "*soba* [noodles]," he made a pun out of the expression 側杖を食う here.

My father also wrote about a dream he had had one night. From this humorous story, I could tell how much he enjoyed preparing packages for me while thinking about me in New York. This particular letter was especially heart-warming because he was fishing—his favorite pastime—even in his dreams.

Excerpts from my father's letter dated November 22, 1977

11/18 (Fri) Fair—The rain that started yesterday has finally cleared up, and we now have a patch of blue sky. It feels like a warm spring day.

Last night I had a dream. I was awakened by a noise—there were peanut rice-crackers, canned food, and mochi cakes buzzing around. I realized I was in the cargo section of a steamship. And I saw on top of the load the cardboard box I had sent to you. Suddenly, the contents of the box began talking, "Luckily, our box was placed on top, so we didn't get crushed! We are happy we are safe!" And they all came out of the box one after another and started shouting one by one: "I can't wait to see Tomoko's happy face!" "I can't wait to meet her!" etc. etc.

The steamship moved forward grandly on the vast ocean.

It was so wonderful that I decided to trawl for fish. But the ship was going so fast that I couldn't catch any. While I was fishing, the package contents came out in a stream to watch me fishing. I said to them, "You'll be in trouble if you don't hurry back inside the cardboard box." I desperately put them back into the box, wrapped the package with paper, and taped it firmly.

Soon I realized that I was doing that work on the gift-wrapping table in my store. I showed the package to your mom and said, "Look! I did a nice job, didn't I?"

Then I was awakened by my own voice. It was all a dream.

[. . .]

I'm doing great as you can see from this story. Your mom and everyone else too. Mihoko is doing well—showing remarkable growth each day.

I hope you had a good laugh reading my letter.

Earlier that year, in February 1977, a daughter (Mihoko) was born to my brother, Hiromi. My parents were so happy to have their first grandchild that they often wrote to me about her. I joyfully and eagerly read about my beloved niece's development. I couldn't wait for her to grow up so that, for example, we could drink saké together.

While blissfully watching their grandchild grow up, naturally, my parents often reminisced about our early childhood. In the following letter, for instance, my father wrote that, although his granddaughter was everyone's focus at the celebration of my parents' thirtieth wedding anniversary, Dad couldn't help thinking about my siblings and me as small children.

Excerpts from my father's letter dated November 27, 1977

As I watch Mihoko's growth, I think about my three children when they were still small—vivid memories come back to me. [. . .] Back then, we didn't have enough helping hands to give the three of you good care. Besides, I was in the middle of rebuilding the family business, which kept me too busy to care for my children as much as I wanted. [See "Rebuilding" in Chapter 3.] But seeing all of my children advancing toward their goals steadily, as a parent, I am so overwhelmed with appreciation that I don't even know how to express my gratitude.

I felt bad after writing about the Japanese feast we had for the celebration, but we'll meet again soon to laugh together eating and drinking to our hearts' content. So, please study hard while looking forward to that day.

> *I took a walk with your mom on the bank of Arakawa*
> *River, enjoying a chat about the good old days. I wonder how many*
> *years ago it has been since we had such a peaceful time together.*
> *Looking at your mom's contented face, I was determined to become*
> *even more dedicated to her from now on as we advance in age.*

Changing Destiny

I grew up in a happy home, but I was suspicious that happiness might be rather fragile and temporary. I often felt that the happiness of my childhood and early adulthood was due to the good luck I was born with. But that luck might be like a bank account that yields no interest. If you spend the money, at some point you'll surely run out.

The question was: "What could I do to keep adding to my fortune so that it would never run dry?" I often wondered about this, especially after entering graduate school. Without having a strong sense of purpose, I felt depressed and disappointed in myself. I lost self-confidence and wondered about my life and what happiness meant, and so forth. I thought my fortune was decreasing.

I also thought about the relationship between myself and the world around me. I wondered why I found life so constantly challenging and exhausting to the point that I felt on the verge of defeat too often.

I began searching for something that would strengthen me, something that might enable me not only to withstand what the world threw at me but maybe even allow me to change that environment. What could I do to begin to feel free enough to live up to my potential without being forever fearful of what might be coming around the corner? I needed fortification.

It was just another ordinary day, but it became one of the most important days in my life. A good friend of mine, also a Japanese student, told me, "I'm a Nichiren Buddhist." He identified himself as a member of a Buddhist lay organization called "*Soka Gakkai*

[Value-Creation Society]." I had no idea what that organization was really all about, but I admit I did have some prejudices against it. I think I inherited them from my parents, who had never explained to me these particular feelings.

I asked my friend a series of questions. The more I asked, the more I was surprised by the clarity of his responses. His explanations made sense to me. I realized I didn't know anything about Buddhism, although I was born in Japan. I felt extremely ashamed of myself for my lack of knowledge about Buddhism and the Soka Gakkai.

My family, from generation to generation, had belonged to the Pure-Land sect of Buddhism—a different denomination from the Nichiren tradition of Buddhism that Soka Gakkai members practice. In my family, however, we had neither learned nor practiced Buddhist teachings. We visited our ancestors' gravesite during the *Bon* [festival honoring the deceased] and equinoctial weeks. My father joined his hands in prayer in front the Buddhist altar at home every morning, and I imitated him when I was a child. That's about it.

Our family often visited Shinto shrines as well.[26] We had never missed going to the Hikawa Shrine in Ōmiya City on the day of the Tōkamachi Festival each year. Our family even had a shrine for *Inari*, the guardian deity, in the backyard of our home.

While my father prayed to Shinto gods, he would also receive and worship a talisman from a Buddhist temple. And don't forget that my parents sent my siblings and me to a Christian kindergarten.

This type of religious coexistence was (and still is) very common in Japan. As it's commonly said, "Japanese get married in a Christian church, go to a Shinto shrine when a baby is born, and go to a Buddhist temple for a funeral." Different religions coexisted in a typical family. Moreover, people did not really learn or practice the

---

[26] *Shinto* [literally meaning "ways of the gods"] is not Buddhism. Shinto is a Japanese religion incorporating the worship of ancestors and nature spirits and a belief in sacred power in both animate and inanimate things. It was the state religion of Japan until 1945.

teachings of any of the religions. In other words, those different religions were for ceremonial purposes only.

But is that the way we should live? I asked myself.

I also thought about my own family and ancestors, who had experienced much misery despite how hard they worked in life. They were also good people, and yet they encountered tremendous misfortune. They were religious in their own way—e.g., having a Shinto shrine at home, visiting and making monetary offerings to Buddhist temples and Shinto shrines, etc.

Why did they have so much misfortune even though they were all very religious and good people? I wondered. I even went so far as to question: *Is it possible that, despite their best intentions, they were actually punished for their practices?*

After speaking with my Buddhist friend, I felt so ashamed of my ignorance that I rushed to the East Asian Studies library in Kent Hall on the Columbia campus. I heard that the president of the Soka Gakkai at the time, Mr. Daisaku Ikeda, had visited Columbia two years before in 1975 and donated a number of books including those authored by him.

At the library, I looked for those books. I began avidly reading them one after another.

What a great human being he is! I was deeply impressed by Mr. Ikeda and his philosophy.

At the same time, I became so interested in Nichiren Buddhism that I decided to pursue it. Then I heard about a visiting professor from Japan who was a Soka Gakkai member. I lost no time in contacting him.

Professor Takada lived with his wife and two small children in an apartment near the Columbia campus. When I called him, he was so welcoming he immediately invited me to come visit his home. I went, expecting him to present some profound Buddhist philosophy. But not quite—we just had a nice familial conversation. As I was leaving, Professor Takada suggested,

"Let's go to a discussion meeting one of these days."

Mrs. Takada also said she would be happy to teach me how to do *gongyō* [sutra reading] and *shōdai* [chanting a Buddhist phrase].

Honestly, I thought, *that's not exactly what I was looking for . . .* But they were being kind, so I accepted both their invitations.

In retrospect, I was looking at religion in general only from a theoretical or ideological perspective. I later learned that the "practice" aspect of religion should be as important as the "study." And, what is "faith"? It has to be cultivated in both "study" and "practice." Each of the three components—faith, practice, and study—is indispensable to the other and an integral aspect of religion.

As promised, Professor Takada took me to a gathering called a "discussion meeting." It was held at an American Buddhist's apartment, where people of different heritages gathered.

First of all, I was shocked to see Americans practicing Buddhism. Secondly, they were men and women from all walks of life—not only different ethnic backgrounds, but also various professions and ages. There were no barriers such as ethnicity, gender, age, profession, education, etc.

How could such different people gather together and hold such a joyful discussion? I wondered.

What was even more impressive was that their eyes seemed to reflect an inner radiance. It made me think: *I have a nice family back in Japan. I'm attending a prestigious school. I probably am more blessed than a lot of the people here, but I don't have the kind of happiness they seem to have. Where does their peace and happiness come from?*

I gradually learned that those Buddhists I met were trying to "revolutionize" their lives through practicing the Buddhism taught by Nichiren, the thirteenth-century priest in Japan, and to achieve absolute happiness. They were also trying to change their "karma" or destiny.

You can change not only your life but also your family's karma as well! I grew excited—finally, I got an answer to the questions that had nagged me so much of my life.

I soon learned that in order to achieve that goal, you must continue chanting "Nam-myoho-renge-kyo." I was dubious. Moreover, I was told that you must recite portions of the Lotus

Sutra assiduously every morning and evening. Again, I simply could not believe that such a practice would lead to one's internal revolution as well as to the changing of one's destiny.

I could see some value in doing activities and holding discussions with other Buddhists in order to improve oneself and one's understanding of the teachings. I did find the studying of Buddhist theory attractive and fascinating. But again, I could not see the necessity or even the sense in the practice of chanting and reading sutras. I really didn't see how it could be effective.

That's hard to believe, I thought in my head. And yet, to reply to Professor and Mrs. Takada's kindness, I decided to give it a try. Since I promised them, I sincerely tried to do gongyō and chant the phrase every day.

I can't believe it. What am I doing? I often wondered.

One morning, I overslept. I rushed to my class without doing my morning prayer. After the class, I was walking along a street. I felt something was strange . . . even wrong. I felt out of rhythm.

No way . . . I said to myself. *That's impossible . . .* I entirely denied it in my head.

Nonetheless, I went back to my dorm room during lunchtime and did gongyō and chanted the phrase. Then strangely, I felt refreshed. I found myself even humming a tune as I went to my afternoon class. It was simply incomprehensible to me.

To make a long story short, although I was in denial about the effect of my Buddhist practice, I decided there was no harm in continuing it.

The spring semester began. Having finished the fall semester with good grades, I was hired as a teaching assistant (TA) by one of my professors. This work gave me a tuition exemption and a small stipend.

"That's your *kudoku* [benefit from the Buddhist practice]," said Arlaana, a Buddhist friend and my fellow Columbia grad student.

I didn't believe her. *Religion is supposed to bring something spiritual, not a benefit like that*, I thought. But soon I realized there was nothing wrong with getting a side benefit. It should be welcomed as long as it makes one's life better. Why not?

As I continued the practice, I began to feel energy that I had never experienced before. This was definitely a welcome benefit. In late-February of 1978, I officially joined the Soka Gakkai organization in New York.

In March, I began to long for my parents. I thought I had become homesick again. This time, however, it seemed different. Whenever I looked at the photo of my parents on my desk, I felt like crying for no particular reason.

My parents continued to send me letters that always opened with: "We are all doing well." I had no reason to believe that there was anything to worry about. The letters were delivered to me as regularly as always.

Comfort bags also kept coming. In early March, for instance, I received a package containing instant *shiruko* [red-bean soup], mochi as well as *hina-arare* [puffy bits of rice cake for the Girls' Festival] so that I could celebrate the *hina matsuri* [the Girls' Festival] on March 3rd. I reminisced about the good old days when my sister and I as young girls had celebrated the festival with our magnificent *hina* dolls of a prince and princess and their court servants displayed on a tiered stand in our house.

My father's letter describing the contents of this particular comfort bag included his haiku:

> *For you too*
> *My princess in America*
> *I send* hina-arare.[27]

I felt a soft spring breeze touching my heart.

Everyone at home was fine. I was doing well at school. My TA job was interesting and enjoyable. And yet, I still felt restless. I became anxious and worried about my parents . . . for no reason.

27　アメリカのお姫（ヒー）様にもひなあられ

In early May, my parents asked me, "Have you made plans for the summer?" I could tell they were anxious for me to come home. I picked up the phone and told them that I would be home in late June. My parents were elated. My father wrote to me after my phone call, "I was so happy and excited that I had trouble falling asleep."

When I said I would be home in June, however, I didn't mean just the summer. I had to tell my parents my real plan in writing.

Excerpts from Tomoko's letter
dated June 6, 1978

> *To tell you the truth, I have decided to take a leave of absence from school. [. . .] I have given a lot of thought to this. Because I was so convinced this is the right thing for me to do, I decided on my own without asking for Dad's advice. I'm sorry for surprising you again with my decision like this as I've done before. Please forgive me. [. . .] I have become uncertain about the field of linguistics, so I want to think about it while taking a year off. My academic advisor was very understanding. I thought I would have to withdraw from the program, but he wouldn't let me quit. Instead, he made arrangements for me to take a leave of absence. He even told me that if I attend graduate school in Japan, he would accept any credits from there too. So, there is not so much to lose.*

It was true—I was beginning to lose interest in linguistics. But that was not the real reason why I wanted to take a leave of absence from school. I was driven by an inexplicable disquiet that had been gnawing at me since March. Even though I couldn't understand what it was, I felt compelled to take a leave of absence and go back to Japan.

Carp on the Cutting Board

In late June of 1978, I arrived at Narita International Airport, which had just opened. It had been a year since I last saw my family.

Imagining a great reunion like the one from a year before, I looked for my family.

There they are! I found them.

As soon as I approached my family and saw my father, I was dumbfounded. With difficulty, I finally opened my mouth,

"What happened to you, Dad? You're so thin . . ."

My father was always well built, but he looked half his normal size, having lost so much weight. He also looked ten years older. Altogether, he looked like a different person.

"I had a bit of stomach trouble. I didn't tell you because I didn't want to worry you. But everything is fine now. Don't you worry," said Dad, smiling.

My mother and sister became silent for a short while, but soon they became chatty, welcoming me home. I was happy to see my family, but I felt dispirited at the same time.

When we were approaching Ōmiya City, I thought of saying, "Let's go see Grandma in Shima," but decided not to. Intuitively, I knew she was no longer living. I knew my parents hadn't told me for the same reason they had not informed me of my grandfather's passing. I also felt at that moment that my family knew what I was thinking.

After finding out about Dad's illness, while sensing my grandmother's passing, I felt disheartened. My homecoming this time made a sharp contrast with the previous year's.

That night, my sister told me the truth. Just as I anticipated, Grandma Tema had been deceased for several months. Reiko also told me about the surgery Dad had had in March of that year. He had a serious case of stomach ulcers, she explained to me.

"Do you remember the week when Dad wrote to you and explained that he might not be able to write a letter the following week? He had surgery soon after writing that letter. 'Don't tell Tomoko about my surgery. It's cruel to make her worry,' he said."

"But I received a letter every week without a fail," I said, utterly shocked, to my sister.

"Of course . . . Do you know what Dad said as soon as the anesthetic wore off? 'I'm going to write a letter to Tomoko.' Then, lying in bed, he grabbed his fountain pen and began writing on airmail stationery, feeling faint the whole time," Reiko explained.

I had no idea. I had read those letters from my father without any suspicion, just as usual.

Later I revisited the letter in question, dated March 19, 1978, in which Dad had expatiated why he had to go on this particular business trip. When I reread it with my new knowledge, I did see this time it was rather odd that he had written two pages explaining he might not be able to write in the following week. He was trying very hard to convince me this trip was so important that he might not have time to write.

As I read it again, I could tell he sounded awkward. He had never missed writing a letter to me no matter where he went or how busy he was. He must have struggled to cover up the real reason why he might not be able to write.

This letter in particular didn't have excerpts from his diary. He concluded it by saying, "Sorry it's gotten so technical that you might find it boring." It was much shorter than usual.

There was a letter from my mother attached to it. She wrote about the plum flowers in full blossom, hyacinth flowers blooming under the eaves, and Dad's azaleas waiting to smile. Her letter was just as usual.

I heard from my mother later what my father had said before the surgery. He said,

"I'm a carp on the cutting board."[28]

He was prepared for the worst. It was indeed a major operation. I was also told that Dad had trouble waking up from the anesthesia, which made his doctor gravely concerned.

What about the letter my dad wrote after the surgery? Well, there was nothing about the business trip he had described at length in the previous letter (which in hindsight may have been suspicious).

---

[28] This expression in Japanese まな板の鯉 [literally "a carp on the cutting board"] means "to be doomed."

Instead, he wrote about the high exchange rate of the Japanese yen, the results of a sumo tournament, etc.

His stories were light-hearted as usual. For instance, he explained why Takanohana, his favorite sumo wrestler, did not win the championship. Dad explained in a humorous way that Takanohana became so nervous that he wasn't able to sleep well before the final match. Then he wrote about "sleep-starved cherry flowers."

Excerpts from my father's letter dated March 26, 1978

Speaking of "lack of sleep," I just remembered, even cherry, peach, and pear trees sometimes suffer from lack of sleep. Have you heard of "sleep-starved cherry flowers"? I'll tell you what. If cherry flowers bloom more than 10 days earlier than usual, the flowers may look the same, but the fruit will be poor. In the opposite case—if they bloom late, the fruit will be much better, I've heard. In the natural world, animals hibernate. As it's written 冬眠 *["winter" + "sleep"—meaning "hibernation"], we may consider it a type of sleep too in the case of flowers. I've just come to realize all this. I wonder if the azaleas at home are at sleep now. In any case, they seem to have good flowers this year again.*

The letter from my mother that accompanied Dad's concluded with "Everyone is doing well."

Reading those letters three months prior to my homecoming, I never imagined that Dad was going through such a horrendous ordeal.

In the morning after I got home, I had a long chat with my father over some green tea before breakfast.

"My stomach ulcer got so bad that I had to have surgery. But the affected area was all removed, so don't worry," Dad said.

I wondered why he had not even gone to see a doctor until his stomach ulcer had worsened to that extent.

Dad was always worried about the health of others, especially Mom's. He frequently took Mom to Iwatsuki Hospital, which was often mentioned in his letters. He had his employees take physical checkups regularly too, whereas he never underwent one himself.

Dad always mentioned in his letters that he was taking good care of his health. Actually, he was too confident in his health. Besides, perhaps due to his army training, he was incredibly tolerant of pain. He would just grin and bear it.

I also remembered that Dad had once said something eerie when I was a child. He had said it when Mom was so sickly that she was often bed stricken.

"I'm strong and sturdy like a big tree. But big trees can be broken down suddenly. Your mom is physically weak. But reeds don't get broken down. Like a reed, she'll live to be over eighty years old."

An image of a big tree falling down came back to me. I hurriedly erased it from my mind.

This is why I came home . . . I finally understood the premonition I had had in March.

Don't Quit School Halfway Through

I had a couple of problems to solve for myself. One was about my education—whether or not I should go to graduate school in Japan. The other was about my religion—I had to tell my family about joining the Soka Gakkai. The latter was a big problem because I could almost hear my father say, "We took great pains to come to terms with your going abroad to graduate school. And you're telling me you joined a new religion?"

It made me anxious to think about it. I was also afraid of causing my father any additional stress as he was already unwell. But soon I remembered why I had chosen to practice Nichiren Buddhism—to change my family's karma and for my own happiness as well as that of my family. I mustered up my courage and told my father why and how I had joined the Buddhist organization.

My father said to me,

"I understand how serious you are about it. You have religious freedom. Give it your best try."

As soon as I received his blessing, I began my Buddhist practice joyfully at home.

In a month or so, my sister was so impressed with my "growth" that she told me she would like to join me in the practice. Happily, the two of us began practicing Buddhism together.

One day, I had a quarrel with my mother over my religious activities. It turned into a long argument. After the heated debate, my mother said definitively,

"Okay, you won. I'll join you."

Mom immediately started practicing Buddhism with my sister and me.

Dad was a bit perplexed—all of a sudden the three women in the household were practicing Buddhism together quite happily. Soon, however, he was overjoyed to see his wife become increasingly healthier and happier, and his older daughter become more cheerful each day. Then, to my pleasant surprise, he even began chanting the phrase "Nam-myoho-renge-kyo."

(My brother, Hiromi, was opposed to our Buddhist practice for eight years. He eventually gave in and joined us. Those eight years saw a lot of drama over the religious issue, which I must skip here. To make a long story short, I was eventually able to convert my entire family to the religion "imported back" from America.)

After my return from New York, Dad regained his strength and seemed to be doing much better. He and I often went fishing. We also enjoyed drinking saké together. We discussed Buddhism too. I would also take him to the hospital in my car. I tried to spend as much time as possible with him.

I began to attend a professional school that trained its students to become simultaneous interpreters for international conferences. I had originally thought of going to graduate school in Japan, but I missed the timing for admission. Instead, when I heard about a famous school opening its doors to future simultaneous interpreters, I decided to give it a try.

As winter approached, it suddenly got cold, and Dad's physical condition started to deteriorate. His weight loss was drastic.

One day in December, I found a note left at my car that was parked near the train station. It was from my brother. It read, "Please stop by my house tonight after school no matter how late it is."

I wondered why. On my way home from school, I stopped by his house.

Hiromi was waiting for me with a look of extreme sorrow. He hesitantly began to reveal his awful secret.

"To tell you the truth . . ."

There was a long pause. Then he continued,

"It's not an ulcer that Dad has."

"What?! What does he have?" I asked, dumbfounded.

"Cancer . . . He has stomach cancer," Hiromi answered.

"But he'll be cured, right?"

"When he had surgery in March, his doctor said it was too late. It's terminal. I wondered whether or not I should tell Dad the diagnosis. I agonized over it. In the end, I decided not to tell him." My brother was holding back his tears.

"You mean, Mom doesn't know either?" I was in complete shock.

"I haven't told her. But I told Reiko the truth yesterday. Dad won't live long. Please prepare yourself."

My brother couldn't speak any longer.

No, no, no! It must be a lie! I screamed in my mind, which became blank. I didn't know what to make of it. I couldn't think. There was a long period of silence between us.

Suddenly, at the heartrending sight of my brother's pained face, the position he had been put in dawned on me.[29]

Over the past nine months, he has been shouldering this devastating burden all by himself . . . I felt my heart torn to pieces.

---

[29] It was common in Japan at that time for medical personnel to let responsible family members decide how much the ill ones should be told.

By the time I got home, it was dark and quiet. Everyone was asleep. When I passed my parents' bedroom, I could hear Dad snoring. I stopped to listen to him. I had started doing that, especially since I found out about his illness in June.

Ah . . . he's alive, I thought, *but the day will come when that snoring will end. How am I supposed to deal with that?*

I went into my room, dove into bed . . . and began crying. Then, my sister came in. Without words, we hugged and cried together.

From the next day on, I had to hide the secret I now knew. I had to deceive my own father. It was excruciatingly painful. My brother had endured this pain for nine long months all by himself. What a nightmare—to be placed in the position to make the decision whether or not the truth should be revealed to his father.

Dad became frail, but he was still worried about his business. He was even trying to take inventory at the end of the year. Hiromi came to help as soon as his winter break began. My brother, sister, and I silently signaled to and encouraged one another, caring for Dad.

On the day before New Year's Eve, Dad said to me out of the blue,

"I want to eat Tomoko's *yakitori* [chicken barbeque]."

He was gradually losing his appetite, so I was overjoyed to hear that he wanted to eat yakitori.

"All right, let me show you my cooking skills. You'll have the special hors d'oeuvre tonight!" I dashed to the supermarket to buy some chicken.

I didn't cook much, but I was good at making hors d'oeuvre to go with saké. Yakitori was my specialty.

As soon as I got some chicken, I began cooking. I barbecued it, sweating all the while. I used the secret recipe that I had inherited from Mom. My mom and sister prepared the other dishes. Then we all enjoyed the feast.

Enjoying the yakitori, Dad kept saying,

"Delicious! Delicious!"

He had more saké and food that evening than usual. His face looked round and showed a healthy complexion. I thought my healthy dad had come back to us. It was the first bright and cheerful dinner we had had in a while.

Dad will regain his health, I said to myself, absolutely convinced. My father looked upbeat and in high spirits all evening.

"A candle flares up brightly before burning out," I once heard. The following morning, Dad didn't feel well. His condition worsened so much that we finally decided to take him to the hospital in the afternoon. He was hospitalized immediately.

In the late evening of New Year's Eve, my father quietly lay on the bed surrounded by the four of us—my mother, brother, sister, and me. What was Dad thinking? Did he know that he was dying?

When we were about to leave for home, Dad looked sad. As soon as my brother sensed it, he said to him,

"Do you want Tomoko to stay?"

Dad gave a big nod. I was happy that I was able to stay with him. Everyone else had a lot of things to take care of at home since it was New Year's Eve. I was free; I didn't have many responsibilities. I stayed with my dad that evening, and the following days without going home at all.

January 1st—After spending New Year's Eve with my father in his hospital room, I welcomed New Year's Day. Other family members came, one after another, and spent time with Dad. They came and went—they all had a lot to take care of at home.

January 2nd—Dad had a little bit of yogurt. He was still conscious but didn't talk much. He seemed to be contemplating something. After taking care of the home front, Mom came and began her stay with me for the coming days without going home.

January 3rd—Dad's doctor wanted to speak to someone in the family. At the time, since I was the only one in the room, I went to speak to him. I must have looked very young, possibly a minor. The doctor asked me,

"Is there an adult member of your family I can speak to?"

Then, my brother came rushing up, looking flustered. I told the doctor I was twenty-three years old. Then he told me to stay there and listen to him.

"Your father has a very strong heart, so he's still alive. But he won't be long. Please prepare yourselves," the doctor said solemnly.

"What do you mean by 'not long'? How long will he live?" Hiromi asked.

"Probably another day or two." The doctor answered.

My brother and I went back to Dad's room without saying a word.

Then, Reiko came and said,

"Dad, your fishing buddy called. The fishing contest has been rescheduled for Sunday, the seventh."

Dad looked disappointed. I said to him,

"You have four more days. You'll get well by then. You can attend the contest. Cheer up, Dad!"

At that very moment, I somehow knew by intuition that January 7th would be the day when Dad was leaving us. His doctor said he would only survive for another day or two, but I was certain that my father would live longer than that. I just wanted him to live as long as possible.

January 4th—Dad could no longer eat. He ate a little bit of yogurt a couple of days before. That was it. I could tell his condition was deteriorating rapidly. He became unconscious. He could no longer talk. It seemed, however, he sometimes heard us; as we talked to him, he occasionally showed his reaction by faintly nodding.

January 5th—According to the doctor, it was a miracle that my father was still living. It was because of his strong heart, the doctor explained. All the other organs, including the liver, had already given up.

January 6th—Informed of my dad's critical condition, relatives came to the hospital one after another. Some of them even conducted a ritual called "*shini-mizu* [wetting the mouth of the person just about to die]," which drove me insane.

January 7th—My brother and sister came early in the morning to join Mom and me. I had been there since New Year's Eve, and

Mom had been there since January 2nd. The four of us gathered there, watching Dad.

Around 9 a.m., Dad started breathing rapidly with difficulty. Hiromi pushed the button to call the doctor.

Oh, no . . . Dad is going to die without regaining his consciousness . . . without saying anything to us!

As soon as I lamented so, Dad opened his big eyes wide. Until that moment, he was so weak, as if in a coma, that his eyes couldn't even focus when they were open.

To everyone's surprise, Dad almost raised his body to sit up. Then he looked into my eyes and said,

"Don't quit school halfway through. Go back to America."

We all heard him clearly. Then, Dad took his last breath.

"Dad!" We continued calling him frantically.

The doctor and nurses came running.

"He's gone," the doctor announced Dad's death.

What a heroic death . . . He mustered up the last ounce of his might and left me with his last words.

When I was a child, I used to say, "I'll die when Dad dies." My sister used to say the same. We loved him that much.

"Grief is the price we pay for love."[30]

It's true. The more you love someone, the greater your grief when you lose that person.

Now Dad was gone. Despite our deepest sorrow, we pledged to him that we would continue to live strong. We knew that's what he wanted and that was the best way to make him happy.

"If we are happy, Dad's happy. Let's live for him."

My brother, sister, and I also pledged to support Mom. In a tiny corner of the hospital we made our promises to one another.

That day, we each drove home separately. On my way home, I thought: *The fishing contest is today. I wonder if Dad knows where to find the fishing rods . . .*

---

[30] Words by Colin Murray Parkes, a British psychiatrist and author

They were in my car trunk. I had kept them since he and I last went fishing together.

I arrived home after being away for one whole week. Everything was chaotic afterwards. We had to get ready for the wake and funeral. We had no time to cry.

My father's friends streamed into the wake. They all shared their rich memories about my father. Then, Dad's fishing buddy, Mr. Matsuo, arrived. Out of breath, he told my sister and me,

"Your dad came to the fishing contest!"

I knew it. Dad went to the fishing contest that day.

Mr. Matsuo explained,

"After the contest was over, we were in a hut warming ourselves at the fire. Then, we heard a car door shut with a bang right outside the hut. I said, 'Who is here so late?' and told a young guy to go see about it. He told us, 'Mr. Takahashi is here.' Knowing your dad was ill, I went outside to tell him, 'Go home. I don't want you to catch cold.' But there was nobody outside. According to the young guy who saw him, your dad wore his usual baseball cap and greeted him with a big smile, saying 'Yo!' and holding his hand up."

As far-fetched as this may sound to some people, this is what I surmised: *Relieved from the physical pain, Dad must have been wandering around with his characteristic curiosity.*

I also wondered: *Was he late for the fishing contest because he couldn't find his fishing rods?*

Then, my childhood friend who lived next door came and said to me,

"I saw your dad in the morning of the day he passed away. I saw him come home in his Nissan entering from the back entrance."

I see . . . he wanted to come home first . . . It suddenly occurred to me why he was late for the fishing contest.

Years later, Mom wrote a poem stating how much Dad loved our home:

Sometime before his passing,
My husband said simply,
"I love our home."[31]

Dad loved fishing. In the letters I had received while I was in the States, he often wrote about fishing—e.g., his fishing trip to Ōhara to catch red snapper, the importance of taking good care of fishing gear, a fishing contest at Oyama Trout Fishing Center, a new fishing center he had found along Route 122, noteworthy stories about fish he had read about in a magazine for fishing lovers, etc.

Anything to do with fishing excited Dad. He remained childlike in his ability to see the world with a pure heart. Well, he was like a child always. He lived a meaningful and full life with a heart so pure that he was able to give his family the best, even though his own upbringing had been so wanting. And with a beautiful mind, he had instilled in all of us a love of learning.

Dad died at age fifty-seven. Although it was a short life, he had lived it to the fullest, making a deep impact on a number of people around him.

My father and I lived parallel lives. He left home to go to Manchuria at age twenty. At the same age, I left home to go to America. When his father, Kiichi, died, Dad was twenty-two. Then, he returned home at age twenty-three to find out about his father's death. I was twenty-three when my father passed away.

Because he was in China, however, Dad didn't get to see his father at his death; he didn't even know his father had died for a while. If I had not taken a leave of absence from Columbia to come home, the same could have happened to me. In reality, however, I was able to spend more than six months of irreplaceable quality time with my father.

When I realized this important difference, I could feel something was gradually changing in my life—I was changing my destiny and revolutionizing my life.

---

[31] 生前に主の残した一言はおれはこの家が大好きなんだ

11. After His Passing

Becoming a Cotton Merchant

After Dad's death, the four of us—my mom, brother, sister, and I—discussed what to do with the family business with no successor.

My brother had graduated from one of the top Japanese universities as an economics major in 1972. Subsequently, he was hired by a major automobile manufacturer in Japan.

Dad said to Hiromi,

"You've entered a business so different from mine. Your business deals with hard stuff made of steel, totally the opposite of cotton."

This was Dad's subtle acknowledgement and permission to his only son—allowing him to work for the automobile company instead of succeeding the family business.

Mom, on the other hand, secretly hoped that her older daughter, Reiko, would marry someone who might take over the family business. Even if that wouldn't be possible, Mom seemed to have been hoping that Reiko would take care of her in her old age.

While I was in college, Mom once wrote to me expressing her wishes for the future.

Excerpts from my mother's letter dated February 13, 1977

I told your brother about my wishes. Then he said, "I don't think it's fair to pressure Reiko like that. But if she marries someone she really loves, and her partner wants to take over the family business, that would be great." I agree with him that

> *parents should not be deciding their child's future in order to fulfill*
> *their own desires. Even though we don't have a successor, your*
> *dad and I are still young. We'll continue working even harder so*
> *that our children will be able to choose their own paths and enjoy*
> *their lives.*

Who would have guessed that Dad would be gone within two years after Mom had written this letter? My father was in his mid-fifties at the time. He also kept saying he was still so young that he would be able to continue working at the business for years.

My sister wished to respond positively to Mom's expectations, but she never rushed to marriage.

Since Dad's business didn't have a successor, the easiest solution would have been to simply close the store, but we all unanimously said to one another,

"Dad was looking forward to the 100th anniversary of the store's founding. So, let's find a way to continue it at least until 1986."

Then, Mom agreed to take over the business as its CEO, and my sister volunteered to assist her. Reiko had never worked before. She had never even touched fabrics for futon, identical to Mom when she had married into the family several decades before.

After graduating from junior college, Reiko went to school to learn the traditional arts of Japanese tea ceremony and flower arrangement—sort of "bridal preparation" for privileged young women in Japan. She became quite skilled at the art of flower arrangement and earned a Grade-A teaching license from the Ikenobo School.

Reiko didn't give up flower arrangement even after beginning to work at the store. I still remember how different she looked when she was going to Tokyo for flower arrangement lessons from when she worked at the store. She looked like two different persons. She sometimes drove a van to the nearby train station. And from that delivery van came out an elegantly dressed lady wearing high heels. She played the dual roles quite well.

I, too, helped at the store. I sometimes delivered merchandise in the store's delivery van. Just like my sister, who continued to go to school, I went to an interpreter's school in Tokyo. Although my transformation wasn't as shocking as my sister's, I, too, played the dual roles of student and merchant.

Dad's great-grandfather Kisuke became a merchant after being a samurai. My father became a salaried employee after being an army officer. I became a store clerk after being a graduate student. Mystically, all the three of us experienced this change after losing our fathers.

Working for the store gave me invaluable experience because I was able to take a peek at Dad's struggles as a young man. I was able to learn more about him and myself as well as about society in general. For instance, I reconfirmed that we should never look at people from discriminating lenses of profession, titles, education, etc.

One day, I delivered some merchandise to a customer. Recognizing me, and surprised to see me delivering her order, the customer asked,

"Aren't you the daughter who went to America to study?"

That reminded me of the time when I, as a child, had observed a customer asking my dad,

"Aren't you the son who became an army officer?"

My father was modest and polite. He had become a futon-store owner through and through. He never boasted about his past. By putting myself in his shoes, I learned many things—e.g., how silly it is to change your attitude depending on the title or education of the person you're talking to, to judge him or her based on his or her appearance, or to cling to one's position or pride.

Sensing a bit of sinister judgment from my customer, I felt like saying, "So, do you have any problem seeing a graduate of an American college delivering a futon mat? Please don't change your attitude like that!" but I didn't.

I responded to her with a big smile,

"Yes! And I now work at the futon store. Thank you for your business!"

Several months after my father's passing, I began to fret over my future.

Is this what I'm supposed to be doing? I asked myself.

As I struggled each day, my father's last words kept echoing in my mind: "Don't quit school halfway through. Go back to America."

It took a lot of courage to go back to New York. Sensing my frustration, my brother said to me,

"It's Dad's will. Go back to America. I'll support you."

Encouraged by him, I finally made up my mind. I wrote a letter to the registrar's office at Columbia to make arrangements to resume my studies.

Two weeks later, I received a reply from the university. What a shock it was . . . I was informed that my leave of absence had already expired. Now that I had lost my matriculation, I became frantic to go back to Columbia.

I wrote to the linguistics department to see if they could give me any advice. I soon received a response from the department secretary, who remembered me quite well. She wrote in her letter: "When I was reading your letter, Professor Hill happened to walk into my office. When I told him about your situation, he asked me to tell you that you should apply to Teachers College."

Professor Hill was affiliated with the Graduate School of Arts and Sciences, but he was, at the time, actually the director of the applied linguistics program at Columbia's graduate school of education known as Teachers College. He remembered me well and encouraged me to apply to his program.

I hurriedly put my application together. And, fortunately, I was accepted into the applied linguistics program at Teachers College. It was already August. I rushed to the US Embassy to renew my student visa. It was a miracle that I got myself ready to leave for the new academic year in time.

Back to New York with a Mission

On September 1, 1979, I left home for New York. I felt my father was watching over me.

Thirty-five years before, in 1944, my dad also left Japan to go back to the battlefield after learning about his father's death. Dad was twenty-three at the time. I was twenty-four when I left home to go back to New York.

My mother and sister sent me off with big smiles showing matching dimples. And, my brother said to me, just as my dad would have,

"*Gambare gambare* [Strive, strive]!"

And here I was back in New York. I didn't feel sentimental this time, however. All I needed to do was to focus on one thing—to finish graduate school by getting a master's degree, just as I had promised my dad.

As soon as I began studying in the MA program in applied linguistics, I was pleasantly surprised. I found my new major extremely interesting; every class was so engaging that I was absorbed into my studies.

In applied linguistics, you literally apply linguistics to something, such as language education. In my case, since I had learned English as a foreign language myself, I found the application of linguistics to language education absolutely fascinating. I became particularly interested in language acquisition research and theories.

The switch from linguistics to applied linguistics, I thought, was brilliant. I felt that my father's death had led me to this fortunate move. Moreover, without his last words, I wouldn't have even made the attempt.

Having been able to transfer the credits I had earned from the linguistics program at the Graduate School of Arts and Sciences, within a year after returning to New York, in May 1980, I was able to receive a Master of Arts degree in applied linguistics. On the graduation day, I felt content. I was fulfilling the promise to my father.

That wasn't the end, however—I decided to continue studying applied linguistics because I had become so absorbed in the field.

A year later, I was about to receive my second master's degree, Master of Education in applied linguistics.

Now what? I asked myself.

I wrote to my brother.

Excerpts from my letter to Hiromi dated March 17, 1981

Thank you for the package. It reminded me of Dad's "comfort bags." [. . .]

I've been pondering over my future. I've mentioned to you some of my ideas, such as working for the UN, going to business school, etc. After much deliberation, I've come to realize that those ideas were an "escape."

I'll be receiving my second master's degree in May. This means, I now clearly see, I'm standing at the crossroads—whether to go into academia or to simply end my study there and pursue a non-academic profession. I think I was afraid of making a commitment. After giving much thought to what I really want to do, I have realized that I want to continue studying in the field of applied linguistics. [. . .]

I've continued studying because I really like this field. My professors are all encouraging me to go on to study in the doctoral program. I think it's a valuable opportunity. [. . .] I promise I will finish the program by 1984. Don't you think it would be fun to have a scholar (or a quasi-scholar) in the Takahashi family?

This was my declaration to go into a doctoral program. At that time, I kept thinking about what my father had said exactly four years before. Just about to graduate from college in 1977, I told my parents I had been admitted to graduate school. Upon hearing that news, my father mumbled in an undertone,

"The Takahashi family will have a scholar . . ."

Excerpts from my letter to Hiromi
dated May 2, 1981

When I was about to graduate from Albertus four years ago, even though I was admitted to Columbia, I really didn't know how I could afford it because it was extremely difficult for international students to receive any financial aid. Realizing how much it would cost, I almost gave up. Dad must have read my mind. He immediately called and said to me, "I would do anything to let you stay in school! Don't you worry!"

Dad also once said to me, "I'll gather your bones" and let me pursue my dreams. Carrying his dreams as well, I have come this far. So, I've got to challenge myself and see how much further I can go. I want to live without regrets. I have reconfirmed that this is my honest desire.

Everything has been going smoothly again this semester. I will be receiving my second master's degree soon. I couldn't have come this far without my family's financial and spiritual support. I am deeply grateful. (I bet the Columbia University president would say to me, "This diploma is for you and your family," just like my kindergarten teacher had said to me, "This perfect-attendance award is for you and your father.") This is definitely the fruit of our teamwork. We are physically far apart, but we are all connected, tied with the pledge we made in a tiny corner of the hospital that day. This spiritual tie gives me a lot of power. I hope we will all stay close and share our happiness and joy with one another for the rest of our lives.

I began my doctoral program in applied linguistics after receiving my second master's degree in May 1981.

My friends' reactions to my continuing into the doctoral program varied. Although most of them were positive, there were some incomprehensible reactions as well.

One of the Japanese male graduate students I knew said to me, "If you become that educated, no man will marry you."

He said it seriously—no kidding. I could not believe how old-fashioned and sexist he was!

On the other hand, another Japanese male friend, Shige, said to me,

"Great! We can continue doing research together!"

He was genuinely happy. Shige and I had been classmates since we met in September 1979. We used to go to a café called "Hungarian Pastry Shop" on Amsterdam Avenue near the Columbia campus and discussed our research for hours and hours. (And today we are still good friends. We have coauthored a number of research papers as well as books and textbooks. We are as proud of our friendship as of our professional relationship.)

Around that time, Mr. Daisaku Ikeda, whom I consider my mentor in life, was visiting the United States, and I had a chance to meet him in New York. He encouraged me to study hard and gave me a book in which he wrote in Japanese:

> *Pursuing the purpose in life,*
> *Praying for youth without regrets.*
> *June 21, 1981, in New York, Daisaku*

I made a promise to him to pursue my doctorate and become an educator to live a contributive life.

In the doctoral program, I finished the required coursework quickly. But it got more challenging afterwards. I had to pass the comprehensive exams and then write a dissertation. Fortunately, I was able to get to the dissertation stage at a surprising speed.

While writing my dissertation, I often became so engrossed in my research that I often forgot to eat. In the morning I would have a bite of toast. Then I would put it on the desk and begin working on my dissertation. Later, I would suddenly feel hungry in the late afternoon at the sight of the cold toast still lying there untouched. That was my life back in 1983.

It was definitely my passion for research that drove me. I finished my work at such an unbelievable speed that I even shocked my dissertation advisors. And I passed the oral examination.

In May 1984, I received my Doctor of Education degree in applied linguistics. I had just turned twenty-nine years old.

My mother came all the way to New York to attend my graduation. Considering the fact that she once was very sickly, I simply could not believe how healthy and strong she had become. She was quite courageous too; she traveled to the JFK all by herself without knowing any English!

Actually, I was certain, Dad was accompanying her in spirit.

"I wish I had attended Tomoko's graduation from Albertus," my dad once said.

He regretted missing my college graduation so much that Mom, and I both felt that he was there at my graduation from Columbia.

I could almost see Dad's big smile looking at me in the doctoral cap and gown. I could also hear his voice,

"Good job, Moko-suke! We do now have a scholar in the Takahashi family!"

After graduation in 1984, I collaborated on research with my former professor, Dr. Leslie Beebe, and received training as a junior scholar. In the field of second language acquisition, Leslie and I produced a series of studies, which became widely published and cited. At applied linguistics conferences, people, recognizing my name, would come to ask me,

"Are you *the* Takahashi of 'Beebe and Takahashi'?"

Those were highlights in my life; I simply loved being associated with my role model and best friend, Leslie.

I also began teaching in the MA in TESOL program at the College of New Rochelle Graduate School. Most of my students were schoolteachers. They were also older than I was.

I must have looked much younger than my real age. As soon as I entered the classroom on the first day of my teaching, everyone looked puzzled, probably thinking, *What is this student here for?*

It took them a short while to realize I was their teacher.

Earlier that day, when I went to the library to drop off some reading materials to be placed on reserve, a librarian asked, mistaking me as a work-study student,

"Who's your professor?"

And, one more episode . . .

I was stopped by a security guard on campus as soon as I got out of my car. He warned me,

"Students can't park there! It's for faculty!"

I responded to him by pointing at my faculty parking-sticker. Well, if I couldn't believe myself that I was a professor, how could he?

Then, I remember, how nervous I was when I taught the first class! Of all things, it was a course in English syntax and pedagogy. Just imagine: a Japanese person—a non-native speaker of English—teaching American schoolteachers both English grammar and how to teach it. I was a nervous wreck!

Closed After 100 Years

On the home front, there were also some changes afoot. The store founded by my great-great-grandfather Kisuke in 1886 was just about to close its doors. In 1986, it had just celebrated its 100th anniversary, which Dad had looked forward to. Takahashi Cotton Store had finally concluded its mission.

To see Dad's store close, we felt as if our hearts would break. Especially, Hiromi as the eldest and only son had mixed feelings. He hadn't taken over the family business after all.

"I couldn't stop shedding tears of appreciation when we decided to close the store, which had supported us for all those years," reminisced Hiromi.

The store was full of our memories. It was the business my father had rebuilt in order to respond to the wish of Grandma Sui, who said, "I want to die here in Haraichi."

And it was the business that my mom and sister had worked so hard to sustain after Dad's death.

We were sure, however, that Dad would be happy because we were closing the business in order for each of us to pursue our own dreams.

To help the going-out-of-business sale, I flew home from America. My merchant's blood tingled with excitement. I felt refreshed driving a van after being a university professor for a while.

My niece, Mihoko (Hiromi's daughter), a nine-year-old artist, drew 100 posters to promote the sale. I realized merchant's blood ran in her body too. Well, she's my dad's granddaughter after all.

My mom and sister had no regrets. They were content after having worked together until that day. Thanks to them, Kisuke's cotton store was able to celebrate its 100th birthday and complete its mission.

My sister, Reiko, got married. She is blessed with two beautiful sons. She never left our hometown. And just as my mom wished, she lives with Reiko and her family. Mom spends much time writing poetry.

My mother, Sachiko, enjoying her retirement (1990)

Mom was hospitalized once after being too engrossed in writing poetry and exhausting herself. At the hospital, nurses and staff gave Mom a nickname, *"Hime* [Princess] on the Third Floor." Not that she was demanding. On the contrary, everyone simply loved Mom for her sweetness. She was such a special patient because she would thank everyone with a poem.

When I heard Mom's new nickname, I thought, she had finally become a real Princess Cinderella.

Kisuke's business didn't vanish completely. After working as a salaried worker for thirty years, at age fifty-three, my brother established a business-consulting firm in 2001—named "Wat's."

This English-sounding name, Wat's, actually came from "Wataya Kisuke," our great-great-grandfather's nickname. Hiromi, of the Fifth Generation, wanted to continue the business spirit of the Founder although his was not a cotton business.

Moreover, Hiromi used the corporate registration of Takahashi Cotton Store as the foundation for his new firm. How could that be possible? Hiromi had kept the Cotton Store's corporate registration for all those years even after the store closure, having renewed the registration each year and even paid taxes, without knowing whether he would ever be able to use this registration in the future. He had kept the company "alive" because he simply did not want to close it entirely.

When Hiromi decided to open his own firm, he immediately thought of using the corporate registration of the Cotton Store and consulted his legal advisor. Hiromi wanted to change the name of the company, renew company assets, etc. He also planned to open his office in Tokyo. He knew he was making the process unnecessarily more complex. It would have been much easier to establish a brand new company, but Hiromi wanted to do it as the Fifth Generation of Takahashi Cotton Store, who had terminated the family business.

Consequently, Hiromi's business-consulting firm started as a company with a long history, although it was established in the twenty-first century. His office is in Tokyo, the city my father loved. I bet Dad is watching over Wat's. I can hear him saying,

"Good job, Hiromi!"

My brother used to be concerned about the fact that the head of our family in each generation, except for Kisuke, had died quite young. Hiromi thus considered as the critical point in his life the age fifty-seven, at which Dad had died. Well, he passed that age long ago. Over sixty, he is thriving.

In 2006, he participated in the New York Marathon and completed the race. What a sight it was—my fifty-eight-year-old brother running in the boroughs of my beloved New York, carrying our dreams, as the CEO of Wat's!

Nowadays, my brother somehow reminds me of Kisuke, the Founder. Looking at Hiromi's forehead, I am beginning to think that he is looking increasingly more like Kisuke, who used to be called "Grandpa Baldy."

(Center: Number 17747) my brother, Hiromi, Age 58, running in the New York Marathon (November 2006)

Living a Contributive Life

After graduation from Columbia, as mentioned, I continued my research and teaching applied linguistics. I loved attending academic conferences and presenting papers. I enjoyed writing research papers quite a bit. In the late 1980s, I began writing books and textbooks as well. Seeing my own writing in print for the first time, I was thrilled.

In 1991, I moved to Southern California. Soon after that, I took a teaching position at the Los Angeles campus of Soka University. The school was emerging as a new American university, and I became one of the pioneers to help establish Soka University of America (SUA). The founder of the university is Mr. Daisaku Ikeda, whom, as I wrote before, I respect as my mentor in life.

The first project I got involved in was to create a Japanese language program open to the community. And the next one was a graduate program; I became heavily involved in these projects as the central person in charge.

Needless to say, it was quite challenging to create something from scratch. At the same time, it was extremely rewarding. Especially in the initial years, we faced many obstacles. But our struggles bore a lot of fruit.

We received generous support from numerous people, for which I am eternally grateful. A number of notable people visited our campus to support the university. The most famous one is Mrs. Rosa Parks, the world-renowned "Mother of the American Civil Rights Movements."

Mrs. Parks came to the Los Angeles campus of Soka University in Calabasas, California, first in December 1992 and again in the following month, January 1993. From that time on, until 2005, when she passed away, I met with her countless times in various places—e.g., Los Angeles, Mexico, Japan, Detroit, Atlanta, Florida, etc. I also became Mrs. Parks's official translator of her books into Japanese.

In May 1994, when Mrs. Parks was eighty-one years old, the SUA Founder, Mr. Ikeda, invited her to Japan. Previously she had not traveled beyond Canada and Mexico. Her decision to go there showed her willingness to experience the unfamiliar. I accompanied her on this trip and saw for myself how she touched the hearts of Japanese people simply by being herself.

I also became good friends with Mrs. Parks's assistant, Elaine Steele. She would call me often. For example,

"Today is Mrs. Parks's birthday. Would you like to stop by on your way home from work?"

Then I would stop by to go see Mrs. Parks at her friend's home in Los Angeles, where she was staying that winter.

One day, as soon as I walked into the house, I looked for Mrs. Parks. I found her in the kitchen. She was slicing tomatoes. And as soon as she saw me, she welcomed me with a big smile and said,

"Hi, Tomoko!"

She looked like a grandmother welcoming her granddaughter. In that moment, I felt I was the luckiest person alive. I have the great fortune to say that there are numerous occasions upon which I have felt that way.

(From left) Elaine Steele, Rosa Parks, Tomoko [author]
(February 1997)

In September 1994, a graduate school was opened at the Los Angeles campus of Soka University. The SUA Founder, Mr. Ikeda, sent a message to celebrate the opening of the Graduate School.

In his message at that occasion, he clearly stated the mission of the school:

> *The mission of Soka University of America is to foster a steady stream of global citizens committed to living a contributive life.*

With the establishment of the graduate program, the school became an independent American institution—Soka University of America. At the same time, I became the Dean of the Graduate School. Because it was a small school, I wore many hats; I was appointed to be in charge of academic affairs (including faculty hires) as well as the recruitment of students.

Tomoko [author] as the Dean of the Graduate School
at the SUA Commencement, wearing the cap and gown from her alma
mater, Columbia University (2002)

Our brand new students of the first entering class came from France, Panama, Japan, and various states of the United States. When I saw them arrive on campus, I screamed inside: *Wow! They are really here!*

I will never forget that sight for the rest of my life.

Once the graduate program began, the growth and happiness of my students and the development of the university became my life. Focusing on student diversity, we tried to recruit students from countries such as China, India, the Philippines, Brazil, etc. I traveled to each country to find excellent students, and welcomed them with financial aid.

That reminded me of myself, who had received a full scholarship to come to America. Whenever I see those international students, I feel as if they were myself a few decades before.

Soka University of America opened its second campus in Orange County in 2001. In the following year, I was appointed as the university's first Provost (Vice President for Academic Affairs), overseeing both the undergraduate and graduate programs of SUA's two California campuses.

As the chief academic officer of the university, one of my responsibilities has been accreditation. In 2005, SUA received accreditation from the Western Association for Schools and Colleges (WASC) by skipping the candidacy level. It was a major victory for us all—students, faculty, staff, and all the supporters of the university. And without the encouragement and support from the SUA Founder, Mr. Ikeda, this wouldn't have been possible.

I'm also deeply grateful for all the encouragement I have personally received from Mr. Ikeda. For instance, in 1998, I was presented with the following poem:

> *The mother of happiness and intellect*
> *Embracing with affection*
> *The Castle of Soka University in America.*

In 2002, my family and I were truly delighted and touched to learn that there would be a tree planted on the campus of SUA in memory of my father. The suggestion was made by the University Founder, Mr. Ikeda. He remembered that I had once written to him about my father.

Twenty-five years before that day, in a dark library room in Kent Hall at Columbia, I devoured those books by Mr. Ikeda. I never thought I would be doing what I'm doing today.

Whenever I see the orange tree planted next to Gandhi Hall on the SUA campus, I thank Mr. Ikeda, and also tell my father,

"Dad, thank you. I wouldn't be here without you and without your last words."

Second Doctorate

In 1996, I was elected to the Board of Trustees of my alma mater, Albertus Magnus College. Honestly, I could not believe it, especially considering the fact that I came to Albertus as an international student from Japan.

In 2006, there was an incident even more surprising. One morning, I received a telephone call from the president of Albertus Magnus College, Dr. Julia McNamara, who said to me,

"We would like you to deliver a commencement address at the upcoming graduation."

I felt extremely honored. I immediately accepted her invitation.

Then she continued,

"We would like to confer upon you an honorary doctorate."

When I heard that, I almost fell off my chair. Extremely surprised, I truly felt, *I'm too young and undeserving for such a great honor.*

At the commencement in May 2006, the reason for this honor was announced as follows:

> *Tomoko Takahashi, you blossomed like the flowers on your native land's sakura tree when you arrived on this campus at the age of twenty. Your life has been filled with distinguished academic achievement, the development of innovative concepts in the field of linguistics, and the forging of groundbreaking links between the diverse Eastern and Western cultures.*
>
> *Your ever-advancing role in the administration of higher education complements the accomplishments you have achieved as scholar and teacher. You have been recognized as leader in the art of translation, which led to your lasting friendship and literary collaboration with the "Mother of the American Civil Rights Movements" Rosa Parks. Thanks to your elegant translations, Mrs. Parks's inspirational texts are now available in your native Japanese.*
>
> *Tomoko Takahashi, Rosa Parks said that each person must live life as a model for others. So you have set a remarkable example by your life and career in ways that render your alma mater proud indeed. [. . .]*

As I listened to this explanation, I reminisced about the day in June of 1975 when I first came to America by myself . . . and also the day in January 1979 when my father passed away, leaving me with his last words: "Don't quit school halfway through."

Dad once said to Mom,

"I wish I had attended Tomoko's graduation from Albertus."

I'm sure he was there in spirit at the conferral ceremony of my second doctorate just like when I received my degree from Columbia University in 1984.

I said in my heart repeatedly,

Thank you, Dad!

Tomoko [author] delivering her commencement address at
Albertus Magnus College, after receiving her honorary doctorate
(May 2006)

Afterword

On the morning of August 19, 2009, as I do every morning, I was looking at the photo of my grandmother Toku and my father as a baby. Then the photo began talking to me. I rushed to my computer to write down what I thought I had heard. The first sentence came to me in Japanese. And once I began writing, I simply could not stop. Unexpectedly, my long-awaited project began; I had always wanted to write about my father. Whenever I found time, I wrote—early in the morning before going to work, and after coming home from work until late at night.

I reread the letters from my father and family—I've kept them all. I also read my letters to them, which my father had filed for me. I called my family in Japan to get more information about Dad. We cried together many times and shed tears of appreciation.

It was quite a journey—a journey of my family history as well. With my brother's assistance, I was able to find out much about our ancestors. As a result, I was able to learn about my own roots. Without them, I wouldn't be who I am today. I am grateful to them.

This writing project also allowed me to live the history of Japan from the Meiji to Shōwa eras. It was a hands-on experience. While imagining how my ancestors might have lived, I was able to revive them—they came alive all of a sudden. I felt strong congenial affinities with them.

I enjoyed having dialogues, for instance, with my great-great-grandfather Kisuke, whom I had never met; what a character he was! I felt it incredibly rewarding to be able to revive my twenty-one-year-old grandmother Toku, who had once vanished from this world . . . and to honor my great-grandfather Yōzaburō, who had been stigmatized and forgotten due to his illness caused by the cruelty of war.

I felt refreshed . . . as if a burden had been lifted. Best of all, I was able to spend quality time with my father again.

Dad still lives, I reconfirmed.

One day, while I was writing the manuscript, I came across a letter from my mother that I had received in 2000. I had forgotten what she had written there:

> *Your father used to say, "After I retire, I would like to write a history of my family. I want to write a book." But he died young before having the chance to realize that dream. I wish he could have written that book and been able to reexamine the life he had created for himself with his sincerity and youthful conviction. It's so regrettable that he was unable to.*

So, it was my father's dream . . .

Five months later, I finished the entire manuscript in Japanese on January 7, 2010—the thirty-first anniversary of my father's passing. And my book『サムライと綿・日本とアメリカ』was published in Japan on Father's Day in June 2010—thirty-five years after my first arrival in the United States.

I immediately began working on the English edition. I'm fortunate that I didn't have to hire a translator; being bilingual in Japanese and English, I was able to do it myself. Well, how could I have even thought of asking someone else to do it? This book project has been too much fun and rewarding.

But I didn't translate the book. Rather, I rewrote it in English. And I wrote it with my dad.

I finished the first draft of the manuscript in English, again, around the time my father's thirty-second memorial was celebrated, in January 2011.

When my father wrote letters, he never ended them with expressions of love. But I knew how much he loved me. He never said, "I love you," but I knew how much he loved his family. I don't remember ever saying, "I love you" to my parents either. That's how it was (and is) in Japanese culture. As a matter of fact, a direct translation of "I love you" into Japanese would sound awkward if it were used by parents to their children and vice versa.

After having lived in the United States for more than thirty-five years, I now feel comfortable saying, "I love you." But I still don't know how to say it in Japanese. So, I have to say it in English,

"I love you, Dad."

And with love, I dedicate this book to Mom, "an eternal eighteen-year-old schoolgirl."

Acknowledgments

My first thanks go to:

My mother, **Sachiko Takahashi**, for all the wonderful episodes she has shared with me since my childhood; and

My brother, **Hiromi Takahashi**, for his enthusiastic help in gathering information about our ancestors and family and for the tremendous amounts of time and effort he spent discussing the content of the book with me.

Special thanks also go to the following individuals for their encouragement, inspiration, and support:

Leslie M. Beebe
MaryAnn Easley
Laurie Golden
Larry Hickman
Mihoko Hirai
Reiko Komagata
Veronica Krisavage
Terrie Mathis
Shigenori Tanaka
Margaret S. Taylor
John F. Walker
Jason J. Yamamoto

Any errors are entirely my own. The names of some persons and places in the story have been changed.

The Nichiren quote at the beginning of the book is from page 52 of *The Record of the Orally Transmitted Teachings* translated by Burton Watson (Tokyo: Soka Gakkai, 2004).[32]

---

[32] English translation of *Ongi Kuden*, records of Nichiren's lectures on the Lotus Sutra that were compiled and put into order by Nichiren's close disciple and successor, Nikko

About the Author

Tomoko Takahashi was born in Japan in 1955; at twenty, she left her home for the United States. She received her BA in English from Albertus Magnus College in New Haven, Connecticut, and earned her doctorate in applied linguistics from Columbia University. She currently serves as the Provost and Vice President for Academic Affairs at Soka University of America, Aliso Viejo, California.

Dr. Takahashi has published more than twenty books, including scholarly books in English and Japanese on language learning, cross-cultural communication, and lexico-semantics; thirteen coauthored textbooks for Japanese learners of English, eight of which have been translated into Chinese and Korean; and Japanese translations of *Rosa Parks: My Story*, *Quiet Strength*, and *Dear Mrs. Parks*.

Glossary[33]

Ansei. A period in the history of Japan (1854–1860). A sub-era in the Edo period (1603–1867). See also ***Edo***.

azuki. Small, round red beans; also spelled *adzuki* or *aduki*.

Alinamin-A. A vitamin drink sold in Japan.

ama-saké.[34] A hot drink made with fresh *saké* lees [yeast deposits]; literally "sweet *saké*." See also ***saké***.

amae. Tendency to depend on someone close, such as one's parent.

AMC. Albertus Magnus College.

ame. A homonym meaning "candy" (pronounced "amé") and "rain" (pronounced "áme").

andon. Lanterns with paper shade.

BA. Bachelor of Arts (degree).

---

[33] Terms introduced in the *Glossary* are all italicized, but italics are used selectively in the text: Common nouns in Japanese are italicized in the text, but most of the proper nouns are not—e.g., names of places, epochs, individuals, groups, etc. Japanese terms that become familiar through repeated use in the text—especially those that have entered the English language (e.g., "samurai" and "haiku")—are italicized only on their first occurrence. If they appear only rarely, italics are retained. Japanese common nouns that are normally italicized appear without italics in italicized quotes.

[34] An acute accent (´) is used to distinguish this word from the English word "sake."

273

Banzai! Hurray! Originally a Japanese battle cry and a form of greeting used to the Japanese Emperor.

Bon. The festival honoring the deceased.

bonsai. A miniature tree or shrub grown in a pot.

chazuke. A simple meal of cooked rice with tea poured on it.

chitose-ame. Sticks of red and white candy for a November festival for children of seven, five, and three years of age.

chon-mage. A topknot—a hairstyle worn by men in pre-modern Japan.

Daikoku. The god of farmers.

daikon. Japanese radish; literally "large root."

daimyo. Powerful feudal lords in pre-modern Japan; literally "big name." A *samurai* class whose fiefdom produced more than 10,000 *koku* each year. See also **han** and **koku**.

dame. No good.

danchi. A housing development.

danna. An old-fashioned honorific used as a polite or respectful way of addressing an older man—"master" or "sir."

dojo. A room or hall in which martial arts are practiced.

Edo. (1) A period in the history of Japan (1603–1867). The era ruled by the Tokugawa family. (2) Present-day Tokyo. The name "Edo" was changed to Tokyo when it became the imperial capital in 1868.

engawa. A wooden strip of floor extending at one side of a traditional Japanese house.

ESL. English as a second language.

furikake. Dried seasoning for sprinkling over cooked rice.

furoshiki. Scarf-like cloth for wrapping and carrying items.

fusuma. Sliding doors.

futon. Traditional-style Japanese bedding consisting of padded mattresses and quilts, which are pliable enough to be folded and stored away during the day.

Gambare. An expression used for encouraging someone to do their very best, even through adversity.

Gogatsu. The month of May.

gongyō. Practice of reciting Buddhist sutras in front of an object of worship.

GPA. Grade point average.

GRE. Graduate Record Examination.

hagoita. A Japanese badminton racket made of wood.

haiku. A Japanese poem of seventeen syllables, in three lines of five, seven and five, traditionally evoking images of the natural world.

han. A fiefdom, domain, or territory of a *daimyo* during the Edo period with an agricultural output assessed at 10,000 *koku* or more. See also **daimyo** and **koku**.

hanami. Cherry blossom viewing.

hanshi. Thin white paper used for calligraphy.

harakiri. Japanese ritual suicide by disembowelment; literally "cutting the belly."

hatamoto. Upper vassals in pre-modern Japan. A *samurai* class in the direct service of the Tokugawa *shogunate* of feudal Japan.

HHH. Helen Hadley Hall, a Yale dormitory.

hime. A princess.

hina ningyō [dolls]. A set of ornamental dolls representing the Emperor, Empress, attendants and musicians in traditional court dress of the Heian period (794–1185) displayed during the Girls' Festival. See also **hina matsuri**.

hina matsuri. The Girls' Festival celebrated on March 3rd.

hina-arare. Puffy bits of rice cake for the Girls' Festival.

hinomaru. The rising-sun flag.

hinomaru bentō. A lunch box stuffed with white rice and a pickled red plum in the center depicting a Japanese flag. See also **hinomaru**.

hokōsha tengoku. A pedestrian zone; literally "pedestrian heaven."

hyōtan. A bottle made out of a hardened gourd or gourd-shaped container.

I-20 (form). A document that provides supporting information for the issuance of a student visa.

I-95. Interstate 95. The main highway on the East Coast of the United States.

Jizō. A guardian deity of children.

Imagawa-yaki. A Japanese muffin containing bean jam.

imon-bukuro. A comfort bag or care package.

kagezen. Meals set out for someone who's away from home.

kago. A Japanese type of litter, suspended by a single crossbeam, carried by two men, usually used to transport one person at a time.

kaimyō. Posthumous Buddhist name.

kanji. Chinese characters.

kashi. Confectionary.

kashiwa-mochi. Rice cakes wrapped in oak leaves.

katakana. A Japanese syllabary. A component of the Japanese writing system used primarily for loanwords.

katsu. A homonym meaning "to win" and "a cutlet."

kendama. A Japanese cup-and-ball toy.

kendo. Japanese fencing.

Kigen-setsu. Imperial Epoch Celebration. Present-day National Foundation Day (February 11th).

kijirushi. A euphemism for *kichigai* [crazy].

kimono. A Japanese traditional garment; literally "thing to wear."

kin-tsuba. An old name for *Imagawa-yaki* muffins; literally "golden sword-guard." See also **Imagawa-yaki**.

koku. A Japanese unit of measurement, approximately 278.3 liters. The *koku* was originally defined as a quantity of rice, historically defined as enough rice to feed one person for one year.

kudoku. Benefit from the Buddhist practice.

Kurisumasu. Christmas.

kusa-mochi. Rice cakes with herbs.

kyōiku. Education.

MA. Master of Arts (degree).

masukotto. Mascot.

Masukotto-jirushi. Mascot brand.

Meiji. A period in the history of Japan (1868–1912).

miso. Soybean paste.

mitsuba. A Japanese herb with a flavor similar to Angelica; leaves are chopped and used to flavor a number of dishes.

mochi. Rice cake.

muri, mura, muda. Excessiveness, inconsistency, and wastefulness.

mushiro. Straw mats.

Nam-myo-ho-renge-kyo. The phrase Nichiren Buddhists chant; also known as *daimoku.* The title of the Lotus Sutra in its Japanese translation is *Myoho-renge-kyo.* But to Nichiren, *Myoho-renge-kyo* was far more than the title of a Buddhist text; it was the expression, in words, of the Law of life, which all Buddhist teachings in one way or another seek to clarify.

neko-kawaigari. Doting on children like cats.

nenneko. A short coat stuffed with cotton to keep the baby warm.

obi. A traditional Japanese sash belt for a *kimono.* See also ***kimono.***

OED. Oxford English Dictionary.

Okaerinasai! Welcome home!

omiai. A meeting for an arranged marriage.

omikoshi. A portable shrine carried around during a festival.

oshiuri. A high-pressure peddler.

o-zōni. Soup with rice cakes. A typical New Year's dish.

Pomade. Brilliantine—a hair-styling product intended to soften men's hair and give it a glossy, well-groomed appearance.

PX. Post exchange—a store at a US military base selling food, clothing and other items.

ronin. (1) In Japan, under the feudal system, a samurai who had renounced his clan or who had been discharged or ostracized and had become a wanderer without a lord. (2) In modern days, a student who spends an entire year, and sometimes longer, studying for another attempt at the entrance examinations.

-saburō. A male name ending meaning "third son."

saké. Japanese rice wine.

sakura. Cherry flowers.

samurai. A member of a military caste in feudal Japan.

Sanzu. A river that the dead must cross; similar to the Styx. It is believed that on the way to the afterlife, the dead must cross the river, which is why a Japanese funeral includes placing six coins in the deceased's casket.

sanzui. Three water-strokes (of a Chinese character).

sashimi. A dish of bite-sized raw fish eaten with soy sauce and *wasabi* horseradish paste.

satsuki. (1) Azalea flowers. (2) The traditional name for the month of May.

sensei. (1) A teacher. (2) A title used as a polite way of addressing a teacher, doctor, etc.

Shakyamuni. Buddha—the enlightened one.

shi, nō, kō, shō. Gentry, farmers, artisans and merchants—the four divisions of society in pre-modern Japan.

shini-mizu. Wetting the mouth of the person just about to die.

Shinto. Japanese religion incorporating the worship of ancestors and nature spirits. The state religion of Japan until 1945.

Shirodasuki-tai. White-sash Corps—a suicide corps formed as the last resort when the Japanese military army reached a dead end during the Russo-Japanese War (1904–1905).

shiruko. Sweet red-bean soup.

shiso. Leaves from a beefsteak plant.

Shodai. First Generation or Founder.

shōdai. Chanting Nam-myo-ho-renge-kyo.

shogunate. A hereditary commander-in-chief in feudal Japan.

Shōwa. A period in the history of Japan (1926–1989).

soba. Japanese noodles made from buckwheat flour.

Soka Gakkai. A lay Buddhist organization; literally "Society for the Creation of Value." The Soka Gakkai was founded in 1930 by Tsunesaburo Makiguchi as a group of reformist educators. Makiguchi drew inspiration from Nichiren Buddhism to develop the organization into a broader-based movement focused on the propagation of Buddhism as a means to enable people to tap their inner potential and ultimately reform Japanese society. Facing oppression from the Japanese militarist government, Makiguchi and his closest follower Josei Toda were arrested and imprisoned in 1943 as "thought criminals." Makiguchi died in prison in 1944. After his release, Toda promoted an active, socially engaged form of Buddhism as a means of self-empowerment. Toda was succeeded as president in 1960 by Daisaku Ikeda, who further developed the Soka Gakkai as a movement of empowered, socially engaged Buddhists. Soka Gakkai International (SGI) was founded in 1975, as a worldwide network of Buddhists dedicated to a common vision of a better world through the empowerment of the individual and the promotion of peace, culture and education. Under Ikeda's leadership, the SGI has developed into one of the largest Buddhist movements in the world.

SUA. Soka University of America.

suiton. Flour dumplings boiled in soup—a typical wartime food.

-suke. An old-fashioned male name ending.

sumo. A Japanese form of heavyweight wrestling.

sushi. A dish consisting of small balls or rolls of vinegar-flavored cooked rice served with a garnish of raw fish, vegetables, or egg.

TA. (1) A teaching assistant. (2) Teaching assistantship.

Taishō. A period in the history of Japan (1912–1926).

tatami. Padded floor coverings.

tempura. A dish of fish, shellfish, or vegetables fried in batter.

TESOL. Teaching English to Speakers of Other Languages.

TOEFL. Test of English as a Foreign Language.

ton-katsu. Breaded fried pork cutlet. See **katsu.**

tonikaku. An adverb meaning "believe it or not," "regardless" or "anyway."

tsuba. A homonym meaning both "a hand guard on a Japanese sword" and "saliva" in Japanese.

udon. Japanese wheat pasta made in thick strips.

waka. A Japanese poem of thirty-one syllables, in five lines of five, seven, five, seven and seven. The term *waka* (literally "Japanese poem") was coined during the Heian period (794–1185).

wataya. A cotton merchant.

WWII. World War Two.

yabuiri. Servants' holidays—a one-day leave (formerly) granted to servants and apprentices working for a store on July 16th and on January 16th.

yagō. A special name or logo for trading.

yakitori. Japanese chicken barbeque—bite-sized pieces of chicken meat skewed on a bamboo skewer and grilled, usually over charcoal.

yama. A mountain.

yoshi. Good.

-zaburō. A variation of the male name ending *-saburō* meaning "third son."